ENDORSEMENTS A

*From the ladies in the Foundations St... sessions in **Embraced, Empowered, Equipped** for their weekly Bible study for three years.*

"Whether you are agnostic, atheist, a new believer, a "seasoned Christian," whether solid in your faith walk or in a season of questioning God, this book is for you! Are you searching for purpose? Struggling with what feels like an attack? Wondering what God´s plan is for your life? Feeling like you don´t have control of your life? Curious about God, but questioning His existence? Hilde has a true God-given talent for digging deep into the Word and helping the reader to uncover gems of learning and understanding for our life, trials, tests, purpose, blessings and God´s gifts for us for our time on this earth. Hilde is anointed to explain life application through Holy-Spirit led teachings about our walk with God. Every session is a vital learning opportunity. The book truly gave me a life-changing perspective, and I challenge you to see if it doesn´t do the same for you."

Mollie Peacock, American living in the Philippines

"Dear reader, I was happy to learn that my friend and Bible study leader Hilde was compiling a book of teachings from our women's Bible study group. As a woman that has personally benefitted from Hilde's insightful lessons, I encourage you to read, open your hearts and let God work within. Over the years, I've had issues with trusting God, and Hilde's teachings have helped me to really understand that God loves ME. His love for me isn't based on my works or worthiness, but because Jesus loves and values me. As a Christian for over 32 years, this basic Christian concept has eluded me. Oh, I've heard it plenty, and I know it's the foundation, this love. That knowledge, however, didn't bring me to a place where trust that God loves me as I am, could begin fresh in my heart. Through Hilde's beautiful, gentle way of teaching, I've been able to grasp this truth, and it has changed the way I view God and our relationship. While this is just one standout benefit for me from her lovely thoughtful teachings of the Bible, there have been many more over the years. My prayer for you that read this book is that you too receive a beautiful nugget from it to apply to your relationship with God. Be blessed."

Wanda Beavers, American living in the Philippines

"As an active, tongues-speaking charismatic Christian for more than 20 years, I felt that coming to the first Bible study of "Foundations Study" might just be another lesson I have heard before. Nonetheless, I felt led to attend and opened up to how it could possibly be fresh for me. And fresh it was. Hilde's perspective and delivery are very Holy Spirit led and acute for every Bible study session I have attended. Each time I think I may already know the topic she brings a freshness through the way she delivers it. It blows me away how much truth and knowledge she delivers in each session. A lot of times her one session is equivalent to my months or weeks of attending church to gather that much understanding and knowledge. Not that the church isn't doing its work but, rather, that Hilde really tries to pour in as much as she can with as little words as possible. She is like a mother trying to feed us with as much as she can possibly give given the time we have together. Personally, I always likened her sessions to "nuggets of gold"—very compact and every bit precious. The sessions drip with wisdom, knowledge and power. They never fail to refresh and lead us each time. Note: Read each lesson over and over again. One reading really isn't enough to capture everything. Looking back, after three years of studies, God used Hilde to refresh my walk in Him. Hilde's day-time Bible study group sustained and fed me spiritually. Her well-prepared lessons and the friendship in the Bible studies have been instrumental in bringing me to another level of growth, even after 20 years as a Christian. I strongly advise spending quiet time in the Word to accompany the lessons, and I am very sure you too will be transformed and renewed in your directions and faith in God no matter where your starting point is. May you and your loved ones be abundantly blessed by this book."

Petra Lau, a Malaysian living in the Philippines

"Hilde's Bible study lessons are not a one day hit wonder. Over the years, I realized her lessons built a strong foundation in us, brick by brick, and surrounded us with the promises of God. At the same time, Hilde opens new windows to shed light on the Word of God, give meaning to the sacrifice of Jesus and new depth to the wisdom of the Holy Spirit. Through her lessons, I went on a journey of discovering His love for me. This gave me new insight and confidence in God, creating a deep relationship with the Father. If we were to compare her teachings of love to a book, this is not romantic, fussy or volatile. She presents God's love in a reassuring, unwavering, gentle and cerebral manner."

Anna Varona, The Philippines

"This is a thorough and grounded book with straightforward lessons on real and foundational topics that helped me learn more about how to have a deeper walk with Jesus. The questions at the end of each lesson help to challenge my comprehension and application of the information so I could begin to live out a real relationship with Him. The short lessons work well into busy lives and give any reader food for thought about the love, ways and workings of Jesus in our world."

A. Leach

"My life has been transformed by learning from Hilde's Bible study teachings. In fact, I converted to become a Christian from being a Muslim because I learned about Jesus from her Bible studies! Her lessons are so hands-on and relate to our daily life. I am forever grateful to have met and learned about Jesus from her. Thanks, Hilde for your knowledge of our Father that you shared with us week after week!"

Dearsy Webb, an Indonesian living in the Philippines

"Hilde Grimstad's Fundamental Bible study lessons teach the important elements about Christianity and the Bible in a way I have not experienced before. She can take a topic like "Forgiveness" and show us what God says about it, quoting Bible verses, and then we further discuss it as a group. I never feel like the topics are too difficult and the message of God's grace is always at the forefront. Through the teachings, I have come to know Jesus, the Lord, and the Holy Spirit in such a personal way. I look forward to each week to learn the next thing, and even if topics are discussed a second time, there is always something new that we take away from our Bible study lessons. The teachings have slowly transformed me. My mind, my heart, my soul, my spirit... are now renewed and changed for good, through Christ Jesus. I would recommend this book to non-believers, new believers, and even Christians who are well into their walk with the Lord. Every person can learn and benefit from the lessons found in this book! They are simply amazing and life changing!"

Lily Beth Soriano, Filipina/American

"I was invited to attend Hilde's Foundation Bible study almost a year ago. I was curious to know what these sessions were all about. I was quite familiar with the Bible and Christian teachings as I had studied the Bible in school throughout my elementary and high school years. However, I found Hilde's Bible Study sessions and approach to be very different from anything I had learned from the past and quite refreshing. Since it's been some years since I've studied and read the Bible, I felt her teachings helped me strengthen my faith in God and in Jesus Christ. During the first session, I felt a very strong presence of the Holy Spirit in the room and found great comfort and support from the ladies. So, I continued to attend the sessions regularly. And in time, I noticed it helped me to rebuild a strong foundation of who I am in God and how to live victoriously through Christ's teachings. The sessions taught me how to worship and love God better, pray better, be more appreciative of God's blessings, choose and fight my battles better with God by my side and understand that I was not a guilty sinner but a true child of God. I felt loved and supported by God again and feel constantly guided by the Holy Spirit. I am so grateful and thankful to have met Hilde and discovered the Foundations Study sessions as I genuinely felt myself changing from the inside out and for the better! I now feel empowered by God's love and grace. Life is truly beautiful...God is good!"

Francesca D. Warnke, Filipina/American

"Infidelity in my family caused me to seek help from a Christian lady, and this is how I ended up in Hilde´s Foundation Study group. Although I had grown up as a Buddhist, I found Hilde´s lessons very touching. I received Jesus as my Savior, and from that point, my life changed a lot. I learned about God´s love, grace and help in every situation. I learned to pray and talk to God just like I talk to my parents. I now love Jesus so much. I thank Hilde and the ladies in the Foundation Study for leading me to find Jesus and a new life! I have now moved to China with my family, but God is here with me and gives me strength every day."

Pat from Thailand

"I have really enjoyed being a part of Hilde's Bible study group and sitting under her teaching. Her sessions are full of truth and revelation but also very practical and easy to apply to everyday life. Every week, each one of us leave her place encouraged, inspired and more in love with Jesus. Every session points us back to Him and unravels another facet of His goodness. We are so happy that Hilde has put this in print for more people to enjoy. Recommended to anyone and everyone! Great job Hilde!"

Katie Orr, Australian living in the Philippines

"My wife and I had the opportunity to go through Embraced, Empowered, Equipped sessions during couples' cell group meetings that truly blessed us as individuals and as couples. Every session was laying in our lives the foundation of practical Christian living pulled out from the Scriptures. The wisdom and life applications we received from each session were profound and changed our lives for the better. Hilde is able to bring to the forefront important Biblical values, which press us to introspect as to where we stand in light of it. Her teachings encourage us to persevere to incorporate the truth into our lives in a gentle yet assertive manner. Her sessions are Holy Spirit inspired. A must read and share with family and friends."

Tenny and Valencia Johnson, Indians living in the Philippines

Embraced

by love

Empowered

by grace

Equipped

for calling and purpose

40 SESSIONS TO KICKSTART YOUR JOURNEY
INTO TRUE IDENTITY, INTIMACY, CALLING
AND PURPOSE IN GOD

Hilde Lundgaard Grimstad

Grimstad Publishing
NORWAY

Grimstad Publishing

Valstadsvingen 28

2013 Skjetten, Norway

www.hildelundgaardgrimstad.com

Book Layout ©2019 BookDesignTemplates.com and Hilde L. Grimstad

Cover design by Danijela Mijailovic based on idea by Christelle Viljoen

Embraced, Empowered, Equipped/ Hilde Lundgaard Grimstad. —1st ed.

ISBN 978-82-93733-00-3

E-book ISBN: 978-82-93733-01-0

For worldwide distribution

CONTENTS

Acknowledgements

All glory and thanks to God for inspiring me to write the lessons in this book. He is the One to be acknowledged above all. However, God depends on people, and there are some in particular who have been instrumental in making this book come to pass. My great friends Katie Orr and Christelle Viljoen have worked on a voluntary basis for an uncountable number of hours to edit and transform my "English second language" into publishing quality language. Christelle even came up with the idea for the book cover. I am forever grateful for their support and hard work. I also want to thank Anna Varona for taking great photos for this book.

I want to thank the ladies in my Bible study group, Foundation Study, who were the ones who encouraged me to compile these lessons into a book. Originally, the lessons were made for them only. This book would never have happened without their great support throughout the whole process.

A special thanks to the pastors and missionaries who read the manuscript before it was finalized and gave their valuable feedback and encouragement to make the book even better.

Finally, I want to thank my husband, kids and friends for always supporting me and believing in me.

Never doubt God's mighty power to work in you and accomplish all this. He will achieve infinitely more than your greatest request, your most unbelievable dream, and exceed your wildest imagination! He will outdo them all, for his miraculous power constantly energizes you.

EPHESIANS 3:20
THE PASSION TRANSLATION

Foreword

PASSIONATE AND DETERMINED. Those are two words that come to mind when I think of describing my friend, Hilde L. Grimstad.

Passionate because when I am with her, she exudes a love and zeal for God that is contagious. The times I have spent with her have really moved my soul and have caused me to yearn more for His presence. I remember hearing her testimony for the first time in a coffee shop. She told it with so much enthusiasm that I felt it was a story that just happened recently. Her laughter and joy at the remembrance of events told me how much her encounter with Jesus meant to her.

Determined because she would pursue God given dreams with a tenacity and a boldness that reflected her faith in the goodness and power of God. She would step out in faith, believing God's Word, whether it was moving to the Philippines, opening a new business or starting a Bible study.

When she first told me about this book, she said she felt nervous and apprehensive at the thought of writing it. But I could see that her heart was to bring out the message of God's empowering love and grace to people. It was a desire burning inside of her. She wanted to see people embraced, empowered and equipped by the gospel of Jesus Christ.

I am glad her passion and determination caused her to pen this book you are now holding in your hands. Reading through it has encouraged me, ministered to me and blessed me beyond measure. It made me realize all the more how the gospel of the Lord Jesus Christ is beautiful and marvelous in its simplicity.

Hilde has put together a book that will inspire and instruct, encourage and equip and, in her own words, "kickstart your journey" into the wonderful plan that God has for your lives.

2 Timothy 3:16-17 declares this:

> *Every Scripture has been written by the Holy Spirit, the breath of God. It will empower you by its instruction and correction, giving you the strength to take the right direction and lead you deeper into the path of godliness. Then you will be God's servant, fully mature and perfectly prepared to fulfill any assignment God gives you.*

Enjoy the book! It is a must read for those who want a solid foundation in the Word of God. It is simple in its approach yet profound in its application. Each page has the potential to minister wisdom and wholeness into your life. I believe every session will speak to your heart. I know they have spoken to mine.

The Cross made all the difference

Mylene Evangelista

Associate Pastor of New Life Alabang, Philippines
Co-founder of Jesus Festival
Co-author of Jesus Focused and Come, Sit and Eat

Introduction

The Background of the Book

In 2015, we moved to the Philippines for my husband´s work. Little did I know what course my life would take in the next few years. This was our second posting in this beautiful, tropical Asian country and I was excited to be back.

My story about this book started when I met Mollie, an American expat living with her family in Manila. She was a new believer in Jesus Christ with a history in New Age beliefs. She was so eager to learn about God, and she was reading and studying any Bible related topic she got her hands on; however, what she learned was kind of random. If compared to building a house, it would be like she was installing a window in the rooftop and creating a balcony on the second floor, but she did not even have walls on her house yet, not to mention the lack of a proper foundation for her "house." Mollie and I met regularly, and I started teaching and explaining to her the basic things we need to understand as believers in Christ. She was so excited about her new revelation and insisted that more people needed to hear this message: "We had to start a group, and I had to teach them!"

When looking back, it had been in my heart for a while to start a Bible study. Throughout the 26 years that I have been a Christian, I have always had a hunger for the things of God. I loved to read and study the Bible, which led me to attend Bible school twice: first with Youth with a Mission in India and the second time in a Pentecostal church in Norway (now Hillsong Norway). In addition to attending church on Sundays, I was consistently reading Christian books and listening to teaching and preaching of the Word. In the end, I felt like I was "constipated" with the Word of God and I felt an increasing urge to start pouring out to others. New believers were particularly in my heart; however, I had to move to the Philippines for it to happen...

As a real soul winner, Mollie gathered a bunch of ladies, mostly expats, and we started the group Foundation Study. The ladies originated from countries all over the world. Some were new believers and others came from traditional church backgrounds or charismatic churches. We also had a Muslim and a Buddhist in the group, who soon received Jesus. Everyone was hungry to learn and grow in the Lord. Wherever they were in their journey with God, they needed a stronger revelation of God´s love, what Jesus had done for them at the cross and their identity and authority in Him. They needed to learn how to live life by God´s grace and the power of the Holy Spirit. They needed to build a strong foundation for their faith and be established in God´s grace and love in the New Covenant.

Embraced, Empowered, Equipped is based on the lessons I made for the Foundation Study group. During the first two years with the ladies, I made a new lesson with a new topic every week. I built truth upon truth—one building block on top of the other from the Word of God. Their knowledge, understanding and revelation grew week by week, and I could see how God gradually transformed them as the Word and God Himself came alive to them.

I never intended for it to become a book, but after a few sessions of Bible study, the ladies proclaimed, "Hilde, this is really great; you have to make a book out of it!" I was reluctant at first, but after having made 40 sessions covering 33 different topics, I decided to go for it! Perhaps it could be a blessing for someone out there...

How Can This Book Change Your Life?

So, what makes the sessions in *Embraced, Empowered, Equipped* so powerful and life changing? Firstly, the love and grace of God infuse every single session of this book. There is no "pointing the finger." You will learn that God is only good, that His great salvation plan was determined from the beginning of time and how He has chosen YOU to be loved and transformed by Him. You will see God´s outstretched, loving arms through Jesus at the cross that will set you free from shame, guilt and condemnation. Jesus came to save us—not condemn us. When you understand that God loves YOU, has called YOU, empowered and equipped YOU it will set you free and take you on a journey into your true identity, intimacy, calling and purpose in Him.

The Holy Spirit plays an essential part in this journey. You will get to know Him in this book: who He is and how He is there to lead you, help you and empower you in every possible way in your life. You will learn how to discover and develop your spiritual gifts, how to hear from God and be led by Him and how to pray powerfully with the help of the Holy Spirit. As you are filled with the Holy Spirit, boldness and confidence will rise inside of you. You will be unstoppable!

To sustain your journey with God, you need to be able to read, understand and apply the Word of God in your life. Don´t worry—you will learn it in this book. Two sessions are covering this in particular. The whole book is, however, filled with life application. You will, for instance, learn how to renew your mind, take control of your thinking and emotions and make the right life choices and priorities with your focus on Jesus and eternal things.

As you follow the sessions in this book, you will grow in your faith and learn the true character of God. As you get a revelation of His grace, you will be transformed and enter into a rest for your soul. You will know deep down that God loves you no matter what. At the same time, this grace will empower you to be everything God intended you to be and do whatever God intended you to do. You will get a revelation of what Jesus actually completed for us at the cross and how the enemy, the devil, was defeated once and for all. As you become aware of your spiritual authority and position in Christ, you will be able to resist the enemy as his dirty schemes are revealed. You can pray based on the victory Jesus already won for you at the cross.

My Denominational Background

You may be wondering where I stand with regard to denomination and theology. I grew up in a traditional Lutheran church; however, my family were not exactly churchgoers. When I received Jesus at the age of 21, I got involved with "Youth with a Mission" where I got a heart for the nations. After I got married, I started attending a Pentecostal church in Oslo, Norway. I learned how to praise and worship the Lord and to enter into His presence. The gifts of the Spirit flowed freely there as well. As we moved to a different part of town, we transferred to Oslo Christian Center, where the Word of Faith was preached with a strong anointing by our pastor, Åge Åleskjær. Around the year 2000, the revelation of God´s abundant grace took the teaching to a new level. Later, the church became a "Hillsong family" church. I am eternally grateful to Oslo Christian Center for the strong foundation that was built in my life based on the Word of God.

In the Philippines, we are attending an amazing church: New Life Christian Center, led by Pastor Paul and Sister Shoddy Chase (Americans), together with Pastor Mylene and Jocel Evangelista as well as other amazing pastors. This church has what all the other churches had combined, and besides that, the prophetic flow is strong. I love my church!

How to Best Use This Book?

How do you best use this book? It is excellent for small groups, but it works just as well for individuals or couples´ Bible study. The book can also be a great resource for evening Bible classes in churches or training for small group leaders, since it is like a mini Bible school covering 33 different topics. Preachers will also find it helpful to find an overview of so many topics in one book.

If you have a small group or are dreaming of starting one, this book is a lifesaver as it provides 40 ready-to-go sessions with questions for discussion included. After a busy day at work, you don´t have to worry that there is no time to prepare. I have prepared everything for you—it is ready to go!

How to use the lessons with the group is up to you as a leader. In my group, we make it simple; we read the lesson out loud together. I add small testimonies or stories when it is relevant. Surprisingly, the members do not find it boring. They actually love to have the session in front of them and follow the teaching and the Scriptures. They take notes in the margins, and they continue to study the lesson at home. It is also an efficient way of covering the whole session in a short time.

To prepare for the discussion afterwards, I often give them 10-15 minutes by themselves to pray, reflect upon and answer the study questions together with God, which takes the discussions to a higher and deeper level since everyone is prepared to share their thoughts. We do not have any homework in our group; however, it is up to you as a leader if you want your small group to read the lesson ahead of the meeting.

When it comes to time, you can easily fit in one session from this book, including the discussion, into a 2-hour small group meeting. In our group, praise and worship, communion and prayer are always part of our meetings as well, so they tend to last a bit longer.

Another great benefit of *Embraced, Empowered, Equipped* is that the sessions build truth upon truth in the right order so the members of the group can grow steadily over time. Due to this, I recommend following the order of the sessions in the book since the foundation is built gradually throughout the sessions. However, nothing can stop you from picking any session if there is an interest in one particular topic.

Embraced, Empowered, Equipped is suitable for both new and mature Christians. The grace and love of God infiltrating the book will lead all believers closer to God´s heart. The book explains spiritual truths in a simple way so new Christians can follow. At the same time, the more mature Christian will appreciate the new perspectives given on the great variety of topics. The sessions have been tested in small groups consisting of both new believers and more seasoned Christians and have been highly appreciated by everyone.

As you go through the sessions in *Embraced, Empowered, Equipped,* I pray you will experience what the Apostle Paul prays in Ephesians 3:16-19 (New Living Translation):

> *I pray that from his glorious, unlimited resources he will empower you with inner strength through his Spirit. Then Christ will make his home in your hearts as you trust in him. Your roots will grow down into God's love and keep you strong. And may you have the power to understand, as all God's people should, how wide, how long, how high, and how deep his love is. May you experience the love of Christ, though it is too great to understand fully. Then you will be made complete with all the fullness of life and power that comes from God.*

Hilde Lundgaard Grimstad

SESSION 1

God's Eternal Love and Salvation Plan through Christ

THE FOUNDATION OF OUR CHRISTIAN FAITH is the person of Jesus Christ. We know that Jesus was on Earth for around thirty-three years. He lived a life entirely free of sin. At age thirty, He started His ministry after being baptized by John the Baptist and receiving the Holy Spirit. He did great miracles, preached the Gospel to the poor and showed us the love of the Father. He died on the cross where He became the perfect sacrifice for the sin of the world and on the third day, He rose from the dead. Because of Him, salvation is available for us today.

This is a very brief summary of Jesus' life on Earth. But when did Jesus Christ actually begin to exist? Was it when He was born in the manger in Bethlehem around 2000 years ago? No, Christ has existed since the beginning of time, before the universe and the Earth were created. In this session, we will hear the redemption story from the very beginning and see how God´s salvation plan—through Christ—has been a red thread throughout the Bible from the very beginning of time.

Christ Has Existed Since the Beginning of Time

In John 1:1-2, we read, *"In the beginning was the Word, and the Word was with God and the Word was God. He was at the beginning with God."*

Here, Christ is called the Word.

Not only did He exist, but He was also very central in the creation of the world. John 1 continues in verse 3, *"All things were made through Him and without Him nothing was made that was made."*

In Colossians 1:16-17, we read, *"For by Him all things were created that are in heaven and that are on earth, visible and invisible, whether thrones or dominions or principalities or powers. All things were created through Him and for Him."*

In Proverbs, Christ Himself describes how He was in Heaven with the Father during creation.

The Lord possessed me at the beginning of His way,
before His works of old.
I have been established from everlasting,
From the beginning, before there was ever an earth.
When there were no depths, I was brought forth.
When there were no fountains abounding with water.
Before the mountains were settled.
Before the hills, I was brought forth;
While as yet He had not made the earth or the fields,
Or the primal dust of the world.
When He prepared the heavens, I was there.
When He drew a circle on the face of the deep,
When He established the clouds above,
When He strengthened the fountains of the deep
When He assigned the sea to its limit,
So that the waters would not transgress His command,
When He marked out the foundations of the earth,
Then I was beside Him as a master craftsman;
And I was daily in His delight,
Rejoicing always before Him,
Rejoicing in His inhabited world,
And my delight was with the sons of men. (Proverbs 8:22-31)

We see that Christ was there already, and He was beside the Father as a master craftsman when creating everything! In my Norwegian Bible, it says He was an artist.

Christ was also involved when creating human beings, together with the Father and the Holy Spirit. In Genesis 1:26, God says, "*Let us make man in Our own image according to our likeness.*"

Why Did God Create Human Beings?

So why did God create human beings? Was the Trinity not content with being just the three of them: The Father, the Son (Christ) and the Holy Spirit?

The answer to this is in the very character of God, in who He is. God is love (see 1 John 4:8), and because He is love, He wanted someone to love and to have a relationship with. God is all about relationship. God the Father also wanted children; He wanted a family! When He created Adam and Eve, they lived in the Garden of Eden and God walked with them in the Garden. They had fellowship. Adam and Eve lived in a totally innocent spiritual state. Their spirit was alive and connected to God's Spirit.

Human Beings Were Given Free Will and Chose to Sin

God could have created human beings programmed to love Him, but He did not. That would not be a real relationship. It would be like trying to have fellowship with a robot—not very satisfying. Therefore, God created human beings with free will and had to take the risk that He was not going to be loved back.

In the Garden of Eden, Adam and Eve could eat from all of the trees, except for one: the tree of the knowledge of good and evil, which was placed there to give them an actual choice to obey or disobey God. The devil (in the form of a serpent) tempted Eve and both she and Adam ate from the tree. However, God knew from the beginning that this was going to happen. He had taken the risk of giving them free will, and now there was a big problem: Sin had entered Adam and Eve's lives, and through them, sin would enter all of humanity. From that moment, all of mankind would be born as sinners with a sinful nature separated from God. Every person born after Adam would be born into this corrupted state: spiritually dead before they ever did anything right or wrong (see Rom. 5:12,18-19). This is why this story is still so relevant for us today, and we are all in need of salvation!

After eating the forbidden fruit, Adam and Eve felt guilt, shame and condemnation for the first time and hid from God in the Garden where they had earlier enjoyed His presence. Their spirit died inside of them, and their fellowship with God was broken.

God´s Great Salvation Plan Is Put into Action

God still loved Adam and Eve, and He did not want them to remain in this state of sin, guilt and condemnation forever. If they stayed in the Garden of Eden, they could eat of the tree of life, which would leave them in this state for all eternity. For that not to happen, He sent them out of the Garden and closed the access to the tree of life (see Gen. 3:22-24).

This must have been heartbreaking for God. Now He had to put into action His salvation plan to win human beings back. He had planned salvation from the very beginning (see 1 Pet.1:20 and Rev.13:8), and Christ, the Son of God, had volunteered to do the job. Christ was willing to leave the perfection of Heaven to be born into our world as a human being so that He could redeem us. When thinking about this fact, we understand His enormous love for us.

However, it took many years from the time God decided to put a salvation plan into action until Jesus actually came to this Earth. God needed a people from whom Jesus could be born. Around 2000 years before the birth of Jesus, God chose a man called Abraham to become His friend and the father of a people from which Jesus Messiah would descend. God entered into a covenant with Abraham with the promise that he would be the father of many, and in him, all the nations of the Earth would be blessed. God promised Abraham and his wife, Sarah, a son, and they gave birth to Isaac at a very old age. The promise and covenant were passed down through the generations, and the people of Israel became God's chosen people from whom Jesus Messiah was going to be born.

God Reveals His Salvation Plan through His Prophets

Down through the centuries, God spoke to the people of Israel about His salvation plan. The Old Testament has so many prophecies about the Messiah who would come to save the people. These prophecies were given more than 600 years before Christ was born and are so accurate! Let us look at a few examples:

> *For unto us a Child is born, Unto us a Son is given; And the government will be upon His shoulders. And His name will be called Wonderful, Counselor, Mighty God, Everlasting Father, Prince of Peace. (Isaiah 9:6)*

Surely He has borne our griefs
And carried our sorrows;
Yet we esteemed Him stricken,
Smitten by God, and afflicted.
But He was wounded for our transgressions,
He was bruised for our iniquities;
The chastisement for our peace was upon Him,
And by His stripes we are healed. (Isaiah 53:4-5)

(Isaiah 53 is a powerful prophetic description of Jesus' finished work at the cross. You can read the whole chapter in your Bible.)

Psalm 22 describes Jesus´ sufferings when the Father turned His back on Him during the outpouring of judgment upon Jesus for our sins. We will look primarily at verse 1 and 16-18:

My God, My God, why have You forsaken Me?
Why are You so far from helping Me, (Psalm 22:1)

They pierced My hands and My feet;
I can count all My bones.
They look and stare at Me.
They divide My garments among them,
And for My clothing they cast lots. (Psalm 22:16-18)

These prophecies all pointed to the coming of the Messiah (Jesus Christ). In the fullness of time, the great plan of salvation was put into action, and Jesus was born into the world by the virgin, Mary. Jesus did not have any earthly biological father, because He was conceived by the Holy Spirit. He was 100 percent human being and 100 percent God at the same time. He lived His whole life without sin.

The Purpose Why Jesus Came to Earth

What was Jesus´ primary purpose on this planet? It was to bring salvation by taking the punishment for all the sin of all human beings by dying on the cross. To be this perfect sacrifice for our sin, Jesus had to be without sin.

When Jesus hung on the cross, all the wrath of God and all punishment for all sins throughout all of history was poured down on Jesus. Before Jesus died, He cried out, "*It is finished*!" (John 19:30). What had Jesus finished? He had finished paying the price for our sin. On the third day, Jesus rose from the dead. He showed Himself to the disciples and others (around 500 people in total) during the forty days before He was taken up to Heaven. God had fulfilled His salvation plan and won us back through Christ's death on the cross and His resurrection.

Salvation Made Available for Everyone Who Believes and Receives

Now salvation is finished and available for everyone who believes and receives Jesus as his or her personal Lord and Savior. Jesus is the ONLY way to God. He says about Himself that *"I am the way, the truth, and the life. No one comes to the Father except through Me"* (John 14:6). Through salvation, we can receive forgiveness for our sin freely as a gift from God. We can get back into a perfect and intimate relationship with Him and experience His presence! Salvation is made available for every person on the planet, but receiving this salvation is still a matter of free will. Remember God wanted a real relationship, so it is up to us to choose to respond to Him. When we do receive this gift of salvation, we are saved from eternal separation from God and brought into everlasting life.

In John 3:16, it says, *"For God so loved the world that He gave His only begotten Son, that whoever believes in Him should not perish, but have everlasting life."*

In John 1:12-13, it says, *"But as many as received Him, to them He gave the right to become children of God, those who believe in His name: who were born not of blood, nor of the will of the flesh, nor of the will of man, but of God."*

So how do we receive this salvation from Jesus?

> *That if you confess with your mouth the Lord Jesus and believe in your heart that God raised Him from the dead, you will be saved. For with the heart one believes unto righteousness and with the mouth confession is made unto salvation. (Romans 10:9-10)*

Romans 10:13 continues, *"For 'whoever calls on the name of the Lord shall be saved.'"*

Salvation is not earned or achieved through good works, but it is received through faith in Jesus Christ. We just believe in what Christ has done for us and then confess this faith with our mouths. We need to accept Him and invite Him into our hearts. He loves us so much and is waiting for us with open arms. He wants to become our Lord and Savior and have a real love relationship with us.

When we receive salvation, we are not only forgiven for our sin, we are also made righteous; our spirit that was dead becomes alive, and we are "born again"; we become children of God and new creations in Christ Jesus. We receive the nature of God, which is like His DNA, and the Holy Spirit comes to live inside of us. Wow! It is all by grace!

We will talk a lot more about these salvation realities in later sessions. However, we know enough already that we can just rejoice and be so happy about this great salvation God has provided for us.

Ephesians 1 (The Message Bible*) sums it up in a beautiful way.

> *How blessed is God! And what a blessing he is! He's the Father of our Master, Jesus Christ, and takes us to the high places of blessing in him. Long before he laid down earth's foundations, he had us in mind, had settled on us as the focus of his love, to be made whole and holy by his love. Long, long ago he decided to adopt us into his family through Jesus Christ. (What pleasure he took in planning this!) He wanted us to enter into the celebration of his lavish gift–giving by the hand of his beloved Son.*
>
> *Because of the sacrifice of the Messiah, his blood poured out on the altar of the Cross, we're a free people—free of penalties and punishments chalked up by all our misdeeds. And not just barely free, either. Abundantly free! He thought of everything, provided for everything we could possibly need, letting us in on the plans he took such delight in making. He set it all out before us in Christ, a long–range plan in which everything would be brought together and summed up in him, everything in deepest heaven, everything on planet earth.*
>
> *It's in Christ that we find out who we are and what we are living for. Long before we first heard of Christ and got our hopes up, he had his eye on us, had designs on us for glorious living, part of the overall purpose he is working out in everything and everyone.*
>
> *It's in Christ that you, once you heard the truth and believed it (this Message of your salvation), found yourselves home free—signed, sealed, and delivered by the Holy Spirit. This signet from God is the first installment on what's coming, a reminder that we'll get everything God has planned for us, a praising and glorious life. (Ephesians 1:1-14 MSG)*

Salvation Prayer

If you want to receive Jesus as your Lord and Savior, you can do that by praying the prayer underneath or you can pray by using your own words. The important thing is that you mean it from your heart.

> *Lord Jesus, I believe that you are the Son of God, that you died on the cross for my salvation, that you rose from the dead and that you live today. I thank you so much that you took the punishment for all my sins. I repent of my sins and receive this gift of salvation today, and I ask you to come into my heart and become my Lord and Savior. Lead me into a personal relationship with you. Thank you, Jesus AMEN!*

If you prayed this prayer for the first time, you are now a new believer in Jesus Christ—a brand new Christian. Welcome to the family of God! In the sessions to come, you will learn a lot about Jesus and the Kingdom of God that will build a strong foundation for your faith in Him!

(*The Message Bible is a Bible Translation in contemporary language which focuses on the meaning of the content instead of being correct word by word. This is an excellent supplement to a Bible like the New King James or New International Version, which are concerned with the actual words by words in the original Bible texts.)

FOR SELF REFLECTION AND GROUP DISCUSSION

> *For all have sinned and fall short of the glory of God, being justified freely by His grace through the redemption that is in Christ Jesus, (Romans 3:23-24)*

1. We all need Jesus for our salvation. Some people consider themselves to be good people, or at least not worse than others. They don't see the need of a Savior. Do you find yourself in this category? Even though you are a good person, you cannot reach up to God's standard of righteousness. You can do this only through receiving Jesus' righteousness by grace. You might find this hard to understand, but you still want God in your life. You feel a need for a deeper meaning, peace and purpose in your life. You can come to Jesus and receive Him just as you are even though you don´t understand.

"But as many as received Him, to them He gave the right to become children of God" (John 1:12)

You can receive Jesus as your Savior right now by praying the prayer of salvation at the end of Session 1.

2. We learned in this session that Christ existed before the Earth was created and that we can read about Him throughout the Old Testament, not only in the New Testament. Were you aware of this before this session? Did your perspective change?

3. Jesus says that He is the ONLY way to God. This means that no other religion can save you, and no spiritual practices that are not based on Jesus as the only Savior can bring you close to God and give you eternal life. What is your reaction to Jesus´ statement? Talk about it in the group.

   Jesus said to him, "I am the way, the truth, and the life. No one comes to the Father except through Me." (John 14:6)

4. The redemption story testifies of God's great love for us. He was willing to give His only Son, Jesus, to die for us and take upon Himself all the punishment for our sin because that was the only way we could be saved. We can receive salvation freely by grace through faith. Meditate on the fact that Jesus has done everything needed for your salvation, so all you have to do is believe and receive. You do not have to try to fix yourself before you come to God.

   SHARE AND DISCUSS WITH THE GROUP

SESSION 2

Introduction to the Bible Part 1

The Background and History of the Bible[1]

OUR CHRISTIAN FAITH is based on the Bible, which we believe is the inspired Word of God. The Bible consists of sixty-six books and letters written by more than forty authors over 1500 years. It is incredible to see the consistency of the message across these books. They don´t contradict each other but, rather, support and supplement each other. The prophesies and foreshadows of the coming Messiah are shining brightly throughout the many books. Only by the inspiration of the Holy Spirit could this be possible.

The Old Testament consists of thirty-nine books and was mainly written in Hebrew with a small part in Aramaic. The Old Testament books are estimated to be written between 1500-1400 BC and 400 BC, and already in 300 BC, they were collected and recognized as official canonical books called the Hebrew Bible, which is what Jesus refers to as the Scriptures in the Gospels.

The New Testament was written during the first century AD. Many letters were circulating in the early church, and not all of them were authentic. The twenty-seven books and letters we find in the New Testament were carefully authenticated and selected by the Council of Nicea in 325 AD and the First Council of Constantinople in 381 AD, based on strict criteria. They had to be apostolic, meaning they had to be written by one of Jesus´ disciples, an eyewitness to Jesus´ ministry or someone like Luke who had interviewed eyewitnesses. Only books and letters written in the first century AD were accepted; they had to be consistent with other parts of Scripture, and they had to be commonly used by the early church before 200 AD.

In 381 AD, they decided on the list of books that were officially accepted as "divinely inspired" to rightfully belong in the Bible and hence to be the only authoritative Word of God. These were called the "Canon of Scriptures."

Around 405 AD, the first edition of the Bible was completed, assembled and translated to Latin by Saint Jerome. This was called the Vulgate and became the Bible translation of the Roman Catholic Church. Already by 500-600 AD, several translations to other languages were completed e.g., Old Nubian (Southern Egypt and Northern Sudan), Coptic, Georgian, the ancient South Semitic language Ge´ek, Gothic and Syriac (a dialect of Armenian). However, the Roman Catholic Church insisted that Latin was the only accepted Bible language, and their claim lasted for almost 1000 years. Only the ordained priests were allowed to read from the Bible (in Latin), and the people were not even allowed to own a Bible, which, of course, meant that they had little knowledge of what the Scriptures actually said. In this way, the Word of God was held captive. There were monks and others who translated parts of the Bible, but the translation of the whole Bible to English only started in 1381-1382 AD with John Wycliffe and associates who, in opposition to the Roman Catholic Church, had a firm conviction that all people should be permitted to read the Bible in their own language.

The printing press made it possible to print Bibles and distribute them widely. In 1455 AD, the first Bible was printed: a Latin Vulgate. New Testaments in Hebrew and Greek were printed early 1500 AD, and full Bible translations were ready for print in French, German (Martin Luther) and English (Tyndale and Coverdale) from 1530-1536, which was part of the ongoing reformation. In 1539, the Great Bible was printed, which was the first English Bible authorized for public use. Not until 1582, did the Roman Catholic church drop its claim of the Latin Vulgate being the exclusive authority as the Bible, and in the meantime, Bible translators were persecuted. Tyndale was, for instance, strangled and burnt on a pole. Ordinary people were persecuted as well just for owning a Bible, and tons of Bibles were burnt by the church authorities. There are many more details to this story. This is only a brief summary of what happened. We can, however, conclude that many brave men and women paid a high price for us to have the Bible in our own languages, and we are forever grateful.

Today, we have several Bible translations for most languages. In our Bible study, you will see that we refer to several of the English translations but mainly the New King James version. The New International Version (NIV), New Living Translation (NLT) and The Message Bible (MSG) are easier to understand with a more contemporary language; however, the Message Bible differs as it focuses on presenting the message of the original text and is not translated word by word like the others. The Amplified Classic Bible (AMPC) explains within the text what certain words mean since there is not one word in English that covers the meaning of the Greek or Hebrew word in the original text. All the translations are considered to be the Word of God, and for us to see the full meaning of a particular Scripture, it can be helpful to compare the different translations. In our digital age, we can have them all in an app on our smartphones.

The Importance of the Word of God in Our Lives

We are so blessed to have the Bible—the Word of God—in our own language. Less than 500 years ago, the public had no access to the Bible.

The Bible is an amazing book. It is like it is multi-layered; you can read it over and over again and see something new each time. Sometimes specific words just stand out on the page and speak to you in a particular way. This is the Holy Spirit who lights up precisely what He wants to say to you from the Word (this is called a *Rhema word*). In general, we need to read the Bible with the help of the Holy Spirit. The Spirit will make the Word come alive and help us understand the meaning of the Scriptures.

What does the Bible say about itself? Firstly, it tells us that the Word of God is powerful. God created the universe with His spoken Word. In the same way, the Word of God is powerful to us.

> *For the word of God is living and powerful, and sharper than any two-edged sword, piercing even to the division of soul and spirit, and of joints and marrow, and is a discerner of the thoughts and intents of the heart. (Hebrews 4:12)*

When we read the Word and believe it, it has the power to transform us. It is a living Word. When reading the Bible throughout the years, I have found many "power verses" that I have underlined and many that I have learned by heart. When we meditate on verses in the Bible and learn them by heart, the Holy Spirit can remind us of the Scriptures when we need them. We can speak them out loud to ourselves, and they help us in particular situations we are facing. The Word of God encourages us and gives us wisdom and guidance. The Word will also transform us to become more and more like Jesus.

For example:

- If you are worried and anxious, meditate on Philippians 4:4-7
- If you are afraid, read Isaiah 41:10
- If you are tired and worn out, read Isaiah 40:28-31

Psalm 119:105 says, *"Your word is a lamp to my feet and a light to my path."* The Word of God will show you what to do and give you direction.

When the enemy (the devil) comes to accuse or attack us, the Word of God is our weapon to fight back; it is our sword.

> *Finally, my brethren, be strong in the Lord and in the power of His might. Put on the whole armor of God, that you may be able to stand against the wiles of the devil.... And take the helmet of salvation, and the sword of the Spirit, which is the word of God; (Ephesians 6:10-11,17)*

In Matthew 4:1-11, you can read how Jesus used Scriptures to fight back against the devil when He was tempted in the wilderness after His baptism.

We can see that the Word of God is vital for us as Christians. Along with worship and prayer, the Word of God is a daily source of refreshment and strength for our lives. It teaches us who God is, who we are in Christ and what His will for us is. We have fellowship with Him through His Word.

An important question, however, is how we read the Word of God. It is such a big book, and it can be quite confusing at times.

In 2 Timothy 3:16-17, it says, *"All Scripture is given by inspiration of God, and is profitable for doctrine, for reproof, for correction, for instruction in righteousness, that the man of God may be complete, thoroughly equipped for every good work."*

In 2 Timothy 2:15, it says, *"Be diligent to present yourself approved to God, a worker who does not need to be ashamed, rightly dividing the word of truth."*

While 2 Timothy 3:16 tells us that all Scripture is profitable for us, 2 Timothy 2:15 says that it is essential for us to divide the word of truth rightly. The Amplified Bible Classic says, *"correctly analyzing and accurately dividing [rightly handling and skillfully teaching] the Word of Truth."*

It is, therefore, essential to have some knowledge about the Bible when you read it. In the rest of this session and in the next session, you will get a brief introduction to the books in both the New and the Old Testament, and you will learn how to read, understand and interpret the Scriptures.

Presentation of the New Testament

The New Testament starts with the four Gospels. They are followed by Acts, twenty-one letters called the Epistles and ends with the Book of Revelation prophesying about the End Times. Let us take a closer look at the different parts of the New Testament.

The Four Gospels

The four Gospels are the Gospel of Matthew, Mark, Luke and John. In the Gospels, we read about the life, ministry and teachings of Jesus on planet Earth: His miracles, His suffering, His death on the cross and the resurrection. Matthew, Luke and Mark write about many of the same things, but from different angles. In these three Gospels, we find the many parables Jesus told to explain the Kingdom of Heaven. They are called the synoptic Gospels since they follow a similar synopsis or outline and use many of the same words and order; hence, they are easy to compare. The Gospel of John is very different from the others as the majority of its content is not found in the other Gospels. John's focus is to reflect on the meaning of Jesus as the divine Son of God.

Acts

This is a story starting with Jesus going to Heaven after His resurrection. Jesus tells His disciples to do nothing until they receive the Holy Spirit. On the Day of Pentecost, the disciples are all baptized in the Holy Spirit, and the church is born. Then we read about the ministry of the disciples and the growth of the church. Furthermore, we learn about Paul who becomes the apostle to the Gentiles and his many mission trips to other countries to spread the Gospel and plant churches.

Paul is the one that receives the revelation from Jesus of the spiritual realities after the cross. Everything changed with Jesus' sacrifice for sin at the cross and His resurrection. We entered into the New Covenant.

On the Apostle Paul's mission trips, he plants churches in many cities in the area around the Mediterranean Sea. Paul writes letters to these churches where he encourages and instructs them as well as teaches them about the life and spiritual truths of the New Covenant.

14 Letters Written by the Apostle Paul

Romans

1 Corinthians

2 Corinthians

Galatians

Ephesians

Philippians

Colossians

1 Thessalonians

2 Thessalonians

1 Timothy

2 Timothy

Titus

Philemon

Hebrews (Many scholars believe it was written by the Apostle Paul)

Other Letters

James

1 Peter

2 Peter

1 John

2 John

3 John

Jude

Most of these letters were sent to one particular church (or person), but they were copied by hand and sent around to all the different churches in the area. The letters address specific situations in the particular church (or person's life), but most of what is written can be used as general enlightenment and instruction for all believers.

Book of Revelation

The New Testament ends with the Book of Revelation, which is a prophetic book about the End times and Jesus coming back to Earth. This is a complicated book to understand, and you might need some help to interpret it. However, what we can be sure of is that since Jesus wins, we win!

In the next session, we will look into the Old Testament and also at general guidelines for interpreting Scripture.

FOR SELF REFLECTION AND GROUP DISCUSSION

1. If you are not familiar with the Bible, open it and find the New Testament with the books presented in this session. It is in the last part of the Bible. If needed, help each other in the group.

2. Think about situations in your life where you need to find promises from God in the Bible that you can hold on to in faith. Share it with the group and help each other to find the Scriptures you need. Learn these by heart and make them your "power verses." If you do not know any verses, you can use the Scriptures presented in this session (Philippians 4:4-7; Isaiah 41:10, 40:28-31).

3. We learned that the Word of God can be our weapon against the enemy (a sword, see Ephesians 6:17). Read Matthew 4:1-11 to see and learn how Jesus uses Scriptures as His weapon to defend Himself when He is tempted by Satan in the wilderness. Also, take notice of how the enemy (the devil) abuses and twists Scripture to try to trick Jesus.

4. Think about and discuss how you can make it a daily habit to read the Bible. The Gospels are a great place to start reading for new believers.

SHARE AND DISCUSS WITH THE GROUP

SESSION 3

Introduction to the Bible Part 2

TO UNDERSTAND THE BIBLE in general, you need to understand the concept of "covenant." A covenant is an agreement, and what makes the Bible covenants special is that God Himself is one of the parties in the covenant. Biblical covenants have three parts[2]:

- a statement about what God brings to the agreement
- a statement about what God expects from humanity in response
- a sign or symbol as a reminder of the covenant

The first covenant in the Old Testament is God's covenant with Adam and Eve and through them with all humanity. God appoints human beings to have dominion over the Earth and be stewards of all creation (see Gen. 1:26, 28).

Secondly, God makes a covenant with the Earth and with Noah, where He promises to never again destroy the Earth with a great flood (see Gen. 9:8-17).

The next covenant is fundamental: the ABRAHAMIC COVENANT (between God and Abraham, the father of faith, and his descendants). In the Abrahamic covenant, one of God's promises is to bless Abraham and to bless all nations on the Earth through him. This blessing is the salvation that will come one day in the future to all nations through the Messiah (see Gen. 12:1-3, 22:15-18). God promises Abraham that he will have as many descendants as the stars in the sky, that he will be a father of many nations and that his descendants will get the land of Canaan as their possession (see Gen. 13:14-18, 15:18-21, 17:4-8). The Abrahamic covenant is unconditional and eternal, and it is passed down to Abraham's son Isaac and grandson Jacob. God repeats the same promises to them as He had given to Abraham (see Gen. 26:2-5, 28:12-15).

The next significant covenant in the Old Testament is the covenant of the Law of Moses (the Old Covenant), where Moses receives the Ten Commandments from God on Mount Sinai. Under the Old Covenant, righteousness had to be earned by following the Law 100 percent, which, of course, nobody could do. Animals were sacrificed repeatedly in the tabernacle and later in the temple to cover the sins of the people. This covenant was based on performance, which meant that there were blessings that followed the people´s obedience to the Law and curses that followed their disobedience. You can read about this in Deuteronomy 28:1-68.

God knew that nobody would be able to keep the Law perfectly; in fact, this is one of the very reasons that the Law was given—to show mankind that we have fallen short and are in desperate need of a Savior (see Rom. 3:19-20).

> *But before faith came, we were kept under guard by the law, kept for the faith which would afterward be revealed. Therefore, the law was our tutor to bring us to Christ, that we might be justified by faith. But after faith has come, we are no longer under a tutor. (Galatians 3:23-25)*

God's plan all along was to send us a Savior—His own Son, Jesus Christ. The Old Covenant was temporary and was replaced by the New Covenant of grace. In this covenant, God puts His law in our hearts and writes it in our minds (see Heb. 10:16).

In John 1:17, we read, *"For the law was given through Moses, but grace and truth came through Jesus Christ."*

In the New Testament, Jesus is called "the Lamb," and He was the perfect sacrifice, paying the penalty for our sins once and for all so that today we can receive eternal forgiveness and redemption. Jesus could be the perfect sacrifice for our sins because He had fulfilled the Law on our behalf by living totally free from sin. In 2 Corinthians 5:21, it says, *"For He made Him (Jesus) who knew no sin to be sin for us, that we might become the righteousness of God in Him."*

The blood of Jesus Christ freed us from the curses we see in the Old Testament, which came upon those who were disobedient. When reading the curses in

Deuteronomy 28:15-68, we should be pleased about that. In Galatians, we read this relieving truth:

> *Christ has redeemed us from the curse of the law, having become a curse for us (for it is written, "Cursed is everyone who hangs on a tree"), that the blessing of Abraham might come upon the Gentiles in Christ Jesus, that we might receive the promise of the Spirit through faith." (Galatians 3:13-14)*

Reading the Bible Based on the Understanding of Covenants

The New Covenant and the new spiritual realities started after Jesus had died on the cross and was resurrected. This means that the Old Covenant was still valid when Jesus was walking around teaching, ministering and doing miracles on Earth. This is surprising to many since Jesus´ life is recorded in the New Testament. Yet, why is this important to understand? It is important to understand when we read the Gospels. In the Gospels, Jesus is still speaking to people living under the Old Covenant Law. He is talking to Jews, and often He is speaking in a furious manner to the Pharisees (religious leaders of the time). When the Gentiles wanted a miracle from Him, He was often reluctant to give it to them because they were not supposed to be included in the Kingdom of God until after the cross. However, Jesus knew that salvation and healing would soon be available to everyone, so He gave the persistent Gentiles a taste of the Kingdom of God, which was about to break forth for all people. The Holy Spirit will help us understand when Jesus is teaching concerning the limitation and end of the Old Covenant and when He points to the New Covenant that would soon come.[3] When reading the Gospels, we need to check the context of the passage and whom Jesus is speaking to.

When we as Christians today read the Old Testament, we always need to remember what Jesus did for us at the cross. We have learned that in parts of the Old Testament God speaks to people who lived under the Law of Moses (the Old Covenant), which was during a time before Jesus had come. The Old Covenant was replaced with the New Covenant when Jesus died on the cross and rose again. After the cross, we entered into a new era: into "the age (or dispensation) of grace," which lasts until Jesus returns. In this era, and in light of the atonement, there is no more judgment, anger or curses from God. When we read about these things in the Old Testament, we can know that this does not relate to us. Jesus took all the judgment, punishment, anger and curses for us at the cross. (However, when Jesus returns, those who have not received salvation will experience the judgment and wrath from God for their sin.)

On the contrary, we can see a lot of promises in the Old Testament, which had as a precondition that the people should obey. For us in Christ there is no precondition to taking part in God's promises; we just believe in the promises and partake of them by faith. All God´s promises are YES and AMEN in Jesus Christ (see 2 Cor. 1:19).

However, the principle of sowing and reaping will always be at work as we see in Genesis 8:22: "'*While the earth remains, seedtime and harvest, cold and heat, winter and summer, and day and night shall not cease.*'" This means that if somebody chooses to live in sin, he or she will reap the consequences, not in the form of God's punishment, but sin in itself has consequences.

As we learned in Session 1, we need to understand the heart of God when we read the Old Testament and see Jesus as a red thread through these books: His salvation plan and great love for us.

Below is a very brief introduction to the books in the Old Testament (not complete) and some guidance on how to read them.

Presentation of the Old Testament

The Pentateuch: The Law

The first five books in the Old Testament are called the "Torah" or the Law, meaning "teachings" (Genesis, Exodus, Leviticus, Numbers and Deuteronomy). These books are written by Moses and are based on the idea of covenant.[2] *GENESIS* starts out with creation and continues with the first period of human beings´ history on Earth until the story of a man called Joseph. In *EXODUS*, you read about Moses and the people of Israel´s escape from slavery in Egypt. Exodus also describes how Moses received the stone tablets with the Ten Commandments at Mt. Sinai. *LEVITICUS* is about the holiness of the people of Israel and the laws regulating their lives and worship. *NUMBERS* is about the people of Israel in their forty years wandering in the wilderness, as well as the miracles of Moses and finally how they prepare to enter the land, which God had promised to give them as their possession. *DEUTERONOMY* is Moses' farewell speech before the tribes enter this promised land, which is the territory of current-day Israel.

History Books

The history books are the books of *JOSHUA, JUDGES, RUTH, 1 AND 2 SAMUEL, 1* and *2 KINGS, 1* and *2 CHRONICLES, EZRA, NEHEMIAH* and *ESTHER.* In these books, you can read stories about the people of Israel entering the promised land and what happened in the hundreds of years that followed. These are quite interesting stories. Be aware that even though these stories are in the Bible, it doesn't mean that God approves of the behavior of the different characters. These stories are just told as they happened.

Poetry and Wisdom

JOB – This book must be read with some guidance since some things Job says in his misery in this book, he takes back in the end, seeing that he was wrong.

BOOK OF PSALMS – There are 150 psalms. Seventy-three of them are written by David, who eventually became the King of Israel. They are very personal and reflect his life in sorrow and joy, battles and victory. They are excellent readings! Psalm 23 is a must-read! (*The Lord is my shepherd...*) It is beautiful to see in the Book of Psalms how David praises and worships God through all of his difficult circumstances.

PROVERBS – This is a book of wisdom written by King Solomon who was the wisest man on planet Earth (see 1 Kings 10:23). Proverbs contain a lot of advice for successful living and warnings for daily life. It is excellent and relevant reading for our lives today.

ECCLESIASTES – This book is also written by King Solomon but take notice of the fact, that he wrote it when he was old and did not adequately serve God anymore but, rather, the gods of his many wives (see 1 Kings 11). He describes how empty and meaningless life is, which refers to his life distant from God. There are still some profound passages in Ecclesiastes but also many passages that relate to his poor spiritual state. The latter is not meant for us to apply to our lives if we live with God!

SONG OF SOLOMON – This is a poetic book of love, which can be seen not only as Solomon´s love for a particular woman but also as an allegory of the love between Christ and His Bride, which is us—His church!

Prophetic Books

In the Old Testament, God spoke to the people through prophets. The prophets spoke into specific situations to the people of Israel and many times warned them of impending judgment because they had left their faith in God and turned to false gods. There are a lot of prophecies about the coming Messiah as well. We need to know <u>whom</u> the prophets are speaking to when we read this as well as the <u>context</u>, and not take it as a word of judgment on ourselves. There are, however, some beautiful passages with great encouraging words we can use for ourselves in between.

The prophetic books were written around 875-500 BC.

THE MAJOR PROPHETIC BOOKS: Isaiah, Jeremiah, Lamentations, Ezekiel and Daniel

THE TWELVE MINOR PROPHETIC BOOKS: Hosea, Joel, Amos, Obadiah, Jonah, Micah, Nahum, Habakkuk, Zephaniah, Haggai, Zechariah and Malachi

Important Guidelines for Bible Interpretation

When we read the Bible, we need to make sure we wear the "eyeglasses of the New Covenant."[3] This means that when we read the Old Testament, we must take into consideration that Jesus has already done everything necessary for our salvation. If we read in the Old Testament about certain things that we need to do to become righteous, we know that does not apply to us. We have received the righteousness of Christ by grace through faith alone. If we read in the Old Testament about certain conditions that we need to fulfill to receive the promises or blessings of God, then we know that in the New Covenant "*all God's promises are yes and amen in Jesus*" (2 Corinthians 1:20). We receive them by grace.

There are some general guidelines we should use when we read the Bible. In her beautiful book *Living the Better Covenant,* Mary Felde suggests these following guidelines[3]:

1. Let Scripture interpret Scripture (e.g., John 15:12 explains John 15:10).
2. Read the context (the full and immediate context).
3. Read the meaning out of the Scripture, not into the Scripture.

4. Be consistent to the selected type of interpretation throughout the Scripture (for example, if a lamb is a type of redemption in the first part of the Bible, then it will also be the type of redemption in the last part).
5. Two or three witnesses are necessary to make a doctrine (a doctrine cannot be made out of a single verse in the Bible).
6. Study to whom a Scripture is written and what time it is written about.
7. Take notice how the finished work of Jesus affects the way we interpret the whole Scripture.

ASK THESE QUESTIONS WHEN YOU READ: Who speaks? To whom is it expressed? What is spoken about? What is the context and situation? How do we understand it in the light of Jesus' finished work on the cross?

For the right interpretation of the Scriptures, it is essential to grasp the intention of what is written. To get the full understanding, we need to know the cultural and historical background of the people it is spoken to. A helpful tool for this is the "IVP Bible Background Commentary"[4] (for both NT and OT), which describes the cultural and historical background for every single passage in the whole Bible.

A Study Bible can be handy when you read as it will give you some explanations in the comments section on the bottom of the page. You can also download study guides and other Bible applications on your electronic devices. Many of these Bibles include references linking to Scriptures speaking on the same topic, which can be very helpful. They usually also contain a paragraph or more at the beginning of each book, describing its content and context.

There are many Bible reading plans you can follow, and many of them will take you through the whole Bible in one year. This can be a good thing; however, you will be spending a lot of time in the Old Testament since it is much bigger than the New Testament.

If you are a first-time Bible reader, I recommend you start by reading through the whole New Testament as well as the Book of Psalms and Proverbs.

It can also be good to develop some kind of routine for your Bible reading to help you read consistently. Just as your body needs food each day, your inner man needs the Word of God each day.

FOR SELF REFLECTION AND GROUP DISCUSSION

1. If you are not familiar with the Old Testament, open your Bible and find the different books mentioned in this session. Get an idea of how the Old Testament is structured. Help each other in the group if necessary.
2. Have you read parts of the Old Testament and gotten confused or scared by what you read, due to warnings and curses mentioned there? Make sure you understand that curses and judgments are not for you as a Christian who lives after Jesus died on the cross.
3. Practice using these questions when you read a text in the Bible: Who speaks? To whom is it spoken? What is spoken about? What is the context and situation? Is this before or after the cross? How do we understand it in the light of Jesus´ finished work on the cross?

SHARE AND DISCUSS WITH THE GROUP

SESSION 4

The Character and Heart of God

MORE THAN ANYTHING, God wants us to get to know Him personally. He wants to have an intimate relationship with each one of us. We get to know Him more and more as we spend time with Him, study His Word, receive His love and listen to what He has to say to us through the Holy Spirit, the Word, creation itself and through our many experiences with Him.

Knowing the heart of God and His character is so important as it affects how we look at ourselves and our relationship with Him. It is also crucial when it comes to how we look at the world around us and how we see other people—both believers and non-believers.

God´s character and heart is a vast topic, but we will focus on three main things in this session:

- God is good.
- God is our Father—we are His children.
- God is love, and He loves the world.

God is Good

Oh, taste and see that the Lord is good; (Psalm 34:8a)
For your goodness and love pursue me all the days of my life. (Psalm 23:6 TPT)

God is good and only good. He wants the best for His children and for the world. Many people think that God is behind disasters, wanting to punish a city or a country. Even insurance companies call disasters an "Act of God." Often, even Christians have claimed that this is God´s punishment for sin in a specific place. This is a big misunderstanding. God is not behind such things. He is not in this time and age punishing and judging cities, nations or people.

Yes, God is a just and righteous God, and in the Old Testament, we see Him many times judging and punishing the people of Israel. (They were punished because they broke the Law they had agreed to follow.) I think this is why many Christians get confused because they see God´s actions in the Old Testament and find it hard to reconcile these actions with a loving God. When people were rebellious, disobedient and worshiping idols in the Old Testament, God sent prophets to warn them and tell them to change their ways, but they did not listen. God could not deny His character of being righteous and just, and so there had to be punishment for sin. Before the cross, people were punished by God for their actions; however, then Jesus came and fulfilled the Law. He took all the sin and all the punishment of the whole world on Himself at the cross. All of God's anger against sin was poured out on Jesus. After the cross, there is no more anger, judgment or punishment of sin from God´s side (in this period called "the dispensation of grace," which lasts until Jesus returns).

> *For God so loved the world that He gave His only begotten Son, that whoever believes in Him should not perish but have everlasting life. For God did not send His Son into the world to condemn the world, but that the world through Him might be saved. (John 3:16-17)*

This is the core of the Gospel. However, so many Christians have not understood this. They think that God is still in the punishing and judgment business today. What they do not realize is that a New Covenant replaced the Old Covenant when Jesus died at the cross and was resurrected. The human race was reconciled to God. There is now peace between God and the world. We are living in the New Covenant of grace.

> *All this is from God, who reconciled us to himself through Christ and gave us the ministry of reconciliation: that God was reconciling the world to himself in Christ, not counting people's sins against them. And he has committed to us the message of reconciliation. We are therefore Christ's ambassadors, as though God were making his appeal through us. We im-*

plore you on Christ's behalf: Be reconciled to God. (2 Corinthians 5:18-20 New International Version)

So, God is not judging the world in this time period. He is in the business of reaching out to people, seeking and saving the lost. He wants the whole world to come to Him since Jesus has already paid the price for their reconciliation. This is our message to the world. God does not hate the world; God loves the world. We should not hate the world or curse the world or people around us. We need to look past sin and see the person behind it. That is what Jesus did. He always took time for the worst sinners, and through His love and goodness, they were transformed.

One day there will be a judgment day, which is one specific day in the future when all people must give account to God for their lives. However, we currently live in the age (dispensation) of grace, when salvation is freely offered to all. For believers, judgment day will not be about Heaven or Hell, since we are saved by the blood of Jesus but, rather, about our reward for being good or bad stewards of our lives, purpose and gifts.

God is good. He wants us to live in health and prosperity. He wants us to be blessed. Many Christians also believe that God is giving people sickness to teach them a lesson or keep them humble. This is so wrong! God is good, and He does not want anyone to be sick. That is why Jesus provided healing as well as salvation at the cross. He does not want anyone to be poor either. Poverty and lack are a curse. God wants us to be blessed and have more than enough so that we can bless others and have more than enough for our own needs.

Many people choose to stay away from God since the message they have heard is that He is judging and punishing people with disasters. They think He is putting sickness on people and wants people to be poor—all to keep them humble. This is far from the truth about who God is.

Besides that, God has been perceived as someone who is condemning of everything that is fun and pleasing: dancing, theatre, movies, sex... a real killjoy. This is not who God is. He is the One who provides for all of these things. God created everything for our pleasure; however, certain things are to be used within God-given boundaries for our own protection.

Even creation itself displays the goodness of God. He could have created the world in black and white, with no colors. He could have made everything very functional. Instead, He created beauty—all different species of flowers, fish, birds and animals with all kinds of shapes, sizes, patterns and colors. He gave us taste buds and made eating a pleasure and a time for fellowship. He designed nature with its seasons, beautiful romantic sunsets, mountains and oceans. All of these things are witnesses of His goodness and majesty.

God Is a Father

In the Old Testament, God was distant from the people. Only a few people came close to God, like Moses, the prophets, David, the patriarchs, Joseph, Daniel, etc. Even though God was called a father in the Old Testament at times, He was a distant father. When Jesus came, it was revolutionary that He called God Abba (Daddy) Father and Himself the Son of God. The people actually thought it was blasphemy.

> *Therefore, the Jews sought all the more to kill Him, because He not only broke the Sabbath but also said that God was His Father, making Himself equal with God. (John 5:18)*

When Jesus made peace between humans and God at the cross, we could become children of God and God could finally have the close and intimate relationship He was longing for with human beings. When we were born again, He became our Abba Father—our Daddy God. Let us look at some Scriptures:

> *But as many as received Him, to them He gave the right to become <u>children of God</u>, to those who believe in His name: (John 1:12)*

> *Behold what manner of love the Father has bestowed on us, that we should be called <u>children of God</u>! Therefore, the world does not know us, because it did not know Him. Beloved, now we are <u>children of God</u>; and it has not yet been revealed what we shall be, but we know that when He is revealed, we shall be like Him, for we shall see Him as He is. (1 John 3:1-2)*

Being a daughter or son of God is the most important identity we have in Christ. This is who we are and has nothing to do with what we do. We are part of the family of God by grace through faith. We need to rest in the assurance of the fact that we are children of God, no matter what. He is our Father, and He is a good Father whom we can have a close relationship with.

> *"But I will tell you plainly about the Father. In that day you will ask in My name, and I do not say to you that I shall pray the Father for you; for the*

Father Himself loves you, because you have loved Me, and have believed that I came forth from God. I came forth from the Father and have come into the world. Again, I leave the world and go to the Father." (John 16:25b-28)

And because you are sons, God has sent forth the Spirit of His Son into your hearts, crying out, "Abba, Father!" Therefore, you are no longer a slave but a son, and if a son, then an heir of God through Christ. (Galatians 4:6-7)

As children, we are also heirs. All the promises of God are ours. The Kingdom of God is ours. We are co-heirs with Christ!

In the New Testament and especially in the letters of Paul, Peter, John, etc., God is often referred to as God the Father. Thinking about God as Father may be difficult for some of you, because you start comparing God with your earthly father. Some of us had good earthly fathers while some of us did not. Maybe you had a father who made you feel like you were never good enough. Maybe your father was violent, absent, never had time for you or made you feel insignificant or unimportant. Our earthly fathers definitely have their limitations and shortcomings, but this is not the kind of father God is.

Our Heavenly Father is perfect. He is always faithful and will never leave you nor forsake you. He always pays attention to you and always wants to spend time with you. He wants to hear what is on your heart and mind, and He always hears your prayers. He has your best interests in mind and has good plans for you. He wants to provide for you and take care of you. He will always work all things together for good for you (see Rom. 8:28). Sometimes, He will correct you but always in a loving way, which will bring forth good fruit. He always receives you with open arms. If you have messed up and fallen into sin, He is waiting for you to come running to Him, so He can help you back on your feet. He never condemns you (see Rom. 8:1). You can tell Him what you did wrong and that you are sorry; then you thank Him for Jesus´ finished work on the cross, where your sin was already punished and taken care of. You can know that you are forgiven by the Father. What a good, good Father!

God Is Love

God is good, and He is a good Father because He is love.

He who does not love does not know God, for God is love. (1 John 4:8)

We see that God not only has love, but He is love. Love is the heart of God and the character of God. He loves His children, but not only His children: He loves the whole world, as we read in John 3:16, "*For God so loved the world...*" When we are children of God and the Holy Spirit lives in us, we too are to love one another and we are to love the world as God loves the world.

Let us read these verses in 1 John 4:7-11:

> *Beloved, let us love one another, for love is of God; and everyone who loves is born of God and knows God. He who does not love does not know God, for God is love. In this the love of God was manifested toward us, that God has sent His only begotten Son into the world, that we might live through Him. In this is love, not that we loved God, but that He loved us and sent His Son to be the propitiation for our sins. Beloved, if God so loved us, we also ought to love one another.*

Verse ten says that in this is love that He loved us first, not that we loved Him! When we know that He loves us so much, we are empowered to love one another.

> *No one has seen God at any time. If we love one another, God abides in us, and His love has been perfected in us. (1 John 4:12)*

> *Whoever confesses that Jesus is the Son of God, God abides in him, and he in God. And we have known and believed the love that God has for us. God is love, and he who abides in love abides in God, and God in him. (1 John 4:15-16)*

The Gospel of John also speaks about us abiding in God and His love. Let us read:

> *As the Father loved Me, I also have loved you; abide in My love. If you keep My commandments, you will abide in My love, just as I have kept My Father's commandments and abide in His love. These things I have spoken to you, that My joy may remain in you, and that your joy may be full. This is My commandment, that you love one another as I have loved you. (John 15:9-12)*

You may be thinking, "But I do not have this love." However, the Scripture says that "*the love of God has been poured out in our hearts by the Holy Spirit who was given to us*" (Romans 5:5). We can trust and lean on this source of love that is already in us. Loving is a decision. Just like when we turn on the tap and water flows out—when we turn on our love tap, love will flow out of us.

So, now we know that God is love and that we are to love one another. But what about the world around us? "There is so much sin. People do such bad things. Should we love them too?" The answer is, "Absolutely." We read earlier that God so loved the world, not only those who are believers. We also read earlier that *"God was in Christ reconciling the world to Himself, not imputing their trespasses to them, and has committed to us the word of reconciliation"* (2 Corinthians 5:19).

Our job is to love the world, pray for the world and bring the grace of God to the world. The arms of the Father are open, and He loves the world so much that He sent His only Son to save them. This is our message. It is the goodness of God that leads people to repentance (see Rom. 2:4).

When we read the Gospels, we see how Jesus treated sinners. He demonstrated grace, compassion and love and gave them hope and a future. His love and grace empowered them to change and embrace a new way of living. Jesus said that He did only what the Father showed Him to do. He who has seen Him has also seen the Father (see John 14:9). We can see the heart of the Father beautifully in the Parable of the Prodigal Son (see Luke 15:11-31). In this parable, the father received his son with open arms and an open heart, with no condemnation—only love and grace. Let the character of God the Father and His heart for the world become your character and heart as well. As you spend time with Him and receive more revelation of His love for you, you will be transformed and become more and more like Him.

So, my dear friend, from this day onwards, know that God is good, God is your Father and He loves you with an everlasting love because God is love.

FOR SELF REFLECTION AND GROUP DISCUSSION

1. God is good and only good. He is not punishing and judging us or the world in this "age of grace." Is this how you have viewed God until now? Meditate on the Scriptures about the goodness of God in this session and ask Him to make them real to you.
2. What does it mean that God has reconciled the world to Himself and given us the ministry of reconciliation? (see 2 Cor. 5:19). How does this

affect the way we see the world and approach people who do not know God yet? Do we bring them the love of God, or do we judge them for their sinful behavior?

3. Meditate on Romans 5:5 that says, "*The love of God has been poured out in our hearts by the Holy Spirit*" and also that you can choose to "turn on the tap" of God´s love in your heart and bring this love to others. How can this revelation change the way you love others?
4. God is your Daddy God—your good, good Father. Is there anything in your relationship with your earthly father that hinders you from viewing God as a good Father? Share with your group if you like and receive prayer for God to heal your heart and set you free so you can receive His love for you.

SHARE AND DISCUSS WITH THE GROUP

SESSION 5

God´s Abundant Grace

WE HAVE LEARNED that when Jesus died at the cross and rose again, the world entered into a new spiritual era: "the dispensation of grace" or "the age of grace" when God no longer holds sin against people. In this period, which will last until Jesus returns, God is waiting with open arms to embrace everyone who receives Jesus as their Savior: *"For 'whoever calls on the name of the Lord shall be saved'"* (Romans 10:13). Salvation is by grace through faith only.

> *For it is by grace you have been saved, through faith—and this is not from yourselves, it is the gift of God— (Ephesians 2:8 NIV)*

The Gospel and the New Covenant are based on the grace of God. The Gospel is called the Gospel of grace (see Acts 20:24). "Grace," which is the Greek word *charis*, means "God´s unmerited favor."[5] Grace is getting what we do not deserve, while mercy is not getting what we do deserve. God meets us with unconditional love. He knows our weaknesses and shortcomings, but He receives us exactly as we are. His throne is called the throne of grace! That is beautiful. Nothing we do or don´t do can make God love us more or less.

Standing Firm in the Grace of God

In this New Covenant of grace, what do we do when we have messed up? We go to God with all our mess, confess what we have done and repent, then thank Him for the forgiveness He has already released at the cross. We can receive it freely. This is so important, because if we try to fix our lives before we go to God, we are basing our Christian life on our own good deeds and self-righteousness. If this is the case, we will never feel good enough to go to God. We will end up living with shame, guilt and condemnation, which make us hide from God, instead of running to Him for help, love and forgiveness. God tells us to come boldly to the throne of grace. He says that our confidence has great reward (see Heb. 10:35).

> *Let us therefore come boldly to the throne of grace, that we may obtain mercy and find grace to help in time of need. (Hebrews 4:16)*

The enemy (the devil) tries to make us doubt the grace of God to keep us in shame, guilt and self-condemnation. However, there is no condemnation for those who are in Christ Jesus (see Rom. 8:1). Grace is one of the most important concepts to understand and embrace in your life. It will bring you into total freedom in Christ. It causes you to look at Him and radiate with joy. You can walk with boldness and with your head held high.

Let us look at some Scriptures about grace:

> *For the law was given through Moses, but grace and truth came through Jesus Christ. (John 1:17)*

> *For all have sinned and fall short of the glory of God, being justified freely by His grace through the redemption that is in Christ Jesus, (Romans 3:23-24)*

> *Therefore, having been justified by faith, we have peace with God through our Lord Jesus Christ, through whom also we have access by faith into this grace in which we stand, and rejoice in hope of the glory of God. (Romans 5:1-2)*

> *For if by the one man's offense death reigned through the one, much more those who receive abundance of grace and of the gift of righteousness will reign in life through the One, Jesus Christ. (Romans 5:17)*

> *Moreover, the law entered that the offense might abound. But where sin abounded, grace abounded much more, so that as sin reigned in death, even so grace might reign through righteousness to eternal life through Jesus Christ our Lord. (Romans 5:20-21)*

> *In Him we have redemption through His blood, the forgiveness of sins, according to the riches of His grace (Ephesians 1:7)*

> *But God, who is rich in mercy, because of His great love with which He loved us, even when we were dead in trespasses, made us alive together with Christ (by grace you have been saved), and raised us up together, and*

made us sit together in the heavenly places in Christ Jesus, that in the ages to come He might show the exceeding riches of His grace in His kindness toward us in Christ Jesus. For by grace you have been saved through faith, and that not of yourselves; it is the gift of God, not of works, lest anyone should boast. (Ephesians 2:4-9)

How Does Grace Work in Our Lives?

God´s grace is so powerful. It saves us, embraces us, empowers us, restores us and sets us free from guilt, shame and condemnation. It helps us to understand and receive the unconditional love of God. When sin is great, grace is greater (see Rom. 5:20). It is the goodness and grace of God that leads us to repentance and a changed life. The grace of God melts our hearts, tears down our walls of defense and sets us free to live the life God has for us. It empowers us to forgive ourselves and others. If we fall and mess up, we do not fall out of grace, but we fall within grace. We get up, receive His forgiveness and keep walking on the path that God has set before us. The grace of God is new every morning.

The grace of God works in us and empowers us to do according to His will and good pleasure (see Phil. 2:13). God starts the good work in us and is able to complete it (see Phil. 1:6). When He calls us to do something, He also gives us grace to do it. That is why we see people going to the worst places on the planet based on the calling of God, but they are the happiest people on Earth. The grace of God has worked in them, so they want to go there, and they are empowered to do the work. The grace of God makes us excited to do His will! Then on top of that, the Holy Spirit gives spiritual gifts to work out supernatural results, which are called "*charisma* gifts" or "grace gifts." (See later sessions for more on that topic.)

To understand more about the grace of God, let us look at the Parable of the Prodigal Son:

To illustrate the point further, Jesus told them this story: "A man had two sons. The younger son told his father, 'I want my share of your estate now before you die.' So, his father agreed to divide his wealth between his sons.

"A few days later this younger son packed all his belongings and moved to a distant land, and there he wasted all his money in wild living. About the time his money ran out, a great famine swept over the land, and he began to starve. He persuaded a local farmer to hire him, and the man sent him

into his fields to feed the pigs. The young man became so hungry that even the pods he was feeding the pigs looked good to him. But no one gave him anything.

"When he finally came to his senses, he said to himself, 'At home even the hired servants have food enough to spare, and here I am dying of hunger! I will go home to my father and say, "Father, I have sinned against both heaven and you, and I am no longer worthy of being called your son. Please take me on as a hired servant."'

"So he returned home to his father. And while he was still a long way off, his father saw him coming. Filled with love and compassion, he ran to his son, embraced him, and kissed him. His son said to him, 'Father, I have sinned against both heaven and you, and I am no longer worthy of being called your son.'

"But his father said to the servants, 'Quick! Bring the finest robe in the house and put it on him. Get a ring for his finger and sandals for his feet. And kill the calf we have been fattening. We must celebrate with a feast, for this son of mine was dead and has now returned to life. He was lost, but now he is found.' So, the party began." (Luke 15:11-24 NLT)

We see in this story that the father never stopped looking for the son. He was always watching out for him, and when he came, the father saw him from afar and ran towards him to embrace, hug and kiss him. It was very shameful for men to run at that time—the father had to pull up his long robe in order to run, but he did not care. All he cared about was the son's return. He had missed him so much. His love for the son was unconditional.

We Should Not Abuse God´s Grace

One last point: The grace of God is not to be abused. We are not to take advantage of the grace of God and live in sin. On the contrary, it is God's grace that enables us to live life victoriously. We do not sin on purpose or do what we know is wrong on purpose, just because we know we will receive forgiveness and grace. No! See, Romans 6:1-2 (NLT) says, "*Well then, should we keep on sinning so that God can show us more and more of his wonderful grace? Of course not! Since we have died to sin, how can we continue to live in it?*"

As new creations in Christ Jesus, we are dead to sin, and we live to follow Jesus and please Him because we love Him. Grace empowers us to live this new life.

Grace flows freely from the finished work of Jesus at the cross. Never stay in self-condemnation, guilt and shame, but always "stand in grace" and keep your eyes on Jesus.

FOR SELF-REFLECTION AND GROUP DISCUSSION

1. Can you give an example from your own life when God met you with grace when you did not deserve it?
2. God wants us to come boldly to His "throne of grace" when we have messed up, not hide from Him. How does this work in your life? Do you try to fix yourself before you go to God or do you bring all your mess to Him?

   It is crucial that we come boldly to God in whatever situation we are in, also when we have sinned, so we can receive His forgiveness and grace as empowerment to move on. We receive His grace and unconditional love freely and undeservingly.
3. Grace is empowerment. Have you experienced receiving special grace from God as empowerment to service or ministry in such a way that others ask you, "How are you able to do this thing or go to this place?"
4. Have you experienced God´s grace at work in you so He makes you want to do His will? See Philippians 2:13 (NLT): *"For God is working in you, giving you the desire and the power to do what pleases him."*
5. Have you experienced God's grace and unconditional love towards you? How has it affected your life?

   SHARE AND DISCUSS WITH THE GROUP

SESSION 6

Self-Righteousness Versus the Righteousness of God

How to Become Righteous before God

RIGHTEOUSNESS CAN BE DEFINED as "having right standing with God." A great question is: How do we become righteous before God? It is crucial to know the answer to this question since being righteous is a precondition to getting into fellowship with God and being filled with the Holy Spirit. God can have close fellowship only with those who are righteous. The Holy Spirit will only live in a temple that is cleansed, holy and righteous. The Bible calls our body a temple of the Holy Spirit (see 1 Cor. 6:19); does that mean that we are considered righteous? What if we do something wrong? Are we still righteous? Do our good deeds add to our righteousness? Do we only receive forgiveness for the things we do before we accept Christ, and then afterwards we need to fix our lives ourselves?

These are important questions because the answers will impact your whole Christian life. If you want to be made righteous before God, and you think you have to earn your righteousness, you may find yourself constantly trying to please God by being "good" and doing good deeds. You may try to be a good person by reading your Bible, praying for a certain length of time and serving in a church—all because you think it is expected of you. These things are all good, but not if they are done in an attempt to earn God´s approval. If this is the case, you will feel like God is watching you and measuring if you are doing enough and doing it well enough. You will compare yourself with others who are doing more than you and consequently always feel that you are falling short. Self-condemnation, guilt and shame will follow you because you never feel good enough as a Christian and you feel that God is not pleased with your effort. So, is this the way we become righteous before God—by our own effort and work? To this question, there is only one big answer, and that is NO!

The struggle I just described is trying to live life according to self-righteousness, which is not the righteousness that God has provided for us. Self-righteousness comes from a religious mindset, which thinks that it is your own efforts and good deeds that make you acceptable to God. All world religions are built on this mindset. Religion says you have to do this and that to please God and be made right with Him, which means you are never really sure if you have done enough, or if you will ever do enough to reach up to His standards. The Gospel of Jesus Christ is not like this. The Gospel is not a religion. It is not based on a set of rules we have to follow to reach up to God. It is all about God coming down from Heaven and doing everything that was necessary for our salvation so that we could get back into a right relationship with Him.

Righteousness Is a Gift from God

Jesus Christ, the Son of God, left His glorious place in Heaven and became a human being so that He could live a perfect life without sin, qualifying Him to be the perfect sacrifice for the sin of all of humanity.

> *God made him who had no sin to be sin for us so that in him we might become the righteousness of God. (2 Corinthians 5:21 NIV)*

At the cross, there was a great exchange happening: Jesus, who had never sinned but had lived a perfect life, took all our sin upon Himself so that we could become the righteousness of God!

Righteousness is given to us as a gift because we believe in Jesus.

> *That if you confess with your mouth the Lord Jesus and believe in your heart that God has raised Him from the dead, you will be saved. For with the heart one believes unto righteousness, and with the mouth, confession is made unto salvation. (Romans 10:9-10)*

For in the Gospel, the righteousness of God is revealed—a righteousness that is by faith from first to last, just as it is written: "The righteous will live by faith." (Romans 1:17 NIV)

This righteousness is given through faith in Jesus Christ to all who believe. There is no difference between Jew and Gentile (see Rom. 3:22).

For if by the one man's offense death reigned through the one, much more those who receive abundance of grace and of the gift of righteousness will reign in life through the One, Jesus Christ. (Romans 5:17)

We can see clearly from the verses above that righteousness is a gift and that it comes by faith alone. When we receive salvation, we become 100 percent righteous before God. This is how He sees us—100 percent righteous! Let me ask you a question: After receiving the gift of righteousness, if we do something wrong, do we lose our righteousness? Or does our righteousness fall from 100 percent to 80 or 60 percent? No! When we fall, we fall IN CHRIST and IN GRACE—we are still 100 percent righteous! It has absolutely nothing to do with what we do or don't do, but with our position before God as a believer.

Don´t Try to Earn Your Righteousness

Why then do so many of us fall into this trap of thinking we need to please God with our own efforts? I think the answer is that it is so natural for our flesh and unrenewed minds to want to earn and deserve what we get. It is a religious mindset that can be so strong in us that we think God is requiring all these things from us. We might be stuck in an Old Covenant mindset, not understanding righteousness in the New Covenant.

God wants us to enjoy the freedom that He has given us through the finished work of Jesus. Through Christ's work on the cross, He has made us 100 percent righteous, holy, accepted and loved by Him. We are free from all of the requirements that were part of the Old Covenant Law of Moses. When it comes to our position before God, sin has been dealt with once and for all AT THE CROSS, where Jesus took the punishment for all our sin upon Himself. That includes all sin that has ever been committed and all sin that will ever be committed in the future.

If we want to earn our own righteousness apart from the finished work of Jesus at the cross, it will cause us problems in our relationship with God. Our salvation and righteousness are based on grace alone. It is a gift. We are to live by faith in His grace, knowing that what Jesus did for us was enough for us to be wholly accepted by the Father. We can come boldly to His throne in praise and prayer, knowing that we are cleansed from all sin we ever committed. God remembers our sins no more. However, if we choose to try to earn our own righteousness by our good deeds and try to reach up to God through our own work and effort, the Bible says we have fallen from grace. This we can see in Galatians 5:4: *"You have become estranged from Christ, you who attempt to be justified by law; you have fallen from grace."*

The whole letter of Galatians in the New Testament is the Apostle Paul's confrontation with the church there, which had come into bondage again for trying to be justified by the works of the law.

In Galatians 2:21, we read, *"I do not set aside the grace of God; for if righteousness comes through the law, then Christ died in vain.'"* What Paul is saying is that if you want to earn your own righteousness, it is as if "Christ died in vain"—this is serious stuff! Jesus paid an extremely high price for our freedom; will we not live in this freedom? The Apostle Paul calls it a bondage to be in this self-righteous state. The fact is that if we want to be made righteous by our own efforts, we have to obey the Law of Moses 100 percent, which no man has ever been able to do. The Law was given to help us understand how high the standards of God are and make us realize that no man can ever reach this standard in his own effort. In Galatians 3:24-25, it says, *"Therefore the law was our tutor to bring us to Christ, that we might be justified by faith. But after faith has come, we are no longer under a tutor."*

We have learned that the Law of Moses is called the Old Covenant. When Jesus lived life on Earth, He fulfilled the Law by living a perfect life, and after His death (which we call His finished work at the cross) and His resurrection, He gave us a New Covenant based on grace and faith. In the New Covenant, we can live a life of freedom, knowing that we are righteous, holy, loved and accepted. We are children of God and co-heirs with Christ, which means that all the benefits and privileges that Jesus has from the Father, we also have. We enter into a rest for our souls, knowing that whatever we do or do not do, we are still righteous, loved and accepted by God.

This rest does not mean that we do not work anymore, but when we work, we work out of a soul that is resting in God. Our souls are at peace, free of stress, fear, condemnation and guilt. This empowers us to work with supernatural efficiency. We can run with confidence and boldness, knowing that God is with us and for us! We can embrace our freedom in Christ and know that we are fully accepted by God.

The most important thing to remember: We do not do good deeds and works to try to make God love us or accept us more, nor do we do it to earn our righteousness. We are already accepted, loved and made righteous through Christ, and whatever we do is out of thankfulness and joy for what we have ALREADY received from the Father. The Holy Spirit will do His work in us so that what we do, we do from our hearts.

When righteousness becomes part of our identity, this will lead to righteous living as well. You become who you already are. You act like the person you already are.

FOR SELF REFLECTION AND GROUP DISCUSSION

1. God made him who had no sin to be sin for us so that in him we might become the righteousness of God. (2 Corinthians 5:21 NIV)
2. God sees you as a righteous person if you have received Christ as your Lord and Savior. Do you see yourself as a righteous person? Meditate on the verse above and ask God to make your righteousness in Christ a part of your identity.
3. Righteousness is your position in God. We are given the righteousness of Christ freely by grace. If you sin, does your righteousness decrease or stay the same? Does your righteousness depend on your actions?
4. What is the difference between self-righteousness and God´s righteousness? Have you been struggling with attempts to please God in your life, while He only wants you to come to Him and receive His grace and righteousness freely?
5. When righteousness in Christ becomes part of your identity, it will lead to righteous living. You will want to do the right thing. You want to act according to your identity. Can you give examples of this happening in your own life?

SHARE AND DISCUSS WITH THE GROUP

SESSION 7

The Power of the Gospel

For I am not ashamed of the gospel of Christ, for it is the power of God to salvation for everyone who believes, (Romans 1:16)

THE POWER IS IN THE GOSPEL! We can learn so many things from the Bible, and we can study so many topics with so many interesting details; however, we always need to come back to the pure Gospel, where we find the power of God to salvation.

What Exactly Is the Gospel?

The central truths in the Gospel are so powerful, but what exactly is the Gospel? Jesus Christ, the Son of God, left His majesty in Heaven—by His own free will, out of love for us while we were still sinners—to become a human being, walk among us and show us who God, the Father is. He did miracles and proclaimed that the Kingdom of God had come close to us.

His purpose was to die at the cross. Why? He had to die to be the perfect sacrifice to God to pay for our sins. Throughout history, since Adam and Eve ate of the tree of good and evil until the cross, all people were sinners. They were slaves to sin. Sin was in their nature. They were spiritually dead and separated from a relationship with God; they tried their best to do good, but whatever they did, it was not good enough to reach up to God´s standard. They were totally lost! (This is still the situation for human beings today who live without Christ.) Animal sacrifices were made to cover their sins, but it was always a temporary solution. The blood of animals could not remove sin; it only covered sin for a while.

When Jesus hung on the cross and shed His blood at Calvary, all the wrath of God was poured down on Him for every sin that has ever been done in history. There had to be punishment for sin because God is a righteous and just God. We were the ones who deserved to be punished, but Jesus Christ took our place! Hallelujah! We will be forever grateful to Jesus!

Jesus died there on the cross, but death could not hold Him, because He was 100 percent righteous. So on the third day, He rose from the dead. Jesus´ death at the cross and His resurrection changed the spiritual realities for human beings for eternity!

The cross is THE central point of time in the whole history of human beings on this Earth. If you can imagine a timeline, you will see that everything before the cross pointed to the Messiah that would come in the future. After the cross, everything points back to Jesus' finished work at the cross!

Let us get back to the starting verse:

> *For I am not ashamed of the gospel of Christ, for it is the power of God to salvation for everyone who believes, (Romans 1:16)*

What Realities in the Gospel Are So Powerful?

When Jesus died on the cross, He cried out, "IT IS FINISHED!" So, what exactly was finished?

Salvation Was Finished.

Anyone who receives Jesus as Lord and Savior will be saved.

> *But as many as received Him, to them He gave the right to become children of God, to those who believe in His name: (John 1:12)*

The Relationship Between Human Beings and God Was Restored.

God had reconciled the world to Himself! We got reconnected to the Father!

> *That is, that God was in Christ reconciling the world to Himself, not imputing their trespasses to them, and has committed to us the word of reconciliation. (2 Corinthians 5:19)*

The Power of Sin Was Broken.

For sin shall not have dominion over you, for you are not under law but under grace. (Romans 6:14)

We Became Righteous before God.

A great exchange took place. Jesus took our sin, and we received His righteousness.

For He made Him who knew no sin to be sin for us, that we might become the righteousness of God in Him. (2 Corinthians 5:21)

We received righteousness as a gift by grace through faith in Jesus. God sees us 100 percent righteous, and it does not depend on what we have done or have not done. Our righteousness is all based on what Jesus has done for us at the cross.

ALL of the Enemy´s Power Was Crushed and Broken by Jesus Christ, ALL Things Are under His Feet!

Having disarmed principalities and powers, He made a public spectacle of them, triumphing over them in it. (Colossians 2:15)

Then we see in Ephesians 1:20-22 that Christ is seated at the right hand of the Father:

In the heavenly places, far above all principality and power and might and dominion, and every name that is named, not only in this age but also in that which is to come. And He put all things under His feet and gave Him to be head over all things to the church.

Healing Was Made Accessible.

Who Himself bore our sins in His own body on the tree, that we, having died to sins, might live for righteousness—by whose stripes you were healed. (1 Peter 2:24)

We Are Freed from the Curse.

Christ has redeemed us from the curse of the law, having become a curse for us (for it is written, "Cursed is everyone who hangs on a tree"), (Galatians 3:13)

If you read the curses of the Law written in Deuteronomy 28, you will be thrilled that you are freed from the curse! You do not need to be afraid of the curses you see in the Old Testament. When Jesus died at the cross, He took all the curses upon Himself. He became a curse for us so we will not be cursed.

No More Condemnation, Shame or Guilt for Those Who Walk According to the Spirit.

> *There is therefore now no condemnation to those who are in Christ Jesus, who do not walk according to the flesh, but according to the Spirit. (Romans 8:1)*

We Became Children of God.

> *The Spirit Himself bears witness with our spirit that we are children of God, (Romans 8:16)*

We Became Kings and Priests before God.

> *But you are a chosen generation, a royal priesthood, a holy nation, His own special people, that you may proclaim the praises of Him who called you out of darkness into His marvelous light; (1 Peter 2:9)*

God´s Presence Moved out of the Holy of Holies, and We Became the Temple of the Holy Spirit on Earth!

> *Do you not know that you are the temple of God and that the Spirit of God dwells in you? (1 Corinthians 3:16)*

In the Old Covenant, God´s presence on Earth was in the Ark of the Covenant in the Holy of Holies in the temple. In the New Covenant, we, as believers, are the temple where God dwells. We are the house of God. God does not live in buildings anymore. He lives in believers! He lives in you! You are a temple of the living God!

We Are Holy in His Sight.

> *And you, who once were alienated and enemies in your mind by wicked works, yet now He has reconciled in the body of His flesh through death, to present you holy, and blameless, and above reproach in His sight— (Colossians 1:21-22)*

We Are Now Saints, Not Sinners.

In the New Testament, Christians are always addressed as saints, never sinners. Look at these examples:

> *To the saints who are in Ephesus, and faithful in Christ Jesus: (Ephesians 1:1)*
>
> *To all the saints in Christ Jesus who are in Philippi, with the bishops and deacons: (Philippians 1:1)*

The Ministry of Reconciliation

After Jesus´ death and resurrection, a New Covenant was introduced between God and human beings! When we have revelation about what Jesus has done for us and who we are in Christ, we will be so bold, so on fire for God, so in love with Jesus, so full of passion and so excited that we belong to Him. We will want to run out to tell other people because God gave us the ministry of reconciliation.

> *Now all things are of God, who has reconciled us to Himself through Jesus Christ and has given us the ministry of reconciliation, (2 Corinthians 5:18)*

Based on this, we urge people to receive the gift of salvation from God because God has already reconciled the world to Himself. Salvation is entirely provided and paid for. This is our message: Mankind is already forgiven and can receive salvation as a free gift. People do not have to fix themselves before they come to Jesus. The Holy Spirit will point out what needs to change after they have given their lives to Jesus.

You Need to Know the Truth of the Gospel to Benefit from Its Realities

The truths in the Gospel are so powerful! The devil does not want us to focus on the Gospel. He knows he has lost and that he is defeated, but as long as we don´t understand who we are or what we have in Christ, he can deceive us. He will keep condemning us and cause us to feel shame and guilt, which takes away our boldness and confidence. If we don't know we are set free, we will keep receiving these lies from the enemy.

When we see who we are in Christ, we will come against the enemy with "the sword of the Spirit," which is the Word of God (see Eph. 6:17), telling Him who we are in Christ and what Jesus has done for us. When we resist the devil, he has to flee. He cannot touch us when we know who we are in Christ—when we know the Gospel truths.

To give you an example: I was a Christian for many years before I understood these realities. I did not realize that God loved me and that He had made me 100 percent righteous before Him. I did not understand the Gospel of grace. I did not know that the righteousness of God was given by grace and received through faith. I thought it was earned through my own good works and effort. I loved God and wanted so much to please Him, but I never felt good enough for Him. I tried my best to be good, to read my Bible and pray, but as soon as my good intentions failed, I felt so condemned and full of guilt. This was, of course, not God condemning me because it says in Scripture that there is no condemnation for those who are in Christ Jesus (see Rom. 8:1). It was based on my wrong mindset about God, which the devil took advantage of. I did not understand that it was the enemy playing with my mind. I tried my best to change, to do well again, read my Bible even more and pray longer. For a while, I felt really good about myself, but then I failed again. I got angry with my husband and my kids, I forgot to pray... and I got back into the ditch of self-condemnation and guilt. My Christian life was like a rollercoaster—up and down. I did not have boldness before God in prayer, because of my guilt and shame.

I started going to a church where the teaching was very different. There, I heard the Gospel truths again and again about God´s grace and that I was righteous by faith, not by works. I started to receive God´s love and let go of the self-condemnation and guilt. I was set entirely free by this message. I began to understand who I was in Christ. I got a revelation about the Gospel realities in the New Covenant, and I entered into the rest of God for my soul! The power that is in the Gospel worked in my life to salvation and freedom. Yes, I was already saved when I went through this rollercoaster struggle, but I did not live in victory; I did not experience the power and the realities of the Gospel. I did not have peace with God in my heart, because of the feelings of condemnation. The enemy had free admission into my life because I did not know what Jesus had done for me at the cross.

We see in Romans 1:16, our opening verse, that the Gospel *"is the power of God to salvation for everyone who believes."* To believe, we have to understand it and get a revelation of it.

So, dig into the Word of God and pray that you will see more and more of what you have in the Gospel and who you are in Christ!

The Apostle Paul prays this prayer in Ephesians 1:17-18:

> *That the God of our Lord Jesus Christ, the Father of glory, may give you the spirit of wisdom and revelation in the knowledge of Him, the eyes of your understanding being enlightened; that you may know what is the hope of His calling, what are the riches of the glory of His inheritance in the saints,*

The Apostle Paul´s prayer is that we see what we already have in Christ and how powerful it is. It is all about understanding what we have and putting it into action. Use your authority and live your life upright, knowing that you are a royal priesthood, a child of the highest God and a new creation in Christ Jesus. The power that raised Jesus from the dead lives in you and works through you! If you do this, you will surely see that the Gospel is the power of God to salvation.

In the next sessions, we will learn more about our identity and who we are in Christ so we can stand firm in this truth.

FOR SELF REFLECTION AND GROUP DISCUSSION

1. At the cross, all of the punishment and judgment that we deserved were poured out on Jesus Christ. Before Jesus died, He said, *"It is finished."* What had Jesus actually finished?
2. Why do we have to understand what Jesus actually provided for us in salvation to benefit from it?

   > *For we have heard the good news of deliverance just as they did, yet they didn't join their faith with the Word. Instead, what they heard didn't affect them deeply, for they doubted. For those of us who believe, faith activates the promise, and we experience the realm of confident rest! (Hebrews 4:2-3 TPT)*

3. You heard my testimony about how I found it life-changing to understand the spiritual realities after the cross. Do you have a similar story to tell, or are you still trying to learn and discover these things for yourself?

If you don´t have a testimony yet, don´t worry; the next sessions will teach you what you need to know.

SHARE AND DISCUSS WITH THE GROUP

SESSION 8

Who Am I? What Gives Me Value?

Do You Let Others Define Who You Are?

WHAT IS MY TRUE IDENTITY? Who am I and what gives me value? Media, advertisements, bloggers, colleagues, friends, family and society in general measure you by certain standards to decide if you are successful in their eyes and if you are interesting and worth spending time with. The general standard of measurement is: Do you have a successful career and a good education? Do you live in the right part of town? Does your home reflect the latest interior design trends? Are you slim, fit and pretty? Is your wardrobe and hairstyle up to date with the new season? Do you drive the right car? Do you have the latest sports equipment? Have you been to the latest holiday destinations? Is your spouse successful? Do you know the right people? Do you have the right number of kids? Are your kids well-behaved and in the right schools? The list is endless. We put our lives on display on social media and try to portray a successful appearance.

The standards for what make you successful and valuable vary in different societies and countries. For instance, in some communities, women are considered successful if they have a great career. If they choose to stay home with their children, they are looked down upon by the majority of people. In other societies, it is the opposite; you are considered a bad mother if you have your kids in childcare and go back to work. If we measure ourselves by these variables and changing standards, we will never feel successful in life. Nobody can reach up to them, and even if we could, our lives would be quite empty and meaningless.

Let God Define Your Identity and Value

We have to be very careful about what we connect our identity and self-worth to. As believers in Jesus Christ, our identity is found in who we are in Christ and our value is found in God's total acceptance and unconditional love for us. We are created in His image with a God-given purpose. Only in God can we find our real value and identity measured by standards that will never change. He is the Rock we can build our lives on.

Even though we are Christians, we might not be aware that we are connecting our identity and value to the wrong things. We might think we have our identity in God, but when we face different circumstances in life, we realize that our identity and value were rooted in something else. This can lead to an identity crisis. For instance, if your identity has been to be a mother your whole adult life, you can experience an identity crisis when your kids grow up and leave home. Your kids have been your whole life. You are left with this big, empty space in your life and heart. Many people experience an identity crisis if they lose their job or get sick since their identity has been so connected to their career and what they do.

Does this really need to happen? Do you have to have an identity crisis? No, you don't. If your identity and value are rooted in who God says you are, you can face any circumstance in life and stand firm.

First of all, as believers, we are not to look at our lives in the same way as the world does. When I say "the world," I mean the common opinion of society, advertising, culture and so on as described in the introduction. We read in Romans 12:2, *"And do not be conformed to this world, but be transformed by the renewing of your mind, that you may prove what is that good and acceptable and perfect will of God."*

What does this mean? It means that we need to find out what God's will for us is through His Word. We read the Bible to see how God sees us and what His will, thoughts and plans are for us. This includes what our true identity in Christ is. When we meditate on these things and speak them out over our lives, we reprogram our minds to think the same thoughts as God thinks. This is what it means when it says in Romans 12:2 to be transformed by the renewing of your mind.

When we are saved, our spirit is born again. The Bible says we become a new creation or a new person! However, it is only the spirit that is born again and becomes new. We consist of body, soul and spirit. Our spirit is born again, but our soul is not—it has to be renewed. By reading the Word of God and listening to teaching and preaching, our will, mind and emotions, including our thinking and thought patterns, will be changed and renewed and come into alignment with the will of God. When this happens, it will affect how we view our identity as well. (We will look more into this in later sessions.)

When you see who you are in Christ and how much God loves you, you will be changed! You will change the way you look at yourself and the way you see God.

Your identity and value will change from being connected to what you do, how skinny you are, what education you have and how successful you are in different areas of your life to being connected to who you are in Christ and how valuable and loved you are by God. This is a process. It might take time, but it is so worth going down that road because your life will be so different when you get a revelation of these things.

The world will still judge you according to the same measurements; however, when you find your true identity and security in Christ and God's love for you, it won't matter to you anymore. You can rest in His love, confident that you are accepted, loved and valuable and knowing that God has a place and a purpose for you in His Kingdom.

Let us read part of Psalm 139. It shows us how special we are to God.

> *For you created my inmost being;*
> *you knit me together in my mother's womb.*
> *I praise you because I am fearfully and wonderfully made;*
> *your works are wonderful, I know that full well.*
> *My frame was not hidden from you when I was made in the secret place,*
> *when I was woven together in the depths of the earth.*
> *Your eyes saw my unformed body; all the days ordained for me were written in your book before one of them came to be.*
> *How precious to me are your thoughts, God!*
> *How vast is the sum of them!*
> *Were I to count them, they would outnumber the grains of sand—*
> *when I awake, I am still with you. (Psalm 139:13-18 NIV)*

In the next sessions, we will learn about our true identity in Christ.

FOR SELF REFLECTION AND GROUP DISCUSSION

1. Have you ever experienced an identity crisis in your life? What was it about?
2. Would it have been different if you were more aware of your identity in Christ and how God looks at you?
3. How can we change from having our value rooted in the things we do, to having our value rooted in who we are in Christ?
4. How can we get away from letting the world dictate our identity?

SHARE AND DISCUSS WITH THE GROUP

SESSION 9

Your Identity in Christ
Part 1

THE PURPOSE OF THESE TEACHINGS is to build a firm foundation for our faith. An essential part of this foundation is to know who we are in Christ and our identity in Him. Knowing who we are and our position in the spiritual world is crucial for us to live victoriously in our Christian walk. The voices of the world, our own low self-esteem as well as the enemy will come to sow doubt and speak lies to us about our identity. We need to be entirely convinced about who we are in Christ so that we can proclaim it when these lies come against us.

Knowing who you are in Christ will affect the way you come to God. It will affect the way you pray. It will affect your self-esteem and your joy. It will change the way you look at your future since it will affect the way you view God. It will strongly influence your confidence.

The Bible tells us that in Christ you are:

- A new creation
- Righteous
- A child of God and an heir with Christ
- A saint, not a sinner (you are holy)
- Seated with Christ in the heavenly places
- Part of the body of Christ
- More than a conqueror

- A temple of the living God
- Citizen of the Kingdom of God
- A royal priesthood
- You are loved!

This is not a complete list, but if you get a revelation of these things and practice them, it will strongly affect your Christian walk. Let us look into it.

You Are a New Creation

Before you received Christ, you were spiritually dead. You were a sinner with a sinful nature. When you accepted Christ as your Lord and Savior, you were born again. You became “a new creation.”

> *Therefore, if anyone is in Christ, he is a new creation; old things have passed away; behold, all things have become new. (2 Corinthians 5:17)*

The new creation is born of God (see John 1:13). It was neither you trying to re-create yourself nor God just cleaning up your old nature, but it was Him creating you to be brand new on the inside. Your spirit came alive, and you were filled with God´s life. When you are born again, the “old things have passed away,” which means that the desires you had before when you were in your sinful nature, have changed. The old has been replaced by a new life that desires the things of God. Your purposes, feelings, desires and understanding are fresh and different. You will see the world differently. Let me give you an example from my own life:

My Testimony of Being Born Again

When I was born again, I had no clue what had happened to me. I´d never heard about being born again or being a new creation. However, my experience was that I felt entirely different on the inside; I felt like a brand-new person. Up until then, I was the party girl who wanted to do crazy things and get really drunk at parties. I was also swearing a lot. I was a student at the time. I did not want to become a Christian, because I did not want to give up my lifestyle. I also found it hard to believe, and I was interested in New Age thinking.

My boyfriend (who is my husband now) was a Christian, and as time went by, he found it problematic to be with a girl who did not share his faith. When he mentioned this to me, my reaction was: "If you break up with me because of God, I will hate God for the rest of my life!" This didn't make it any easier for him.

My boyfriend´s family was secretly praying for me during this period. In the months leading up to the night when everything changed, the prayers had softened my heart, and I got this sudden interest and urge to ask questions about God. I could feel that God was in the room when we talked about Him. However, I still resisted becoming a Christian. I felt that many of the Christians whom I had met in my life had been pointing the finger at me, and it provoked me because I felt that they thought they were better than me. In my opinion, they were really boring people who did not join in on any of the fun. At the time, I had not really met any Christians full of the love, joy and life of God. I definitely did not want to become like the Christians I´d grown up with. I did not want to be boring like them! However, when I was a child, I used to go to Sunday school, and I also learned about Jesus at school. Seeds of faith were planted in my heart, and I loved Jesus as a child. The seeds had been well buried up until that time, but they were still there.

One night, my boyfriend and I had a discussion, and I asked him, "What is really the difference between you and me? You say you are a Christian and I am not, but we live the exact same way?" (He did not really have a Christian lifestyle at that time). Then he answered me with the question: "Do you believe Jesus is the Son of God and that He died to take the punishment for all of your sins?" I was quite irritated at this stage of our discussion and yelled, "Yes, I believe that." "Well, then you are a Christian," he replied. My reaction was more like, "Yeah right..." However, what happened next was so powerful.

The next day, I felt totally different on the inside. I felt like a brand-new person. I had no clue what was going on with me. At the time, college was starting a new semester, and I met up with a Christian girlfriend (who was not boring, by the way). One of the first things I said to her was, "Ingrid, I think I am becoming religious—it is like God is everywhere inside of me!" That was the words I used as I had no clue about anything regarding being born again. She asked me what had happened, and I told her about the previous night's discussion with my boyfriend. She could explain that I had confessed the little faith I had in my heart by saying "yes" to my boyfriend's question. In her Bible, she showed me these verses in Romans 10:9-10:

> *If you confess with your mouth the Lord Jesus and believe in your heart that God has raised Him from the dead, you will be saved. For with the heart one believes unto righteousness, and with the mouth, confession is made unto salvation.*

The little faith I had confessed was enough for God—He had just been waiting for the opportunity to come into my heart. What amazing grace!

Ingrid and I went to buy my first Bible, and when I started to read it, the words were ALIVE! It made sense to me, and it touched my heart deeply. Nobody told me to start reading the Bible, but the "new creation" girl in me was so hungry and could not get enough. Ingrid and I read the Bible and prayed together at any opportunity. Nobody told me to stop getting drunk and stop swearing, but the "new creation" girl did not have any other desire than pleasing Jesus, my new-found love. My conscience had come alive like never before. I could sense in a new way what was right and wrong. I also experienced and saw the world in a new way—the colors were brighter, and I could see the glory of God in creation everywhere. I had a new love and compassion for people as well. The new creation reality was so powerful and present even though I had no idea or knowledge about it.

This is my experience. You have your own unique testimony about what the Lord did for you. Most people don't have such a revolutionary change overnight in their lives as I did, but you are still born again and a Christian.

What If You Sin When You Are Born Again?

When you are born again, you are set free from your sinful nature. So, what if Christians sin? None of us will ever be able to live a life entirely free of sin, but as a new creation, you are no longer a slave to sin. Through the grace of God, you are empowered to say "no" to sin. Sin no longer has power over you (see Rom. 6:6-7). You don't have to "*let sin reign*" in your life anymore, but you count yourself "*dead to sin, but alive to God in Christ Jesus*" (Romans 6:11-12 NIV).

We learned in the previous session that it was our spiritual being that was born again, not our soul. The Bible tells us to renew our mind (soul) so that our thinking, feelings, dreams, attitudes, etc. will be aligned with the Word of God and His will. We are to "put off our old self" and "put on the new man" in the attitude of our mind.

Romans 12:2 describes it very well:

> *And do not be conformed to this world, but be transformed by the renewing of your mind, that you may prove what is that good and acceptable and perfect will of God.*

In Ephesians 4:20-24 NIV, we learn the following:

> *That, however, is not the way of life you learned when you heard about Christ and were taught in him in accordance with the truth that is in Jesus. You were taught, with regard to your former way of life, to put off your old self, which is being corrupted by its deceitful desires; to be made new in the attitude of your minds; and to put on the new self, created to be like God in true righteousness and holiness.*

As we behold Jesus, focus on Him and who He is, read the Word of God, listen to teaching and preaching and spend time in God's presence in praise, prayer and worship we will be transformed—all by the grace of God working in us by the Holy Spirit. Our part is to submit and allow Him to do His work in us.

> *But we all, with unveiled face, beholding as in a mirror the glory of the Lord, are being transformed into the same image from glory to glory, just as by the Spirit of the Lord. (2 Corinthians 3:18)*

> *If then you were raised with Christ, seek those things which are above, where Christ is, sitting at the right hand of God. Set your mind on things above, not on things on the earth. (Colossians 3:1-2)*

As your thinking is transformed (your mind is renewed), it becomes more and more aligned with the Word of God, thereby enabling you to discern the will of God. Your soul will agree with your "new creation-man," and it will allow the Holy Spirit to empower you to live in victory over sin and temptation.

FOR SELF REFLECTION AND GROUP DISCUSSION

1. Do you have a testimony about how you became born again and a "new creation in Christ Jesus"? Describe the changes in your life.
2. Why do we have to renew our mind even though we are born again?

3. Describe your own process of how your mind has been renewed after you became a Christian. How have your thinking patterns and mindset changed?

   SHARE AND DISCUSS WITH THE GROUP

SESSION 10

Your Identity in Christ Part 2

IN THE NEXT TWO SESSIONS, we will continue looking into our true identity in Christ.

You Are Righteous

Righteousness was given to you as a gift through salvation. It does not come from your own works. It is all by grace. You were made righteous by God. You received the righteousness of Jesus. When this revelation sinks into your heart, it will change the way you approach God big time! All shame, guilt and condemnation will leave, and you will approach the Father boldly with full confidence. As you embrace righteousness as your identity, it will lead to righteous living as well. You become who you already are. (This topic was covered thoroughly in Session 6.)

You Are a Child of God

When we were born again, we became sons and daughters of God the Father. We got the DNA of God in our newborn spirit—in our spirit man.

> *Having predestined us to adoption as sons by Jesus Christ to Himself, according to the good pleasure of His will, (Ephesians 1:5)*

> *Beloved, now we are children of God; and it has not yet been revealed what we shall be, but we know that when He is revealed, we shall be like Him, for we shall see Him as He is. (1 John 3:2)*

> *For you did not receive the spirit of bondage again to fear, but you received the Spirit of adoption by whom we cry out, "Abba, Father." The Spirit Himself bears witness with our spirit that we are children of God, (Romans 8:15-16)*
>
> *For you are all sons of God through faith in Christ Jesus. (Galatians 3:26)*
>
> *And because you are sons, God has sent forth the Spirit of His Son into your hearts, crying out, "Abba, Father!" Therefore you are no longer a slave but a son, and if a son, then an heir of God through Christ. (Galatians 4:6-7)*

We come to the Father as sons and daughters. A good earthly father would provide for his children, protect them, guide them, prepare for their future, discipline them, embrace them with love and confirmation and surprise them. God the Father is just like this towards us as His daughters and sons. We are adopted into His family, and He will take care of us the same way as an earthly father would but, of course, much better and in a perfect way! He knows exactly how He has created us and equipped us. He will take care of each one of us in a very individual way.

You Are a Saint Not a Sinner – You Are Holy

After you are born again, you are not a sinner anymore—you are a saint! The Apostle Paul greets the churches in many of his letters by addressing them as saints.

> *To all who are in Rome, called to be saints: (Romans 1:7)*
>
> *To the church of God which is at Corinth, to those who are sanctified in Christ Jesus, called to be saints, with all who in every place call on the name of Jesus Christ our Lord, both theirs and ours: (1 Corinthians 1:2)*
>
> *To the church of God which is at Corinth, with all the saints who are in all Achaia: (2 Corinthians 1:2)*
>
> *To the saints who are in Ephesus, and faithful in Christ Jesus: (Ephesians 1:1)*
>
> *To all the saints in Christ Jesus who are in Philippi, with the bishops and deacons: (Philippians 1:1)*
>
> *To the saints and faithful brethren in Christ who are in Colosse: (Colossians 1:2)*

If you look through the New Testament, the Christians are always called saints, never sinners. Jesus loved to be with sinners when He was on planet Earth, but when He called them sinners in the Gospels, they were not saved yet.

So, what does it mean to be a saint? In the New Testament, a saint is a "holy one"—someone who is set apart for God´s special purposes. Every follower of Jesus Christ is a saint. How can this be? It is based on our position before God after the cross. In Christ, we were sanctified and made holy!

> *But of Him you are in Christ Jesus, who became for us wisdom from God—and righteousness and sanctification and redemption— (1 Corinthians 1:30)*

In the NIV version of the Bible, the word "holiness" is used instead of "sanctification."

> *It is because of him that you are in Christ Jesus, who has become for us wisdom from God—that is, our righteousness, holiness and redemption. (1 Corinthians 1:30 NIV)*

Jesus became our sanctification and holiness! He made us saints, and He made us holy! This is our position before God. All who are identified with Jesus Christ by faith are given the status of "holy" before God because of what Jesus has done for us.

So, how should this affect our lives and lifestyles? We have learned that as we have been made righteous by God through salvation, it will lead to righteous living. We become who we already are. In the same way—as we get the revelation that we have been made holy and saints before God—this will be reflected in the way we live our lives. The Holy Spirit is at work in you to transform your life so that you reveal the ultimate righteous and Holy One—the Lord Jesus Christ.

You Are a Member of the Body of Christ

We are not lonely riders as saints; we are a part of the body of Christ, which is the church. We have our place to fill in the body of Christ.

> *For as the body is one and has many members, but all the members of that one body, being many, are one body, so also is Christ. For by one Spirit we were all baptized into one body—whether Jews or Greeks, whether slaves*

> *or free—and have all been made to drink into one Spirit. (1 Corinthians 12:12-13)*

> *For as we have many members in one body, but all the members do not have the same function, so we, being many, are one body in Christ, and individually members of one another. (Romans 12:4-5)*

We, the church, are the body, and Christ is the head of the body.

> *And He put all things under His feet and gave Him to be head over all things to the church, which is His body, the fullness of Him who fills all in all. (Ephesians 1:22-23)*

As a believer and a member of the body of Christ, it is essential to be part of a local church. It is not enough to just be part of the universal church as many Christians tend to believe these days with so much teaching, preaching and worship music available online. Many choose to sit in their own living room and listen to a preacher on TV or the internet instead of going to church. Listening to online teaching and preaching is great, but it cannot substitute physically attending a local church.

The Apostle Paul told the church in Corinth that they may have many teachers in Christ but not many fathers (see 1 Cor. 4:15). In the local church, you will consistently be fed with the Word by pastors who care for you. You have a community of believers who encourage you and whom you are accountable to through fellowship. You can also meet in small groups, get involved in ministry and grow in your spiritual gifts. We are meant to be part of the body, the church, and function there, not be a "lonely body part" content by itself. So, I encourage you to find a local church where you feel at home.

You Are Seated with Christ in the Heavenly Places

According to Ephesians 1:20-21, Christ is seated at the right hand of the Father *"in the heavenly places, far above all principality and power and might and dominion, and every name that is named, not only in this age but also in that which is to come."*

Christ is seated in the heavenly places but what is OUR spiritual position? Where does this place us? Physically, we are here on Earth, but when it comes to our spiritual position, we are much more than that. Let us read in Ephesians again:

But God, who is rich in mercy, because of His great love with which He loved us, even when we were dead in trespasses, made us alive together with Christ (by grace you have been saved), and raised us up together, and made us sit together in the heavenly places in Christ Jesus, that in the ages to come He might show the exceeding riches of His grace in His kindness toward us in Christ Jesus. (Ephesians 2:4-7)

Wow! We are seated together with Christ in the heavenly places in Christ Jesus. Try to visualize what we read earlier—that Christ is seated far above all principalities and powers. This is really powerful, but there is still more; all things are under His (Christ Jesus´) feet. When Christ is the head of the body and we are a part of the body, all things are under our feet as well! In the name of Christ Jesus, we have authority over principalities and powers, might and dominion and every name that is named (see Eph. 1:20-21).

Let us stand strong in our spiritual position and authority and learn how to exercise it in our daily life. Let us live, act and think out of this heavenly position we have been given in Christ Jesus.

FOR SELF REFLECTION AND GROUP DISCUSSION

1. You become a child of God when you are born again. Describe what situations and needs you want your good, good Father to solve and take care of for you. Try to imagine that it is your child who has needs and how you would do everything in your power to help your child. How much more will your Heavenly Father do the same for you?
2. Until now, have you called yourself a saint or a sinner? Meditate on the fact that God calls you a saint—that you are holy in His sight. Feel how it empowers you to be the person God wants you to be.
3. Are you part of a local church community? If not, why? Help each other in the group to find a good local church to attend.
4. Make a drawing that shows how you are spiritually seated with Christ in the heavenly places far above all principality and power and might and dominion, and every name that is named (see Eph.1:20-22 and Eph.2:4-7). All the enemy´s power is under Jesus´ feet (and your feet).

SHARE AND DISCUSS WITH THE GROUP

SESSION 11

Your Identity in Christ Part 3

IN THIS SESSION we will finalize the teaching about your identity in Christ. You will learn that you are more than a conqueror, a temple of the living God, a citizen of the Kingdom of Heaven, a royal priesthood and you are loved by God.

You Are More Than a Conqueror

> *Yet in all these things we are more than conquerors through Him who loved us. (Romans 8:37)*

This verse is part of a passage in Romans 8:31-39 that describes different things that we can go through in life; however, in all these things we are more than conquerors.

It starts by saying, *"If God is for us who can be against us He who did not spare His own son, but gave Him for us all, how shall He not with Him also freely give us all things?"* (Romans 8:31-32).

It ends by saying, *"For I am persuaded that neither death nor life, nor angels nor principalities nor powers, nor things present nor things to come, nor height nor depth, nor any other created thing, shall be able to separate us from the love of God which is in Christ Jesus our Lord"* (Romans 8:38-39).

Whatever happens to us, God is able to take everything and turn it into something good.

> *And we know that all things work together for good to those who love God, to those who are the called according to His purpose. (Romans 8:28)*

That makes us more than conquerors.

Christ has already fought the fight for us and won when He defeated all principalities and powers at the cross...

> *Having disarmed principalities and powers, He made a public spectacle of them, triumphing over them in it. (Colossians 2:15)*

Our fight against the enemy is based on the victory Jesus has already won. We do not have to fight a battle against the enemy. We just "stand on" and proclaim what Jesus has already done—His victory! That makes us more than conquerors.

You Are a Temple of the Living God

In the New Covenant, you are a temple of the living God.

> *Do you not know that you are the temple of God and that the Spirit of God dwells in you? (1 Corinthians 3:16)*

In the Old Covenant, God´s presence on Earth was in the Ark of the Covenant in the innermost room of the temple (or tabernacle) called the Holiest of All. The Ark was covered with gold on all sides, and above it was the cherubim of glory overshadowing the mercy seat. The Ark of the Covenant contained the stone tablets with the Ten Commandments Moses got from God on Mt. Sinai, a golden pot with manna (the heavenly food the people of Israel ate in the desert) and Aaron´s staff, which budded as a sign for the people of Israel in the wilderness (see Heb. 9:1-5).

A thick veil was covering the entrance to hinder anyone from entering the Holiest of All. Only the High Priest could enter the Holiest of All once a year to offer sacrifices for the sins of the people (see Heb. 9:7). If anyone else entered, they would die. We can clearly see the great separation between God and the people. However, when Jesus died on the cross, a significant thing happened—the thick veil that was separating the Holiest of All (and God) from the people was torn from top to bottom with no human hands involved (see Mark 15:38).

When Jesus shed His blood and made peace between God and the world, <u>God moved out of the Holiest of All</u> and <u>out of the temple</u>. By tearing the veil, God showed the people that from then on, everybody who believes in Jesus could enter into the Holiest of All, which is His presence. Jesus became our eternal High Priest.

But Christ came as High Priest of the good things to come, with the greater and more perfect tabernacle not made with hands, that is, not of this creation. Not with the blood of goats and calves, but with His own blood He entered the Most Holy Place once for all, having obtained eternal redemption. (Hebrews 9:11-12)

In the New Covenant, we as believers are the temple where God lives. We are the house of God. God does not live in buildings anymore; He lives in believers! He lives in you! You are a temple of the living God!

You Are a Citizen of the Kingdom of Heaven

For our citizenship is in heaven, from which we also eagerly wait for the Savior, the Lord Jesus Christ, who will transform our lowly body that it may be conformed to His glorious body, according to the working by which He is able even to subdue all things to Himself. (Philippians 3:20-21)

Here on Earth, we are from different nations with different cultures, but above this, we are citizens of the Kingdom of Heaven. That means the culture of the Kingdom is what should influence our thinking—more than the culture in our earthly home country, especially if they are not in agreement. We might not feel at home anywhere if we have lived in several places or in several countries, which makes it especially great to know that we are citizens of the Kingdom of Heaven. We have an eternal home in Heaven that is waiting for us when we leave this planet one day.

You are a Royal Priesthood

But you are a chosen generation, a royal priesthood, a holy nation, His own special people, that you may proclaim the praises of Him who called you out of darkness into His marvelous light; (1 Peter 2:9)

To Him who loved us and washed us from our sins in His own blood, and has made us kings and priests to His God and Father, to Him be glory and dominion forever and ever. Amen. (Revelation 1:5b-6)

"And have made us kings and priests to our God; And we shall reign on the earth." (Revelation 5:10)

In Christ, we are "royalty" because we belong to the King! This is all about mindset. We need to leave our pauper mentality behind and embrace our royal identity in Christ.[6] Let your royal identity influence your dignity, character, feeling of significance and the way you carry yourself. This will create confidence, which will empower you to do what God has called you to do.

We are also priests and are all called to minister to the Lord through praise and worship. In the Old Covenant, there were appointed priests who ministered on behalf of the people. In the New Covenant, we can all come to the throne of God anytime due to our righteousness in Christ Jesus. We all minister to the Lord in praise, worship and prayer.

> *"But the hour is coming, and now is, when the true worshipers will worship the Father in spirit and truth; for the Father is seeking such to worship Him. God is Spirit, and those who worship Him must worship in spirit and truth." (John 4:23-24)*

We are given the Holy Spirit so we can worship in spirit and truth! There is a fountain that runs out of our inner man, our spirit. Let it flow!

You Are Loved!

God the Father loves you so much. You are totally loved and accepted by Him. He gave up His only Son to save you and bring you back into relationship with Him.

John 3:16 says it all:

> *For God so loved the world that He gave His only begotten Son, that whoever believes in Him should not perish but have everlasting life.*

He loves YOU. He sees YOU. He knows everything about you. He has a plan for you...

Summary

Now that we know more about our identity in Christ and our position in Him, we can live our lives with our heads held high because we know what Christ has done for us and who we are in Him.

We can come boldly to His throne in prayer and worship because we are 100 percent righteous in Christ Jesus. We can be confident that He has accepted us, He loves us and hears us. We are free of all condemnation, guilt and shame because we know Jesus took the punishment for all of our past, present and future sins at the cross 2000 years ago. We can live a life out of rest in our soul.

We can resist the evil one with certainty that we have authority over the powers of darkness. The Bible says that as we resist him, he must flee from us (see James 4:7). When the devil comes against us with his lies, we can speak out who we are in Christ, using the "*sword of the Spirit*" (see Eph. 6:17).

This is all by the grace of God. At the same time, as we are fully aware of our identity in Christ, our focus is not on ourselves but on Christ Jesus, who is the center of our lives and the center of it all...

FOR SELF REFLECTION AND GROUP DISCUSSION

1. Perhaps you thought that God lives in church buildings, but He does not. He lives in believers; He lives in YOU! He is as close to you as is possible. Talk to God right now while you think about how near He is. You can use your own words and tell Him whatever you want. It is not hard to believe that He hears you when you know that He lives inside of you and that you are a temple of the Holy Spirit!
2. We are called to be a royal priesthood and minister to the Lord with thanksgiving, praise and worship. What does that look like in your life?
3. Meditate on the fact that God loves you so much!

SHARE AND DISCUSS WITH THE GROUP

SESSION 12

Water Baptism

BEFORE JESUS WENT TO HEAVEN, He gave us the Great Commission. This is our primary purpose and goal as Christians while we are on Earth.

> *And Jesus came and spoke to them, saying, "All authority has been given to Me in heaven and on earth. Go therefore and make disciples of all the nations, baptizing them in the name of the Father and of the Son and of the Holy Spirit, teaching them to observe all things that I have commanded you; and lo, I am with you always, even to the end of the age." Amen. (Matthew 28:18-20)*

In this session, we will learn about water baptism. We see in the Great Commission how this is part of God´s plan; we bring people to faith, disciple them, baptize them and teach them...

What Is Water Baptism?

In Mark 16:16 (NIV), we read, *"Whoever believes and is baptized will be saved, but whoever does not believe will be condemned."*

Baptism is connected to believing. It is a natural and important next step to take after receiving Christ, although it is not a requirement to be saved and go to Heaven. Many of us were baptized as babies with water sprinkled on our heads. This is the way some traditional churches practice baptism, but when we look in the Bible, this is not the way baptism is described. Baptism, as described in the Bible, is when the whole body goes under the water and rises up again. Why is this so? Because the meaning of baptism is that we bury our old lives with Jesus in the "grave of the water" and we are raised up again from the water to live a new life for Him, just like He was resurrected. We become one with Jesus' death when we are buried in the water and one with His resurrection when we are raised out of the water. We do this out of our faith in Jesus Christ who died for us on the cross and was resurrected from the dead on the third day.

We get baptized to outwardly and publicly show the whole world what has already happened on the inside. It is how we physically confirm that we want to belong to Christ with an outward act of faith and obedience. Let us look into some Scriptures that explain what baptism is about:

> *Or don't you know that all of us who were baptized into Christ Jesus were baptized into his death? We were therefore buried with him through baptism into death so that, just as Christ was raised from the dead through the glory of the Father, we too may live a new life. For if we have been united with him in a death like his, we will certainly also be united with him in a resurrection like his. (Romans 6:3-5 NIV)*

See how these verses in Romans 6 talk about the burial of our old lives and resurrection to a new life through baptism.

> *Having been buried with him in baptism, in which you were also raised with him through your faith in the working of God, who raised him from the dead. (Colossians 2:12 NIV)*

> *For all of you who were baptized into Christ have clothed yourselves with Christ. (Galatians 3:27 NIV)*

We clothe ourselves with Christ! We put on the "new man" (the new creation man) and leave the "old man" behind.

In 1 Peter 3:20-22 (NIV), we read the following:

> *To those who were disobedient long ago when God waited patiently in the days of Noah while the ark was being built. In it, only a few people, eight in all, were saved through water, and this water symbolizes baptism that now saves you also—not the removal of dirt from the body but the pledge of a clear conscience toward God. It saves you by the resurrection of Jesus Christ, who has gone into heaven and is at God's right hand—with angels, authorities and powers in submission to him.*

Here baptism is compared to the water that held the ark of Noah. Noah and his family entered the ark and were saved. Our ark is Christ. We enter Christ through receiving salvation. It is Christ´s finished work that saves us, but baptism is the water that sustains our faith. Let us look at the Amplified Bible:

> *And baptism, which is a figure [of their deliverance], does now also save you [from inward questionings and fears], not by the removing of outward body filth [bathing], but by [providing you with] the answer of a good and clear conscience (inward cleanness and peace) before God [because you are demonstrating what you believe to be yours] through the resurrection of Jesus Christ. (1 Peter 3:21 AMPC)*

We are demonstrating what we already believe out of a good and clear conscience before God. We have a good and clear conscience because we are already saved through our faith in Jesus, but according to this verse, baptism saves us from inward questioning and fears. You give all of this to Jesus in your baptism.

When Is the Right Time to Get Baptized?

So, when is the right timing to get baptized? When we look at the book of Acts, we see that baptism was done <u>immediately</u> after people received salvation. They did not wait for months or years, thinking about whether they were ready or not. It was a natural thing to do after accepting Christ. Let's look at some Scriptures:

> *Then Peter said to them, "Repent, and let every one of you be baptized in the name of Jesus Christ for the remission of sins; and you shall receive the gift of the Holy Spirit." (Acts 2:38)*

We will read the whole story of the Ethiopian eunuch in Acts 8:26-40 to get full understanding:

> *Now an angel of the Lord spoke to Philip, saying, "Arise and go toward the south along the road which goes down from Jerusalem to Gaza." This is desert. So he arose and went. And behold, a man of Ethiopia, a eunuch of great authority under Candace the queen of the Ethiopians, who had charge of all her treasury, and had come to Jerusalem to worship, was returning. And sitting in his chariot, he was reading Isaiah the prophet. Then the Spirit said to Philip, "Go near and overtake this chariot."*
>
> *So Philip ran to him, and heard him reading the prophet Isaiah, and said, "Do you understand what you are reading?"*

> *And he said, "How can I, unless someone guides me?" And he asked Philip to come up and sit with him. The place in the Scripture which he read was this:*
>
> *"He was led as a sheep to the slaughter;*
> *And as a lamb before its shearer is silent,*
> *So He opened not His mouth.*
> *In His humiliation His justice was taken away,*
> *And who will declare His generation?*
> *For His life is taken from the earth."*
> *So the eunuch answered Philip and said, "I ask you, of whom does the prophet say this, of himself or of some other man?" Then Philip opened his mouth, and beginning at this Scripture, preached Jesus to him. Now as they went down the road, they came to some water. And the eunuch said, "See, here is water. What hinders me from being baptized?" Then Philip said, "If you believe with all your heart, you may."*
>
> *And he answered and said, "I believe that Jesus Christ is the Son of God."*
>
> *So he commanded the chariot to stand still. And both Philip and the eunuch went down into the water, and he baptized him. Now when they came up out of the water, the Spirit of the Lord caught Philip away, so that the eunuch saw him no more; and he went on his way rejoicing. But Philip was found at Azotus. And passing through, he preached in all the cities till he came to Caesarea.*

We see that immediately after the Ethiopian eunuch believed, he was baptized.

Saul, who became the Apostle Paul, also received baptism immediately after accepting Christ.

> *And Ananias went his way and entered the house; and laying his hands on him he said, "Brother Saul, the Lord Jesus, who appeared to you on the road as you came, has sent me that you may receive your sight and be filled with the Holy Spirit." Immediately there fell from his eyes something like scales, and he received his sight at once; and he arose and was baptized. (Acts 9:17-18)*

Let us look at some other situations in Scripture where baptism was encouraged:

So they said, "Believe on the Lord Jesus Christ, and you will be saved, you and your household." Then they spoke the word of the Lord to him and to all who were in his house. And he took them the same hour of the night and washed their stripes. And immediately he and all his family were baptized. (Acts 16:31-33)

And now why are you waiting? Arise and be baptized, and wash away your sins, calling on the name of the Lord. (Acts 22:16)

Different Types of Baptism

And it happened, while Apollos was at Corinth, that Paul, having passed through the upper regions, came to Ephesus. And finding some disciples, he said to them, "Did you receive the Holy Spirit when you believed?"

So they said to him, "We have not so much as heard whether there is a Holy Spirit."
And he said to them, "Into what then were you baptized?"
So they said, "Into John's baptism."
Then Paul said, "John indeed baptized with a baptism of repentance, saying to the people that they should believe on Him who would come after him, that is, on Christ Jesus."
When they heard this, they were baptized in the name of the Lord Jesus. And when Paul had laid hands on them, the Holy Spirit came upon them, and they spoke with tongues and prophesied. (Acts 19:1-6)

In these verses, Paul talks about three types of baptisms. The first one was the baptism of the Holy Spirit, which is available for all believers. The second one is John the Baptist´s baptism, which we read about in the Gospels. This was a baptism of repentance that prepared the people to receive salvation later. This does not apply to us today, because Jesus has come already. The baptism we are talking about in this session is the third kind—baptism in the name of the Lord Jesus. So, we see this is different from John the Baptist's baptism in the Gospels.

We can see clearly that baptism belongs together with salvation. It is not a suggestion from God; it is something He wants us to do as an outward confirmation of what has happened to us on the inside. You could compare it to a wedding ceremony where you publicly, and before God, proclaim that you have decided to love and stay with your spouse for the rest of your life. You already love each other. The relationship is already there, but the wedding ceremony is a confirmation and proclamation of your decision before God and men. It is the same with water baptism. You have decided to follow Jesus, and your relationship with Him is already there, but you make it public and confirm it through baptism. You leave your former life and all your junk in the grave of the water. If you ever feel doubts, you can look back to your day of baptism and be reminded that your old life was actually buried with Christ in the water and you were raised up to a new life in Christ. There is no turning back. You belong to Him forever.

Perhaps you were baptized as a baby and wondered if that is a valid baptism? Well, that needs to be determined by your conscience and conviction before God. I was baptized as a baby as well, but when I received Christ at the age of twenty-one, I learned about baptism according to the Bible. I felt a strong urge on the inside to get baptized. I wanted to obey God and to show the whole world that I have decided to follow Jesus. I wanted to bury my old life in a visible physical way so I could rise up to live a new life with Jesus. I found a church where I could do it, and it was a great day. In my entire life, I had never felt so clean on the inside.

I repeat—being baptized is not a suggestion from God. Even though baptism is not a pre-requisite for salvation, it is actually something He wants us to do. Baptism is a powerful proclamation to the spiritual realm as well. You tell all of the enemy´s army that you belong to Jesus and that there is no turning back.

Take Action

After reading this, you might feel the Holy Spirit pulling on your heart to get baptized. Talk to your pastor and leaders to make arrangement for it to happen. If there is not a church where you can do it, you can have your own baptism ceremony in your Bible study group. Baptism can be done in a river, a lake, the sea, a swimming pool and even in a bathtub at home if that is your only option. For our Bible study group, we have had two beautiful ceremonies in our garden with baptism in our pool. We invited the families and made it into a celebration. The ladies who were baptized shared their testimonies, and they received prayer together with their families before they went into the water. The presence of God was very tangible. After the baptism, we celebrated with food and fellowship. We chose to have baptism within our group instead of in the church, since the ladies went to different churches and there were several of them wanting baptism at the same time. We invited pastors from the church to come, though.

SESSION 13

The Holy Spirit
Part 1

THE HOLY SPIRIT IS SENT from our Father in Heaven to live inside of us to be our Helper. In the New Covenant, God can be with every believer at the same time through the Holy Spirit. He lives in us, and He can work supernaturally in us, through us and for us.

The Holy Spirit as a Person in the Trinity

God is one God, but, still, He is three persons: Father, Son and Holy Spirit. We call this the Trinity. The Holy Spirit is one of the three persons in the Trinity. Just like the Father and the Son, the Holy Spirit wants us to know and recognize Him as a person and develop a relationship with Him. He wants us to get to know Him and His character and become familiar with the ways He works and how He wants to minister to us and through us.

The Holy Spirit in the Old and New Covenant

The Holy Spirit worked differently in the Old Covenant before the cross than He does now in the New Covenant after the cross. In the Old Covenant, the Holy Spirit was not for all people. He came upon only the prophets, the kings and the priests. The Holy Spirit did not live inside of them but came upon them, anointing them to function in their particular office. God´s presence dwelled only in one place on Earth in the Old Covenant, which was in the Ark of the Covenant in the Holiest of All in the temple. When Jesus died on the cross, the thick curtain (veil) that separated the Holiest of All from the people was ripped wide open from top to bottom by the hand of God. He moved out!

> *And Jesus cried out with a loud voice and breathed His last. Then the veil of the temple was torn in two from top to bottom. (Mark 15:37-38)*

In the New Covenant, we are the temple of the Holy Spirit. He lives in each one of us who have received Jesus as our Lord and Savior. The Holy Spirit is now available for all believers.

Jesus and the Holy Spirit

When Jesus came to planet Earth as a human being, it is quite interesting to see that He did not start His ministry and He did not perform any miracles until after He had received the Holy Spirit. Jesus received the Holy Spirit after He had been baptized by John the Baptist.

> *And the Holy Spirit descended in bodily form like a dove upon Him, and a voice came from heaven which said, "You are My beloved Son; in You, I am well pleased." <u>Now Jesus Himself began His ministry at about thirty years of age,</u> (Luke 3:22-23)*

> *<u>Then Jesus returned in the power of the Spirit</u> to Galilee, and news of Him went out through all the surrounding region. And He taught in their synagogues, being glorified by all.*
> *So He came to Nazareth, where He had been brought up. And as His custom was, He went into the synagogue on the Sabbath day, and stood up to read. And He was handed the book of the prophet Isaiah. And when He had opened the book, He found the place where it was written:*
> *"The Spirit of the Lord is upon Me,*
> *Because He has anointed Me*
> *To preach the gospel to the poor;*
> *He has sent Me to heal the brokenhearted,*
> *To proclaim liberty to the captives*
> *And recovery of sight to the blind,*
> *To set at liberty those who are oppressed;*
> *To proclaim the acceptable year of the Lord."*
> *Then He closed the book and gave it back to the attendant and sat down. And the eyes of all who were in the synagogue were fixed on Him. And He*

> *began to say to them, "Today this Scripture is fulfilled in your hearing" (Luke 4:14-21)*

All the miracles and everything supernatural Jesus did on Earth were by the power of the Holy Spirit. He could not do anything supernatural by Himself—He only did what the Father showed Him and only by the power of the Holy Spirit.

At the end of Jesus' ministry and life on Earth, He told the disciples that it would be to their benefit that He left. If Jesus stayed, He could physically be at only one place at a time because He was limited to a physical body. When He left, He could send the Holy Spirit to all believers.

> *Nevertheless I tell you the truth. It is to your advantage that I go away; for if I do not go away, the Helper will not come to you; but if I depart, I will send Him to you. (John 16:7)*

> *And I will pray the Father, and He will give you another Helper, that He may abide with you forever— the Spirit of truth, whom the world cannot receive, because it neither sees Him nor knows Him; but you know Him, for He dwells with you and will be in you. I will not leave you orphans; I will come to you. (John 14:16-18)*

After Jesus' death and resurrection, salvation was made available for all human beings. Those who believed were now cleansed and ready to receive the Holy Spirit.

> *Then, the same day at evening, being the first day of the week, when the doors were shut where the disciples were assembled, for fear of the Jews, Jesus came and stood in the midst, and said to them, "Peace be with you." When He had said this, He showed them His hands and His side. Then the disciples were glad when they saw the Lord. So Jesus said to them again, "Peace to you! As the Father has sent Me, I also send you." And when He had said this, He breathed on them, and said to them, "Receive the Holy Spirit." (John 20:19-22)*

This was the moment when the disciples were born again. They were born of the Spirit.

The Baptism of The Holy Spirit on the Day of Pentecost

Jesus had so much more in store for them! He did not want them to live the Christian life in their own strength and power. He had always planned to send them (and us) power from above. He intended to send the Holy Spirit to come and live inside each one of them. The disciples were told to WAIT until they had received this power.

One of the last things Jesus said to the disciples before He went to Heaven was this:

> *"And now I will send the Holy Spirit, just as my Father promised. But stay here in the city until the Holy Spirit comes and fills you with power from heaven." (Luke 24:49 NLT)*

> *And being assembled together with them, He commanded them not to depart from Jerusalem, but to wait for the Promise of the Father, "which," He said, "you have heard from Me; for John truly baptized with water, but you shall be baptized with the Holy Spirit not many days from now." Therefore, when they had come together, they asked Him, saying, "Lord, will You at this time restore the kingdom to Israel?" And He said to them, "It is not for you to know times or seasons which the Father has put in His own authority. But you shall receive power when the Holy Spirit has come upon you, and you shall be witnesses to Me in Jerusalem, and in all Judea and Samaria, and to the end of the earth." (Acts 1:4-8)*

> *John answered, saying to all, "I indeed baptize you with water; but One mightier than I is coming, whose sandal strap I am not worthy to loose. He will baptize you with the Holy Spirit and fire." (Luke 3:16)*

In Acts 2:1-18, we read how the Holy Spirit came on the Day of Pentecost. It happened like this:

> *When the Day of Pentecost had fully come, they were all with one accord in one place. And suddenly there came a sound from heaven, as of a rushing mighty wind, and it filled the whole house where they were sitting. Then there appeared to them divided tongues, as of fire, and one sat upon each of them. And they were all filled with the Holy Spirit and began to speak with other tongues, as the Spirit gave them utterance*
> *And there were dwelling in Jerusalem Jews, devout men, from every nation under heaven. And when this sound occurred, the multitude came together, and were confused, because everyone heard them speak in his own language. Then they were all amazed and marveled, saying to one another, "Look, are not all these who speak Galileans? And how is it that we hear,*

each in our own language in which we were born? Parthians and Medes and Elamites, those dwelling in Mesopotamia, Judea and Cappadocia, Pontus and Asia, Phrygia and Pamphylia, Egypt and the parts of Libya adjoining Cyrene, visitors from Rome, both Jews and proselytes, Cretans and Arabs—we hear them speaking in our own tongues the wonderful works of God." So they were all amazed and perplexed, saying to one another, "Whatever could this mean?"
Others mocking said, "They are full of new wine."
But Peter, standing up with the eleven, raised his voice and said to them, "Men of Judea and all who dwell in Jerusalem, let this be known to you, and heed my words. For these are not drunk, as you suppose, since it is only the third hour of the day. But this is what was spoken by the prophet Joel:
'And it shall come to pass in the last days, says God,
That I will pour out of My Spirit on all flesh;
Your sons and your daughters shall prophesy,
Your young men shall see visions,
Your old men shall dream dreams.
And on My menservants and on My maidservants
I will pour out My Spirit in those days;
And they shall prophesy."

Peter continues this with a lengthy sermon, which you can read for yourself in Acts 2.

Peter, who had denied Jesus a few days earlier, was now filled with the Holy Spirit, and suddenly He became so <u>bold</u> and preached to all the people. That day, 3000 people were saved in Jerusalem. The church of Jesus Christ on planet Earth was born.

FOR SELF REFLECTION AND GROUP DISCUSSION

1. How did the Holy Spirit work in the Old Testament and how does He work in the New Testament after the cross?
2. Why didn´t Jesus start His ministry or do any miracles until after He had received the Holy Spirit?
3. Why were the disciples told to wait in the city until the Holy Spirit would fill them with power? (See Luke 24:49 and Acts 1:4-8 in the session.)

4. In what ways did the disciples change after they were baptized with the Holy Spirit?

   SHARE AND DISCUSS WITH THE GROUP

SESSION 14

The Holy Spirit Part 2

The Ministry and Character of the Holy Spirit

ON THE DAY OF PENTECOST, the Holy Spirit came to Earth to stay. He became available to all believers. The Holy Spirit came to remain in us, with us and work through us. He will never leave us.

> *And I will pray the Father, and He will give you another Helper, that He may abide with you forever— (John 14:16)*

This explains what Jesus meant when He said that it was for our benefit that He leave us, because through the Holy Spirit, He can now be with all of us at the same time! He is always there for each one of us 24/7. He is not bound by a physical body.

The Holy Spirit is a person, and when we give Him attention and get to know Him, we can benefit from all of the things He wants to do for us and through us. He wants to have close fellowship with us and help us, but He is a gentleman, so we need to ask Him to help. If we let Him, He is always there to minister to us, reveal Jesus to us and glorify Him, comfort us, guide us, remind us, encourage us, correct us, lead us, strengthen us and give us power.

> *But the Helper, the Holy Spirit, whom the Father will send in My name, He will teach you all things, and bring to your remembrance all things that I said to you. (John 14:26)*

> *I still have many things to say to you, but you cannot bear them now. However, when He, the Spirit of truth, has come, He will guide you into all truth; for He will not speak on His own authority, but whatever He hears He will speak; and He will tell you things to come. He will glorify Me, for He will take of what is Mine and declare it to you. All things that the Father has are Mine. Therefore, I said that He will take of Mine and declare it to you. (John 16:12-15)*

John 14:26 calls the Holy Spirit a *HELPER*. The Amplified Bible provides an explanation of the original meaning of the word "Helper" in John 16:7:

> *However, I am telling you nothing but the truth when I say it is profitable (good, expedient, advantageous) for you that I go away. Because if I do not go away, the Comforter (Counselor, Helper, Advocate, Intercessor, Strengthener, Standby) will not come to you [into close fellowship with you]; but if I go away, I will send Him to you [to be in close fellowship with you]*

Let us look at each of the seven meanings of the Holy Spirit as our Helper:

COMFORTER: He will lift you up from your situation, increase you and give you a higher perspective so that you can count all your blessings. There is vision and life when the Comforter comes to minister to you!

COUNSELOR: He is wonderful in counsel and excellent in guidance (see Isa. 28:29 AMPC). He brings us into the supernatural. To be effective in this world, we need His counsel. He will lead us and give us the right timing for things. God has planned everything for us and laid it out already, so we can follow Him step by step.

HELPER: He is the One who comes when you are crying out for help. You can expect support when you ask, and you have access to the resources of Heaven. Circumstances will turn around because you will be given insight into situations and the time we live in.

> *The Lord is my Helper; I will not be seized with alarm [I will not fear or dread or be terrified]. What can man do to me? (Hebrews 13:6 AMPC)*

STRENGTHENER:

> *I can do all things through Christ who strengthens me. (Philippians 4:13)*

STANDBY: He is ready to help and is always there.

> *God is our refuge and strength, A very present help in trouble. (Psalms 46:1)*

ADVOCATE: One who pleads for another in front of a judge. Jesus is your advocate in Heaven (see 1 John 2:1-2). The Holy Spirit is your advocate on Earth as He reminds you of who you are in Christ. (This is what gives you boldness before God.)

INTERCESSOR:

> *Likewise the Spirit also helps in our weaknesses. For we do not know what we should pray for as we ought, but the Spirit Himself makes intercession for us with groanings which cannot be uttered. Now He who searches the hearts knows what the mind of the Spirit is, because He makes intercession for the saints according to the will of God. And we know that all things work together for good to those who love God, to those who are the called according to His purpose. (Romans 8:26-28)*

The Spirit makes intercession for us when we pray in the Holy Spirit, which means that we pray in tongues. This is a prayer language that we get as a gift from God when we are baptized in the Holy Spirit. When we pray in the Spirit (in tongues), we are joining in the symphony of what the Holy Spirit is praying for us.

Speaking in tongues was a sign that the disciples had been baptized by the Holy Spirit on the Day of Pentecost. It is also a gift with many benefits to the believer. When we pray in tongues, we stir up our inner man. In 1 Corinthians 14:4 we read that "*He who speaks in a tongue, edifies himself.*"

The Disciples After Pentecost = Us After Pentecost!

It is interesting to see the change in the disciples after Pentecost when they had been baptized in the Holy Spirit. They became witnesses for Jesus and preached the Gospel with great boldness.

Peter preached, and 3000 people were saved the same day. From the Day of Pentecost onwards, the disciples were empowered to minister in power by the Holy Spirit as Jesus Himself had done. See how Peter and John healed a lame man in Acts Chapter 3.

Throughout the entire book of Acts, we can see how bold and brave the disciples were and how they ministered in the power of the Holy Spirit. The Gospel was demonstrated through healings and miracles. Demon-possessed people were set free. We can see that the disciples wanted to be used by God in this way. See how they prayed:

> *"Now, Lord, look on their threats, and grant to Your servants that with all boldness they may speak Your word, by stretching out Your hand to heal, and that signs and wonders may be done through the name of Your holy Servant Jesus."*
>
> *And when they had prayed, the place where they were assembled together was shaken; and they were all filled with the Holy Spirit, and they spoke the word of God with boldness. (Acts 4:29-31)*

In the same way this power was given to them, it is given to us! If we are baptized in the Holy Spirit, we have access to the same power. The power is provided so we can be witnesses of Jesus and bring the Gospel to the world.

So, how does this work? First, we need to trust that it is true. We need to believe that the Holy Spirit lives in us. Then we need to be willing and have an open ear and heart to hear His voice and to do what He says. When He gives us a prompting to do something, we should do it. For example, He may prompt you to pray for someone who needs healing, to share the Gospel, to call someone or to go somewhere. The Holy Spirit will give gifts of the Spirit, so we can minister to people supernaturally. We will learn more about this in a later session. Most importantly, we need to stay connected to Jesus—abide in Him and remain in the vine—so His life and power can flow through us (see John 15).

Jesus said He will do greater things through us than He did Himself (see John 14:12)!

In Mark 16:17-18, Jesus says, *"And these signs will follow those who believe: In my name they will cast out demons; they will speak in new tongues; they will take up serpents; and if they drink anything deadly, it will by no means hurt them; they will lay hands on the sick, and they will recover.'"*

This is what we are created for: to live by the Holy Spirit! Let us open our hearts and receive His power and fire in our lives. Let us get to know the Holy Spirit and let Him lead us into the life He has designed us to live. Let Him lead us in everyday life. Let Him work through us with His power when we reach out to minister to people on His behalf.

How do we receive the baptism of the Holy Spirit? We ask God for it. In Luke 11:13, we read, *"If you then, being evil, know how to give good gifts to your children, how much more will your heavenly Father give the Holy Spirit to those who ask Him!'"*

You can also receive it by the prayer and laying on of the hands of another Spirit-filled believer. This is what happened to Timothy when the Apostle Paul laid hands on him: *"Therefore I remind you to stir up the gift of God which is in you through the laying on of my hands" (2 Timothy 1:6).*

Let Us Pray

> *Lord Jesus, we thank you for sending the Holy Spirit to us. Thank you that you have come to live in us by the Holy Spirit. We open our hearts for the Holy Spirit's work in us and through us. We pray that you will manifest your Word today by filling us and baptizing us all with your Holy Spirit. Amen.*

FOR SELF REFLECTION AND GROUP DISCUSSION

1. Why was it to our benefit that Jesus went back to Heaven to be with His Father instead of staying on Earth with us after He was resurrected? Who was sent instead of Jesus to be with every believer on Earth?
2. Review the different ways the Holy Spirit is your Helper and think of testimonies from your own life when He has been your Comforter, Counselor, Helper, Strengthener, Standby, Advocate and Intercessor.
3. Have you experienced the baptism of the Holy Spirit? Do you speak in tongues as a prayer language? If not, do you want to receive it? Then ask God for it (see Luke 11:13) and let another Spirit-filled believer lay hands on you and pray for you to receive the baptism of the Holy Spirit.

   SHARE AND DISCUSS WITH THE GROUP

SESSION 15

Forgiveness in the New Covenant

FORGIVENESS IS A KEY that unlocks our lives. The forgiveness we have received, and keep receiving from God daily, is like a life source released. It sets us free from guilt, shame and condemnation so that we can live our lives in freedom with a clean conscience before God. When we think about the amazing grace God has given us and keeps giving us, we are filled with gratitude.

God Has Already Forgiven You

The reason why God can forgive us is because Jesus took all punishment for our sin upon Himself when He died on the cross. He became the perfect sacrifice for sin once and for all, so there is no more punishment for sin or no more sacrifices needed (see Heb. 7:27, 9:12, 10:12). We can come to God through Christ and receive forgiveness freely. Forgiveness was already provided at the cross 2000 years ago. We come to God with a heart of repentance (we are sorry for what we did and determined not to do it again).

> *If we confess our sins, He is faithful and just to forgive us our sins and to cleanse us from all unrighteousness. (1 John 1:9)*

We do not have to beg God for forgiveness. The moment we bring our wrongdoings, bad attitudes and weaknesses to God, we can thank Him for the forgiveness Jesus already provided for us and receive it freely. What amazing grace! When we have sinned, we should not hide from God but run to Him. He wants us to fully trust in His grace and come boldly to His throne!

> *For we do not have a High Priest who cannot sympathize with our weaknesses, but was in all points tempted as we are, yet without sin. Let us therefore come boldly to the throne of grace, that we may obtain mercy and find grace to help in time of need. (Hebrews 4:15-16)*

It is very tempting to try to hide from God if we have failed and sinned since we feel guilty and ashamed of ourselves; however, God wants us to come boldly to His throne of grace! He knows everything about us, and He is not condemning us. We receive forgiveness, but at the same time, we pray that the Holy Spirit will work in our areas of weakness and empower us to change our bad patterns, habits and attitudes. As we just read in Hebrews, Jesus sympathizes with our weaknesses and wants to help us. At the throne of grace, we will find help in our time of need. It is important to note that we cannot keep doing the same things over and over again on purpose, counting on God's forgiveness. We cannot abuse grace (see Rom. 6:1-2). We must not forget that even though forgiveness is free for us, it came with a very high price for Jesus.

Ask Forgiveness and Make It Right with Others

It is not enough to just ask God for forgiveness when we have sinned—we need to make things right with the people we have hurt and offended as well. God wants us to humble ourselves and be quick to ask for forgiveness from others.

When we have received forgiveness from God and people, we need to move on. We are not supposed to keep digging up the same sin again and bring to God what has already been forgiven. In Jeremiah 31, we find a prophecy about the New Covenant (the covenant we live in today). One of the main stipulations of the New Covenant is that God will remember our sins no more.

> *"But this is the covenant that I will make with the house of Israel after those days, says the Lord: I will put My law in their minds, and write it on their hearts; and I will be their God, and they shall be My people. No more shall every man teach his neighbor, and every man his brother, saying, 'Know the Lord,' for they all shall know Me, from the least of them to the greatest of them, says the Lord. For I will forgive their iniquity, and their sin I will remember no more." (Jeremiah 31:33-34)*

When God has forgotten about it, we need to move on as well. Sometimes the issue is that we have a hard time forgiving ourselves...

Forgive Others Just as You Were Forgiven by God

The grace and forgiveness we have received, God wants us to release to others. In the New Covenant, there is no precondition for forgiveness like there was in the Old Covenant, where you were forgiven only if you forgave first. After the cross, forgiveness is received by grace. In the New Covenant, we forgive others just as we have ALREADY been forgiven in Christ Jesus. See how these verses speak about forgiveness in the past tense:

> *And be kind to one another, tenderhearted, forgiving one another, even as God in Christ forgave you. (Ephesians 4:32)*

> *Therefore, as the elect of God, holy and beloved, put on tender mercies, kindness, humility, meekness, longsuffering; bearing with one another, and forgiving one another, if anyone has a complaint against another; even as Christ forgave you, so you also must do. (Colossians 3:12-13)*

It can be tough to forgive someone who has hurt you badly, especially if the person repeatedly does the same thing. In Matthew 18:21-22, Jesus tells us to forgive not only seven times but seventy times seven times.

To forgive someone does NOT mean that you excuse what the person did, or that what the person did was not wrong. It also does not mean that you were not hurt by what happened or that you give the person permission to do it again. Forgiveness is a choice to let go of what you are holding against another person. You no longer keep an offense against him/her.

God wants us to forgive even if the other person does not ask for our forgiveness. The person who hurt you might not even be aware of what he/she did. You may try to talk to the person who offended you, but even then, the person may be too proud to ask for forgiveness. Regardless of the attitude of the other person, we should forgive because of the great grace we have received from God.

If you choose not to forgive, the one trapped in pain, hurt, bitterness and offense is you, regardless of the other person's attitude. You will be the victim of your own unforgiveness. Forgiveness will set you free on the inside and start a healing process in your heart. When you are willing to forgive and let go, God is there with His Spirit to empower you by His grace to do it. It might not happen overnight, but God will take you through a process of forgiveness, healing and restoration.

Relationships are restored through forgiveness; however, when trust has been broken, it has to be won back. This takes time and has to be proven.

If you have been a victim of physical abuse or you live in such a relationship, forgiveness does not mean you should stay in that situation and allow it to continue. That is not what Jesus meant by forgiving seventy times seven times. We need to be wise to protect ourselves and get out of the situation. When it comes to friendships, you don't have to stay best friends with a person who keeps hurting you and doesn't seem to care. We need to take care of ourselves and get out of destructive relationships. (If this is a marriage, counseling is advisable.) My point is that forgiveness does not mean that we let someone repeatedly take advantage of us.

Forgiveness is essential in the matter of guarding our hearts and not letting any bitter root grow up and ruin our lives (see Heb. 12:15).

> *Guard your heart above all else, for it determines the course of your life. (Proverbs 4:23 NLT)*

FOR SELF REFLECTION AND GROUP DISCUSSION

1. Read and meditate on the two Scriptures in Colossians 3:12-13 and Ephesians 4:32. Think about all of the things God has forgiven in your life. Think about the fact that God remembers it no more and thank Him for it. Think about the freedom you can enjoy with a clean conscience, knowing that God holds nothing against you.

   > *And be kind to one another, tenderhearted, forgiving one another, even as God in Christ forgave you. (Ephesians 4:32)*

   > *Therefore, as the elect of God, holy and beloved, put on tender mercies, kindness, humility, meekness, longsuffering; bearing with one another, and forgiving one another, if anyone has a complaint against another; even as Christ forgave you, so you also must do. (Colossians 3:12-13)*

2. Read again Hebrews 4:15-16:

For we do not have a High Priest who cannot sympathize with our weaknesses, but was in all points tempted as we are, yet without sin. Let us therefore come boldly to the throne of grace, that we may obtain mercy and find grace to help in time of need. (Hebrews 4:15-16)

What do you tend to do if you sin? Do you hide from God or run boldly to the throne of grace to receive forgiveness? If you tend to hide from God and stay away from Him, keep meditating on these Scriptures until you have revelation and confidence to approach God boldly in every situation of your life.

3. The next step is to pray that the Holy Spirit will reveal to you anything or anyone that you need to forgive. Talk to the Lord about it and ask Him to help you come to the point where you are able to forgive and let go. Write about it in your journal.

4. Forgive yourself! God forgave you, but have you forgiven yourself? Do you keep "beating yourself up" for things God has forgiven and forgotten? Write in your journal and ask Jesus to help you forgive yourself.

SHARE WITH THE GROUP AND ASK THEM FOR PRAYER IF YOU NEED IT. KEEP PRAYING ABOUT THESE QUESTIONS AT HOME.

SESSION 16

Guard Your Heart

GOD HAS GIVEN US THE RESPONSIBILITY to guard our hearts carefully. We are asked to guard, watch over and keep our hearts clean and soft. Our heart is like a garden, and we need to watch over it so that weeds, thorns and thistles do not overtake it. We cannot allow bitterness, unforgiveness, resentment, insults or misunderstandings to take root in the garden, as these things will harden the soil of our hearts. We need to ensure our hearts are the good ground where the seed of God's Word can bring forth a great harvest in our lives.

This is very well stated in Proverbs 4:23. Let us look at it in different translations to understand its full meaning:

> *Keep your heart with all diligence, For out of it spring the issues of life. (NKJV)*
>
> *Guard your heart above all else, for it determines the course of your life. (NLT)*
>
> *Above all else, guard your heart, for everything you do flows from it. (NIV)*

Why Guard Your Heart?

The first reason why we should guard our hearts is that the condition of our hearts will determine how we live our whole life. The state of your heart will affect your choices, priorities and the direction of your life. It will affect your behavior and reactions. Hurt people hurt others, and cold, hard-hearted people have no empathy or sympathy for others; they only think about themselves. We know that bitterness, hurt, unforgiveness, jealousy, greed, revenge, etc. can make people do the most horrible things.

As "good Christians" we might not live in these extremes. However, in Song of Songs 2:15 (NIV) we read, *"Catch for us the foxes, the little foxes that ruin the vineyards, our vineyards that are in bloom."*

We see from this verse that there are little foxes that ruin the vineyards. So, we need to be aware of the little things that sneak up on us. We might start spinning on a small negative thought about somebody, and as we keep thinking that thought, it becomes a thought pattern that turns into a negative attitude against that person, which will affect your whole relationship. Marriage is a common breeding ground for this. We need to take our wrong thoughts captive (see 2 Cor. 10:5) and choose to focus on the good things (see Phil. 4:8). This kind of "thought management" plays a critical role in guarding our hearts.

> *For the weapons of our warfare are not carnal but mighty in God for pulling down strongholds, casting down arguments and every high thing that exalts itself against the knowledge of God, bringing every thought into captivity to the obedience of Christ, (2 Corinthians 10:4-5)*

> *Finally, brethren, whatever things are true, whatever things are noble, whatever things are just, whatever things are pure, whatever things are lovely, whatever things are of good report, if there is any virtue and if there is anything praiseworthy—meditate on these things. (Philippians 4:8)*

There are situations every day that can cause misunderstandings, hurt feelings, jealousy, resentment, offense and many other negative things. If we don't clean up "our garden" daily by taking it all to God in prayer AND sorting things out with the people involved, our hearts will get hard and bitter. Our "garden" will become full of weeds, thorns, thistles and bitter roots. The ground will get hard, and nothing good will grow there. Our relationships will be affected—both towards other people and God.

Pride plays a big part in it since that is usually what keeps us from sorting things out with people. We want justice for ourselves, and we do not want to be the first one to say sorry. As time goes by, it gets worse and the roots get bigger and stronger. The soil gets harder. This is not a nice place to be.

> *"God resists the proud, But gives grace to the humble." (James 4:6)*

If you find yourself in this situation, God has a way out for you through repentance, humility and making things right with people... the Holy Spirit is there to help you.

Be Good Ground for the Word of God

In the Gospels, Jesus told a parable about a sower going out to sow seed. We find this parable in Mark 4, Matthew 13 and Luke 8. In the parable of the sower, Jesus tells us how the condition of our hearts will determine whether the Word of God sown into our lives will bring forth a harvest or not. Let us read:

> *"Listen! Behold, a sower went out to sow. And it happened, as he sowed, that some seed fell by the wayside; and the birds of the air came and devoured it. Some fell on stony ground, where it did not have much earth; and immediately it sprang up because it had no depth of earth. But when the sun was up it was scorched, and because it had no root it withered away. And some seed fell among thorns; and the thorns grew up and choked it, and it yielded no crop. But other seed fell on good ground and yielded a crop that sprang up, increased and produced: some thirtyfold, some sixty, and some a hundred." And He said to them, "He who has ears to hear, let him hear!" (Mark 4:3-9)*
>
> *The Parable of the Sower Explained: And He said to them, "Do you not understand this parable? How then will you understand all the parables? The sower sows the word. And these are the ones by the wayside where the word is sown. When they hear, Satan comes immediately and takes away the word that was sown in their hearts. These likewise are the ones sown on stony ground who, when they hear the word, immediately receive it with gladness; and they have no root in themselves, and so endure only for a time. Afterward, when tribulation or persecution arises for the word's sake, immediately they stumble. Now these are the ones sown among thorns; they are the ones who hear the word, and the cares of this world, the deceitfulness of riches, and the desires for other things entering in choke the word, and it becomes unfruitful. But these are the ones sown on good ground, those who hear the word, accept it, and bear fruit: some thirtyfold, some sixty, and some a hundred." (Mark 4:13-20)*

We see in this parable how the Word of God needs good ground in the heart to bring forth a great harvest. Seeds are designed to multiply, but a seed is at the mercy of the soil it is planted in. When the Word of God is sown in good ground, you will reap a harvest in your life—a harvest of the grace and knowledge of Jesus Christ. The Word that is planted in your heart continues to work in you and becomes a well and a river of salvation that flows inside of you. It will produce an increase in whatever area of your life that specific Word relates to. A force of faith will come out of this Word that is planted in your heart, which will keep you strong through any trials you face.

The planted Word brings revelation, faith, trust and hope. We act on the Word and become a demonstration of the Word. As we abide in the Word, many people will be blessed by our lives. We will be sensitive to the voice and the leading of the Holy Spirit, so we do not walk off-track but stay right in the will of God. We are quick to repent, forgive and ask for forgiveness so that our relationship with people and God is flourishing. Our soft hearts easily submit to God's ways, so we grow in character and maturity in Christ. What a flourishing life! No wonder it says in Proverbs 4:23 that we should guard and keep our hearts above all else! Because it really determines the whole course of your life!

FOR SELF REFLECTION AND GROUP DISCUSSION

1. Ask the Holy Spirit to search your heart and reveal to you any bitter root or unforgiveness. Pray about these issues and ask God to cleanse your heart and help you to forgive and let go.
2. Do you consider your heart to be soft and receptive to God? If not, what is making it hard and not responsive?
3. Thought management—how is your thought life? Do you actively manage your thoughts and guard what is allowed to settle in your mind and become a mindset or a stronghold? (See 2 Cor. 10:4-5.)
4. What are some examples of "the little foxes" which sneak in to ruin the vineyard?

   Catch for us the foxes, the little foxes that ruin the vineyards, our vineyards that are in bloom. (Song of Songs 2:15 NIV)

   SHARE AND DISCUSS WITH THE GROUP

SESSION 17

Praise and Worship

PRAISE AND WORSHIP is our hearts´ language towards God. It is the way we thank Him and respond to His goodness, mercy, holiness, grace, love, faithfulness and so much more in our lives. Our God is perfect, almighty, holy and righteous. He is the Creator of all things and is the only One who is worthy of our worship. He wants us to worship Him only, not idols. He wants to be the center of our lives and the center of our worship and praise, because He loves us so much and wants to be loved back.

Why Praise and Worship?

Through praise and worship, we have relationship and fellowship with the Lord. The Lord is always there to hear our prayer requests, but He appreciates that we also thank Him for everything He has already done for us and praise Him for all that He is to us. It says in Psalm 100:4:

> *Enter into His gates with thanksgiving,*
> *And into His courts with praise.*
> *Be thankful to Him, and bless His name.*

In the Message Bible, it says that we enter with the password: "Thank you!" This means that whenever we want to pray, we should always start by first thanking and praising Him for who He is and what He has already done for us.

> *Therefore by Him let us continually offer the sacrifice of praise to God, that is, the fruit of our lips, giving thanks to His name. (Hebrews 13:15)*

PRAISE is thanking Him for what He has already done for us. Everybody can do that. However, *WORSHIP* is at a deeper level and is a very spiritual act. It comes from an overflow of awe and adoration of the greatness of God and who He is to us. It comes from a place within us that knows that if God would never do anything for us again, we would still worship Him because of who He is.

In John 4:23-24, Jesus explains this to the Samaritan woman at the well.

> *"But the hour is coming, and now is, when the true worshipers will worship the Father in spirit and truth; for the Father is seeking such to worship Him. God is Spirit, and those who worship Him must worship in spirit and truth."*

We need the Holy Spirit to worship since we cannot worship in spirit and truth from our flesh. If we are born again, we have received the Holy Spirit. We have a "*fountain of water springing up into everlasting life*," and from our inner man shall "*flow rivers of living water*" (John 4:14, 7:38). The Holy Spirit is there to help you and lead you in worship. He will glorify and reveal Jesus to you, so worship comes as a natural response.

Through praise and worship, you enter into the presence of God. You enter into the spiritual realm—into the supernatural. You are not the only one worshiping in this heavenly realm; the angels and the saints in Heaven are constantly worshiping as well. The Lord will respond to your praise and worship in a great way. He loves your devotion, and it truly touches His heart. In His presence, anything can happen.

Praise and worship bring joy into your life. The joy of the Lord is your strength. Your praise and worship will bless you just as much as it exalts the Lord.

> *You have turned for me my mourning into dancing; You have put off my sackcloth and clothed me with gladness, To the end that my glory may sing praise to You and not be silent. (Psalm 30:11-12)*

How to Praise and Worship God

Praise and worship come in many forms—it can be singing, clapping, playing instruments, shouting, proclaiming His power and might, telling Him how beautiful He is, how much you love Him and so much more... It can take place with others in a group or in church, or it can just be you, alone with the Lord. The Book of Psalms speaks a lot about praise and worship. Here are a few examples:

Oh, clap your hands, all you peoples! Shout to God with the voice of triumph! (Psalm 47:1)

Sing praises to God, sing praises! (Psalm 47:6)

Oh come, let us sing to the Lord!
Let us shout joyfully to the Rock of our salvation.
Let us come before His presence with thanksgiving;
Let us shout joyfully to Him with psalms.
For the Lord is the great God,
And the great King above all gods. (Psalm 95:1-3)

Make a joyful shout to God, all the earth!
Sing out the honor of His name;
Make His praise glorious.
Say to God, "How awesome are Your works!
Through the greatness of Your power... (Psalm 66:1-3)

The Holy Spirit has many ways of leading us in worship. One way is to put a song in our hearts that we really want to sing to the Lord, or He leads us to pray or sing in the Spirit. In several places in the Book of Psalms, we are encouraged to sing a new song to the Lord (see Psalm 96 and 98). This is a new song birthed in the Spirit right at that moment, and it might be prophetic, which means that you sing the things you want to see in the future, inspired by the Holy Spirit.

We see that there are many ways to praise and worship the Lord. Being a worshiper of God is a decision, and it is a lifestyle. We make a choice to be a worshiper of the Father—a worshiper of Jesus!

Praise and Worship Strengthen Your Faith

Abraham is our father of faith, and he was a worshiper. Abraham received promises from the Lord that could not come to pass naturally. He was very old and did not have any children, but God promised him that he would have a son and become the father of many nations. Sarah, his wife, was far past child-bearing age. But Abraham stayed firm in his faith, and he did not waver. Do you want to know the secret to his strong faith and trust in the Lord? The answer is found in Romans 4:20-21:

> *He [Abraham] did not waver at the promise of God through unbelief, but was strengthened in faith giving glory to God, and being fully convinced that what He had promised He was also able to perform.*

This is really interesting; as Abraham spoke out his praises and worship to God, it built faith in Him. Abraham heard himself proclaiming the promises of God and God's unlimited ability to make them come to pass again and again, and we know that *"faith comes by hearing and hearing by the word of God"* (Romans 10:17). The same thing will happen to us when we worship and give glory to God. Our faith will be strong! We will stand firm on His promises.

Choose to Praise and Worship God in Spite of Your Situation

We do not always feel like praising God, but we choose to praise and worship Him because He is worthy and because we know it is the solution to our problems.

In Psalm 103, we see that David speaks to his own soul and commands it to bless the Lord. He chooses to praise the Lord.

> *Bless the Lord, O my soul;*
> *And all that is within me, bless His holy name!*
> *Bless the Lord, O my soul,*
> *And forget not all His benefits (Psalm 103:1-2)*

David was a true worshiper. He was a man after God's own heart. When we read the Psalms of David, they are full of praise and worship to God. David did not care what the people thought of him. When the Israelites were bringing the Ark of the Covenant to Jerusalem, the Bible says, *"Then David danced before the Lord with all his might; and David was wearing a linen ephod"* (2 Samuel 6:14)—which means he was dancing in his underwear in public. His wife, Michal, despised him for it, but he proclaimed to her, *"It was before the Lord, who chose me instead of your father and all his house, to appoint me ruler over the people of the Lord, over Israel. Therefore I will play music before the Lord. And I will be even more undignified than this, and will be humble in my own sight"* (2 Samuel 6:21-22).

The Apostle Paul knew the secret of worship as well. On one of Paul and Silas' mission trips, they delivered a young slave girl from an evil spirit of divination.

Her master became very angry because he had earned money from her fortune-telling services. Paul and Silas were beaten with rods and thrown into the inner prison, and their feet were fastened in the stocks. You can read the story from Acts 16:16 onwards. What is interesting to take notice of here is Paul and Silas' response to the situation. They had every reason to complain and murmur, but what did they do?

> *But at midnight Paul and Silas were praying and singing hymns to God, and the prisoners were listening to them. Suddenly there was a great earthquake so that the foundations of the prison were shaken; and immediately all the doors were opened, and everyone's chains were loosed. And the keeper of the prison, awaking from sleep and seeing the prison doors open, supposing the prisoners had fled, drew his sword and was about to kill himself. But Paul called with a loud voice, saying, "Do yourself no harm, for we are all here." Then he called for a light, ran in, and fell down trembling before Paul and Silas. And he brought them out and said, "Sirs, what must I do to be saved?" So they said, "Believe on the Lord Jesus Christ, and you will be saved, you and your household." (Acts 16:25-31)*

When they chose to worship in spite of the circumstances, God got to work and solved their problem. Notice too that because the two of them worshiped, the prison doors for all the prisoners opened. Worship and prayer is so powerful, it affects not only you but the people around you as well!

We praise and worship before we see the answer because that is what will bring us the solution. We praise and worship in the midst of our trials and challenges. In our praises, we thank God for who He is, what He is able to do and everything He has already done for us. It strengthens our faith and helps us to focus on the One who will bring the answer.

I encourage you to decide today to praise and worship the Lord in all circumstances! As you do, you will see your situation turn around, your "chains fall off" and you will enter into a more intimate relationship with the Lord. You will experience His joy and His presence in a stronger way, and praise and worship will lead your prayer life into a whole new dimension and flow in the Holy Spirit! You can worship anywhere: in the shower, car, bedroom, when you are exercising... You are the temple of the Holy Spirit in which prayers, praise and worship will go on and on and on—to the Lord!

Let us end with the words of Jesus in John 4:23-24:

"But the hour is coming, and now is, when the true worshipers will worship the Father in spirit and truth; for the Father is seeking such to worship Him. God is Spirit, and those who worship Him must worship in spirit and truth."

FOR SELF REFLECTION AND GROUP DISCUSSION

1. What has been your attitude to worship until now—did you think of it as just singing some songs and "what's the point"? Or did you put your heart into it to truly worship God? Did today's lesson put worship in a new perspective for you?
2. Meditate a while on the fact that God is longing for your worship and to have fellowship with you. How does that make you feel? Meditate on the fact that God wants us to seek His face, not only His hands (seek Him for who He is, not only for what He can do for you). Write down any thoughts you get. Based on this lesson, is there anything you will change in your personal time with the Lord?
3. Strengthen your faith through worship. Revisit the Scripture in Romans 4:20-21.

   He [Abraham] did not waver at the promise of God through unbelief, but was strengthened in faith giving glory to God, and being entirely convinced that what He had promised He was also able to perform.

   Think of a situation in your life where you can take on a new strategy to strengthen your faith and to worship and thank God for His willingness and ability to do what He has promised in your situation.

   Take some time to worship and thank Him in the area or situation you thought of above.

   SHARE AND DISCUSS WITH THE GROUP

SESSION 18

The Sovereignty of God

Is God in Control?

THERE IS A LOT OF CONFUSION around the sovereignty of God. We continuously hear statements like "God is in control" and "everything happens for a reason" and "nothing happens without God allowing it." Many people are living by fate, not by faith. You hear this kind of talk a lot among Christians as well. This raises an important question: If our faith is in fate, where does that put God? If God is in control of everything, then He would be the one behind disasters, murder, sickness and disease, massacres, rape... you name it. If God is the one allowing these things to happen, then He is definitely not a good God. If God is like this, how can we trust Him with our lives? If God controls everything, why should we pray?

We have already learned in previous sessions that God is good and only good. This raises the following questions: Why are all these tragic things happening in the world? How can a good God allow these things to happen? How can these things happen if God is in control? This is very confusing for many people, and it becomes a stumbling block for their faith.

When we say that God is sovereign, what does it really mean? When we look in Scripture, some translations of the Bible (especially the NIV) use "sovereign Lord" repeatedly, while most translations use only "Lord"; for instance, the New King James Version. This shows that the focus in these Scriptures should be on God being "Lord."

The New Spirit Filled Life Bible beautifully describes the sovereignty of God in its commentary[7]:

> The necessary beginning point of studying the theme of "the kingdom of God" is the Bible's opening verse. Here we meet the Sovereign of all the Universe, whose realm, reign and regency are described as the outset.
>
> 1) His realm (or scope of His rule) is transcendent; that is, not only does it include the entire physical universe, but it exceeds it. He existed before all creation, He expands beyond it, and by virtue of having begotten it, He encompasses all that it is. 2) His reign (or the power by which He rules) is exercised by His will, His word and His works. By His own will He creatively decides and designs; by His own word He speaks creation into being; and by His own works His Spirit displays His unlimited power. 3) His regency (or authority to rule) is in His preexistence and holiness. He is there before creation "in the beginning". Thus as its Creator, He deserves to be its Potentate. His benevolent intent in creating things "good" reveals His holy nature (that is complete and perfect), and thus His moral right to be creation´s King. All power and authority flow from Him.

Wow! This is awesome reading about the sovereignty of God, but it might confuse us even more. Shouldn't this mean that God is "in control"? To get an answer to this question, we need to study Genesis 1 as there are several keys in this chapter that will unlock the answers to our questions.[8] First, we need to know that God created everything good. We see repeatedly in the creation story that *"God saw that it was good."* God also created human beings good. Adam and Eve were good from the beginning. However, a second important key here is that God chose to give Adam and Eve free will. He wanted a love relationship with them based on free will. He chose not to control them like robots, because love has to be a choice. The third important key is that human beings were created in the image of God, and just as God has the ability to rule, He gave human beings the ability to rule, reign and make choices. Not only did God give man the ability to rule, but He also chose to delegate His authority and dominion over the Earth to human beings! See what the Bible says in Genesis:

> *Then God said, "Let Us make man in Our image, according to Our likeness; let them have dominion over the fish of the sea, over the birds of the air, and over the cattle, over all the earth and over every creeping thing that creeps on the earth." (Genesis 1:26)*

During creation, God had already said this about human beings: Let THEM have dominion over all the Earth. God could have chosen to include Himself and said, "Let US have dominion," but He did not. He excluded Himself and gave dominion on Earth to human beings. He chose to limit Himself and His sovereignty.[8] Why did He do that? He wanted to give humans the opportunity to be good stewards of the Earth through a relationship with Him. They were to be productive and fruitful, radiating God's glory on the Earth.

A fourth important key is to understand that God is bound by His own Word. He chooses to limit Himself by His Word.[8] If He breaks His own Word, He is no longer trustworthy. God does not take back what He said in Genesis 1:26. Dominion and authority of the Earth was given to human beings. However, the story did not stop there.

Adam and Eve Lost the Authority over the Earth to the Devil

Adam and Eve's ability to effectively sustain their role as delegated rulers depended on their submission and obedience to God's rule as King of all.[7] They were meant to use their free will to choose the ways of God and draw on God's wisdom and power to exercise their dominion on the Earth and in doing so, bring the Kingdom of God to the Earth (as we pray in the Lord's prayer). However, Adam and Eve did not end up using their free will to obey God. They chose to listen to the serpent (the devil) instead of God and ate of the tree of good and evil. The moment they ate of the fruit of this tree, they lost their authority over the Earth and gave it to the serpent. Mankind became sinners with a sinful nature. Even creation was cursed because of Adam and Eve's fall.

> *Then to Adam, He said, "Because you have heeded the voice of your wife, and have eaten from the tree of which I commanded you, saying, 'You shall not eat of it':*
> *"Cursed is the ground for your sake;*
> *In toil you shall eat of it*
> *All the days of your life.*
> *Both thorns and thistles it shall bring forth for you,*
> *And you shall eat the herb of the field.*
> *In the sweat of your face you shall eat bread" (Genesis 3:17-19a)*

The administration of this fallen and cursed Earth now came under the authority of the devil. Mankind had lost their connection with God and became easy prey for the enemy with their sinful nature. They continued to use their free will to do many evil things that were against God's will, and they still continue to do so up to this day.

It is essential to understand that God did not create the Earth as it is today with natural catastrophes, droughts, famine, etc. He created all of the Earth good, but the Earth changed when it was cursed after the fall of man in the Garden of Eden. Human beings have added to this condition through bad stewardship of the planet. However, one day the Earth will become new. (see Rev. 21:1 and Rom. 8:20-22).

Jesus Won Back the Authority

The good news is that when Jesus died on the cross, He conquered the devil and disarmed him. At the cross, He triumphed over all principalities and powers!

> *Having disarmed principalities and powers, He made a public spectacle of them, triumphing over them [at the cross]. (Colossians 2:15)*

> *When he raised Christ from the dead and seated him at his right hand in the heavenly realms, far above all rule and authority, power and dominion, and every name that is invoked, not only in the present age but also in the one to come. And God placed all things under his feet and appointed him to be head over everything for the church, which is his body, the fullness of him who fills everything in every way. (Ephesians 1:20-23 NIV)*

In the book of Revelation, we read that Jesus took back the keys of Hades and Death from the devil when He went down to Hades after His death at the cross. See what Jesus says:

> *I am He who lives, and was dead, and behold, I am alive forevermore. Amen. And I have the keys of Hades and of Death. (Revelation 1:18)*

The devil could not keep Jesus there in Hades (death), since He was without sin. That is why the resurrection is so important. (Hades is a temporary place where dead unbelievers are kept until the final judgment day.) [9]

In the Great Commission, Jesus tells us to go out into all the world based on His authority:

> *Then Jesus came to them and said, "All authority in heaven and on earth has been given to me. Therefore, go and make disciples of all nations, baptizing them in the name of the Father and of the Son and of the Holy Spirit,*

and teaching them to obey everything I have commanded you. And surely I am with you always, to the very end of the age." (Matthew 28:18-20 NIV)

Jesus has won back the authority and power in the spiritual realm. However, we still need to use our free will to choose Him. As Christians, we have accepted Jesus, received Him and made Him Lord of our lives. When we pray and declare the Word of God, we exercise His authority on the Earth. There are, however, still a majority of people on this planet who do not have Jesus as their Lord. These people use their free will every day to make good, bad or evil choices and decisions. As Christians, we do not always make the right choices either. The devil is still there with his demonic influence on the planet, trying to bring as much destruction and distraction as possible. In John 10:10 (NIV), we read that *"The thief comes only to steal and kill and destroy; I have come that they may have life, and have it to the full."*

God Depends on Cooperation with Us

We see from this that God is not "in control" on planet Earth in the sense that He is behind everything that happens. Neither is He the one allowing bad things to happen. God is definitely not behind evil; it is the devil that uses people as his tools. People use their free will to do evil things. God is not behind sickness and disease either. Natural disasters, sickness and disease are part of the cursed and fallen creation. (However, Jesus took all sickness and disease upon Himself at the cross as well, so we can receive His divine healing and health today.)

God will not overrule people's free will. That means God will not intervene or interfere on the planet unless He is asked to or "given permission" by us. This is where prayer and the declaration of God's Word and promises come in. When we pray, we invite God to do His work on the planet. We exercise the authority Jesus bought back for us at the cross, and when we do this, the devil must flee. (The next session, "The Purpose of Prayer," explains this in more detail.)

Therefore submit to God. Resist the devil and he will flee from you. (James 4:7)

God is still as powerful and sovereign as He was at creation. It was Him who chose to limit His sovereignty by giving human beings free will and by delegating the dominion of the Earth to us. This dominion was always meant to be exercised through the empowerment and wisdom of God. As His children—living in relationship with our Daddy God—we can be the stewards and "rulers" of the

Earth that God intended us to be from the beginning. We can contribute to "*[His] kingdom come [His] will be done on earth as it is in heaven*" (Matthew 6:10).

Can we still trust God and put our lives in His hand if He has chosen to limit His sovereignty? Absolutely! God is entirely in charge of our situation when we put our lives in His hands. His promises to us are dependable and trustworthy, and God is who He says He is.

There will always be questions we will not get answers to in this life. Why did this happen even though I prayed? Why didn't this person get healed? One day in Heaven we will get all the answers.

> *And we know that all things work together for good to those who love God, to those who are the called according to His purpose. (Romans 8:28)*

Even though bad circumstances are not orchestrated or sent by God, He will always turn it around into something good for us when we pray and give the situation to Him.

Most importantly, from what we have learned in this session, we see how important prayer is. God needs us to exercise the authority Jesus won back on the cross and cooperate with Him through Spirit-led prayer and intercession for the world, our families and loved ones as well as our own lives. Also, we need to let God's empowering grace work in us and through us as we are stewards of the things in our domain on planet Earth.

FOR SELF REFLECTION AND GROUP DISCUSSION

1. How was this session an eye-opener to you when it comes to the sovereignty of God and the thought that He is "in control" etc.? Until now, did you think that "everything happens for a reason," thinking God was behind even the wrong things? How has this session changed your view of God?
2. Meditate on the fact that God gave human beings, including you, dominion over planet Earth. Are there areas where you have passively accepted circumstances, where you should have been rising up and "taking dominion and authority?" Explain.

3. God's delegated dominion and authority to us are empowering when we realize its implications. Take a stand and make decisions to rise up from now on and use your authority in prayer and in action.

SHARE AND DISCUSS WITH THE GROUP

SESSION 19

The Purpose of Prayer

PRAYER IS AN ESSENTIAL PART of our lives as believers. In prayer, we talk to God and have fellowship with Him; we also receive instructions, guidance, encouragement and strength. We give Him our burdens and concerns in faith that He will take care of it. There are many promises regarding God answering prayer in the Bible. In this session, we will look at the actual purpose of prayer and why prayer is so important. It is much more than fellowship with God and laying off our burdens. As we learned in the last session, God has made Himself dependent on our prayers to intervene on planet Earth.

Why is Prayer so Important?

To understand the principle and purpose of prayer, we need to understand certain things about the Kingdom of God and the character of God.

God is sovereign, but when it comes to God's sovereignty, He is as sovereign as His Word.[8] When God speaks, it becomes law. God will never violate His Word; hence, He has chosen to limit Himself by His own Word. If God would break His own Word, we could not trust Him, but God is 100 percent trustworthy and faithful. We can say that God is sovereign until He speaks. When He speaks, He has to stick to what He says,[8] so let us see what He said:

> *Then God said, "Let Us make man in Our image, according to Our likeness; let them have dominion over the fish of the sea, over the birds of the air, and over the cattle, over all the earth and over every creeping thing that creeps on the earth." (Genesis 1:26)*

We learned in the previous session that God delegated the dominion on Earth to human beings. Human beings are therefore the only ones with "legal right" to operate on Earth. This means that for God to get anything done on Earth, He has to cooperate with human beings. He needs their prayers to get "legal right" to interfere on Earth. Prayer invites and asks God to come into the domain of humans and bring His Kingdom in. We could say that prayer is giving God license to interfere on planet Earth.[8]

In the Bible, God always used and cooperated with humans when He wanted to do something. In the Old Testament, when He had seen the outcry from the sinful cities of Sodom and Gomorrah and wanted to destroy the two cities, Abraham negotiated with God and God listened to him. Let us read in Genesis 18:20-33:

> *And the Lord said, "Because the outcry against Sodom and Gomorrah is great, and because their sin is very grave, I will go down now and see whether they have done altogether according to the outcry against it that has come to Me; and if not, I will know."*
>
> *Then the men turned away from there and went toward Sodom, but Abraham still stood before the Lord. And Abraham came near and said, "Would You also destroy the righteous with the wicked? Suppose there were fifty righteous within the city; would You also destroy the place and not spare it for the fifty righteous that were in it? Far be it from You to do such a thing as this, to slay the righteous with the wicked, so that the righteous should be as the wicked; far be it from You! Shall not the Judge of all the earth do right?"*
>
> *So the Lord said, "If I find in Sodom fifty righteous within the city, then I will spare all the place for their sakes."*
>
> *Then Abraham answered and said, "Indeed now, I who am but dust and ashes have taken it upon myself to speak to the Lord: Suppose there were five less than the fifty righteous; would You destroy all of the city for lack of five?"*
>
> *So He said, "If I find there forty-five, I will not destroy it."*

Abraham negotiated with God down to ten righteous people. The Lord listened to Abraham; however, the cities of Sodom and Gomorrah were destroyed. There were not even ten righteous people to be found in the cities.

Another example is when the people of Israel had been led out of Egypt and were in the Sinai desert. Moses was up on the mountain, speaking to God for many days. In the meantime, the people got sick of waiting for Moses, and they asked Aaron to give them another god they could worship. He made them a golden calf out of melted earrings and gold they had in the camp. Then they worshiped the calf. God got very angry with them and wanted to destroy them, but see what happened:

> *And the Lord said to Moses, "I have seen this people, and indeed it is a stiff-necked people! Now therefore, let Me alone, that My wrath may burn hot against them and I may consume them. And I will make of you a great nation."*
>
> *Then Moses pleaded with the Lord his God, and said: "Lord, why does Your wrath burn hot against Your people whom You have brought out of the land of Egypt with great power and with a mighty hand? Why should the Egyptians speak, and say, 'He brought them out to harm them, to kill them in the mountains, and to consume them from the face of the earth'? Turn from Your fierce wrath, and relent from this harm to Your people. Remember Abraham, Isaac, and Israel, Your servants, to whom You swore by Your own self, and said to them, 'I will multiply your descendants as the stars of heaven; and all this land that I have spoken of I give to your descendants, and they shall inherit it forever.'" So the Lord relented from the harm which He said He would do to His people. (Exodus 32:9-14)*

God needs us to impact our city. Prayer is not an option—it is a necessity. God needs a human to pray in order for Him to interfere. He has given us the keys to the Kingdom.

> *"I will build My church, and the gates of Hades shall not prevail against it. And I will give you the keys of the kingdom of heaven, and whatever you bind on earth will be bound in heaven, and whatever you loose on earth will be loosed in heaven." (Matthew 16:18b-19)*

Jesus said He would give us the keys to the Kingdom. Keys are principles. We need to use the right key in the right lock to open the door. Matthew 18:18-20 says:

> *"Assuredly, I say to you, whatever you bind on earth will be bound in heaven, and whatever you loose on earth will be loosed in heaven."*

> *"Again I say to you that if two of you agree on earth concerning anything that they ask, it will be done for them by My Father in heaven. For where two or three are gathered together in My name, I am there in the midst of them."*

From verse 20, we see the power of united prayer or prayer based on agreement.

The Model Prayer

There was only one thing the disciples asked Jesus to teach them according to Luke Chapter 11—they asked Him, "Lord, teach us to pray"! They had observed how Jesus spent a lot of time in prayer, and they understood that this is where He got the power and direction for all of the powerful miracles that happened as He ministered during the day. Jesus taught them what is commonly known as *"The Lord's prayer"* or *"The model prayer"* (Matthew 6:9-13):

> *In this manner, therefore, pray:*
> *Our Father in heaven,*
> *Hallowed be Your name.*
> *Your kingdom come.*
> *Your will be done*
> *On earth as it is in heaven.*
> *Give us this day our daily bread.*
> *And forgive us our debts,*
> *As we forgive our debtors.*
> *And do not lead us into temptation,*
> *But deliver us from the evil one.*
> *For Yours is the kingdom and the power and the glory forever. Amen.*

In both Luke and Matthew, Jesus says, "*When you pray.*" He does not say, "If you pray." This tells us again that prayer is not an option; it is a necessity.

> *But you, when you pray, go into your room, and when you have shut your door, pray to your Father who is in the secret place; and your Father who sees in secret will reward you openly. And when you pray, do not use vain repetitions as the heathen do. For they think that they will be heard for their many words. "Therefore do not be like them. For your Father knows the things you have need of before you ask Him." (Matthew 6:6-8)*

This prayer is a model prayer for us. The New Spirit Filled Life Bible puts it like this in its commentary[10]:

> Jesus' words "Your kingdom come" are more than a suggestion to pray for a distant millennial day, for everything in this prayer is current. This prayer is not a formula for repetition so much as it is an outline for expansion. Worship is to be longer than a sentence. Petitions are not confined to bread. Forgiveness is to be requested in specifics, not generalities, and prayer for the entry of God's kingdom into present earthborn situations is not accomplished in a momentary utterance. The word mood and tense of "Your kingdom come" essentially says, "Father, let Your kingdom come here and now!" Such prayerful intervention is called intercession. Motivation toward such prayer occurs when we recognize the importance Jesus placed on prayer in helping us service in our rules as "kingdom administrators". Without the intervention of God's kingdom rule through prayer, Earth's circumstances will succumb to inevitable consequences. Earthly scenes of need must be penetrated by God's "will here as in heaven." Either the weakness of man's rule (the flesh) or the viciousness of hell's work (the Devil) will prevail. God's power alone can change things and bring heaven's rule (kingdom) instead, and the honor and the glory for prayer's answer are His. However, the praying is ours to do: unless we ask for the intervention of His kingdom and obey His prayer-lessons, nothing will change. All kingdom ministry begins with, is sustained by, and will triumph through prayer.

How important our prayers are! No wonder there are so many Scriptures in the New Testament that encourage us to pray and promise an answered prayer.

We just read that the model prayer is an "outline of expansion." We fill in this outline with our own specific prayer requests.

Guidelines for Prayer

> *So I say to you, ask, and it will be given to you; seek, and you will find; knock, and it will be opened to you. For everyone who asks receives, and he who seeks finds, and to him who knocks it will be opened. (Luke 11:9-10)*

We see in this verse in Luke 11:5-6 that our prayers should be followed by actions; we pray, we seek, and we knock at "the doors."

We pray in faith and expect to receive what we ask for.

> *So Jesus answered and said to them, "Have faith in God. For assuredly, I say to you, whoever says to this mountain, 'Be removed and be cast into the*

> *sea,' and does not doubt in his heart, but believes that those things he says will be done, he will have whatever he says. Therefore I say to you, whatever things you ask when you pray, believe that you receive them, and you will have them." (Mark 11:22-24)*

Have a clean heart before God when you pray. Forgive whoever you need to forgive.

> *And whenever you stand praying, if you have anything against anyone, forgive him, that your Father in heaven may also forgive you your trespasses. But if you do not forgive, neither will your Father in heaven forgive your trespasses. (Mark 11:25-26)*

Be aware that here, Jesus speaks before the cross. In the New Covenant, we are already forgiven. However, we still need to make our hearts right before God and people and forgive as Jesus says in this verse.

So, who do we pray to? The Bible tells us to pray to the Father in Jesus' name. We don't pray to Jesus but to the Father in Jesus' name.

> *Most assuredly, I say to you, he who believes in Me, the works that I do he will do also; and greater works than these he will do, because I go to My Father. And whatever you ask in My name, that I will do, that the Father may be glorified in the Son. If you ask anything in My name, I will do it. (John 14:12-14)*

Let your prayers be led by the Holy Spirit.

> *Praying always with all prayer and supplication in the Spirit, being watchful to this end with all perseverance and supplication for all the saints— (Ephesians 6:18)*

> *Likewise the Spirit also helps in our weaknesses. For we do not know what we should pray for as we ought, but the Spirit Himself makes intercession for us with groanings which cannot be uttered. Now He who searches the hearts knows what the mind of the Spirit is, because He makes intercession for the saints according to the will of God. And we know that all things work together for good to those who love God, to those who are the called according to His purpose. (Romans 8:26-28)*

These verses refer to both prayer led by the Holy Spirit and prayer in tongues. Prayer in tongues is your own personal prayer language, while Spirit-led prayer is allowing your prayer in your known language to flow as led and inspired by the Holy Spirit. Any prayer that is directed, inspired and sustained by the Holy Spirit is a prayer that is prayed in the Spirit. You yield to the Holy Spirit as you pray and listen to what is on God's heart for a person or situation (instead of just speaking out of your own opinion). This is how you can intercede efficiently since you cooperate with the Holy Spirit in bringing God's will and Kingdom into situations. This is when prayer gets exciting!

Have a heart of prayer. Pray continuously, without ceasing. This means that you are online with the Holy Spirit all the time and in every situation throughout the day, bringing everything to the Father in prayer. You ask for wisdom, guidance and God's supernatural help and interference in everything. The "antenna" of your spirit is always up and ready to receive signals from the Holy Spirit regarding people or situations that need prayer. All of this goes on while you are working, driving, exercising, socializing... Let prayer and communication with God be a natural part of your daily life, not just limited to your prayer time in the morning.

What If Your Answer to Prayer Is Delayed?

Never give up praying even though the answer is delayed. Jesus talks about this in Luke 18:1-8 in the Parable of the persistent widow (NIV):

> *Then Jesus told his disciples a parable to show them that they should always pray and not give up. He said: "In a certain town there was a judge who neither feared God nor cared what people thought. And there was a widow in that town who kept coming to him with the plea, 'Grant me justice against my adversary.'*
>
> *"For some time he refused. But finally he said to himself, 'Even though I don't fear God or care what people think, yet because this widow keeps bothering me, I will see that she gets justice, so that she won't eventually come and attack me!'"*
>
> *And the Lord said, "Listen to what the unjust judge says. And will not God bring about justice for his chosen ones, who cry out to him day and night? Will he keep putting them off? I tell you, he will see that they get justice, and quickly. However, when the Son of Man comes, will he find faith on the earth?"*

In the book of Daniel, we get insight into what is happening in the spiritual world when we pray. God immediately hears our prayers and is ready to send His angels out on their mission, but there can be a battle... This is the archangel Gabriel speaking:

> *Then he continued, "Do not be afraid, Daniel. Since the first day that you set your mind to gain understanding and to humble yourself before your God, your words were heard, and I have come in response to them. But the prince of the Persian kingdom resisted me twenty-one days. Then Michael, one of the chief princes, came to help me because I was detained there with the king of Persia. Now I have come to explain to you what will happen to your people in the future, for the vision concerns a time yet to come." (Daniel 10:12-14 NIV)*

This passage is from the Old Testament before Jesus Christ had conquered the enemy and his demonic forces. These forces are, however, still at work trying to stop God's will, which can cause delays for us. We need to learn how to pray out of the victory Jesus has already won and use the authority in Jesus' name.

Sometimes delays in answered prayers are because God's plans and timing are different than ours. We can be so impatient when we want to see something happen. There might be a reason why there needs to be specific timing for certain answered prayers in our lives.

Everything that you are learning in this book will be a strong foundation for your prayer life. You know who you are in Christ and your position in Him, you know the Word and God's promises for your life and you know that you are righteous and loved by God. You have full access to God in prayer. You know what Jesus completed at the cross. You are filled by the Holy Spirit. These things are so important.

When the Apostle Paul prays for the saints in the letters in the New Testament, he prays that they will get a revelation of what they already have in Christ. You can read this for yourself in Ephesians 1:15-21 and Galatians 1:9-12. Knowledge and understanding of spiritual things will help you a lot when you pray.

Be encouraged by the words in James 5:16b-18 (NIV):

> *The prayer of a righteous person is powerful and effective. Elijah was a human being, even as we are. He prayed earnestly that it would not rain,*

and it did not rain on the land for three and a half years. Again he prayed, and the heavens gave rain, and the earth produced its crops.

FINALLY: Prayer belongs together with praise and thanksgiving—a grateful heart.

Let's end with this well-known passage:

Be anxious for nothing, but in everything by prayer and supplication, with thanksgiving, let your requests be made known to God; and the peace of God, which surpasses all understanding, will guard your hearts and minds through Christ Jesus. (Philippians 4:6-7)

FOR SELF REFLECTION AND GROUP DISCUSSION

1. How is your current prayer life? (Be honest.) How did this lesson change your view of the importance of prayer?
2. See in the two stories in this session how both Abraham and Moses made God change His mind. They were very bold in their requests to God. What does this teach you about the way you can approach God? Could you be bolder in your prayers?
3. How have you experienced delayed answer to prayer in your life but, still, you did not give up? Share about both the breakthroughs with answered prayers and prayers you are still waiting for the fulfillment of.

SHARE AND DISCUSS WITH THE GROUP

SESSION 20

Do Not Worry But Trust in the Lord

Leave Your Burden with God

ONE OF THE MOST IMPORTANT THINGS in our Christian walk is to trust in the Lord and rest in Him. Faith and trust go hand in hand. Faith is a lot about trusting that what the Lord says in His Word is true even though our circumstances might be telling the opposite. We tend to give everything to the Lord in prayer and hand over all our burdens to Him, and the next minute we take it back and start to carry it ourselves again. We feel like we must help the Lord a bit, and the way we do it is through worry. We let things nag us over and over again, and we worry about the outcome of our situation. We might pray about the same thing repeatedly, but we are still unable to leave it with God and let Him take care of it. This is not how God wants us to be. Let us look at a familiar verse:

> *Be anxious for nothing, but in everything by prayer and supplication, with thanksgiving, let your requests be made known to God; and the peace of God, which surpasses all understanding, will guard your hearts and minds through Christ Jesus. (Philippians 4:6-7)*

In this verse, the word "supplication" is used. Let us look this up in the New Spirit Filled Life Bible[11]:

> Supplication is more than petitioning but suggests an intensity of earnestness in extended prayer—not to gain merit by many words, but to fully transfer the burden of one's soul into God's hands. Prayer and

peace are closely connected. One who entrusts cares to Christ instead of fretting over them, will experience the peace of God to guard him from nagging anxiety.

So, we are to leave our burden with God, not take it back and keep worrying about it.

Trust That God Is Who He Says He Is

We can trust that God is who He says He is. As we walk in faith and get to know the Lord more and more, we will experience God's faithfulness in our lives. Our trust should, however, not be based on experience but on the Word of God. The Word tells us that God does not want us to worry, because He knows our situation and what we need. We do not have to fear, because (as much as we allow Him) He has our future in His hand.

One thing we tend to worry about is our provision, both in our current situation and also for our future. God says very specifically that we do not have to worry about these things:

> *"Therefore I say to you, do not worry about your life, what you will eat or what you will drink; nor about your body, what you will put on. Is not life more than food and the body more than clothing? Look at the birds of the air, for they neither sow nor reap nor gather into barns; yet your heavenly Father feeds them. Are you not of more value than they? Which of you by worrying can add one cubit to his stature?*
>
> *So why do you worry about clothing? Consider the lilies of the field, how they grow: they neither toil nor spin; and yet I say to you that even Solomon in all his glory was not arrayed like one of these. Now if God so clothes the grass of the field, which today is, and tomorrow is thrown into the oven, will He not much more clothe you, O you of little faith?*
>
> *"Therefore do not worry, saying, 'What shall we eat?' or 'What shall we drink?' or 'What shall we wear?' For after all these things the Gentiles seek. For your heavenly Father knows that you need all these things." (Matthew 6:25-32)*

God says that He knows that we need food, housing and clothes and He promises to take care of us. This passage continues with this important key to access God's provision:

But seek first the kingdom of God and His righteousness, and all these things shall be added to you. (Matthew 6:33)

But seek his kingdom, and these things will be given to you as well. (Luke 12:31 NIV)

This is very important! Our first priority and focus are not on material things but on the Kingdom of God and His righteousness. Our part is to seek the Kingdom of God and seek the person of God—seek His face. When we do our part, God will do His part which is to add all these other things unto us. When we seek His face, we also get His hand to help us and provide for us.

In Peter's first letter, we are also told to transfer our cares to God.

Therefore humble yourselves under the mighty hand of God, that He may exalt you in due time, casting all your cares upon Him, for He cares for you. (1 Peter 5:6-7)

Let us look at 1 Peter 5:7 in the Amplified Bible:

Casting the whole of your care [all your anxieties, all your worries, all your concerns, once and for all] on Him, for He cares for you affectionately and cares about you watchfully.

"Cast" is the Greek verb *epiript,* which means "to propel something from one place to another, throw."[12] It also means "to transfer one´s concerns, cast upon." This is a very active word. I think of it in terms of "throw," "propel," "eject," "remove violently" and "send worry as a projectile far from you."

So often, we tend to nurse our fears and dwell upon them. Even at night, we allow them to disturb our sleep. Peter tells us to "throw" them to God. We do that through prayer.

Let us look at another word in 1 Peter 5:7 (NIV):

Cast all your anxiety on him because he cares for you.

Peter tells us about God's concern for us. "Cares" is the Greek verb *melo:* "be an object of care, be a cause of concern."[13] You are an object of concern to God. He is concerned for your welfare. He wants you to be whole and healthy. He feels your pain and sadness. God paid the penalty for your sins and has set you free from condemnation. God HIMSELF cares for you! Wow! Why should we cast our anxieties His way? Because He has real concern for us. Let Him bear your worries, for He has deep concern and interest in everything you face.

> *Cast your cares on the Lord and he will sustain you;*
> *he will never let the righteous be shaken. (Psalm 55:22 NIV)*

FOR SELF REFLECTION AND GROUP DISCUSSION

1. What are the things you tend to worry about? What do the promises of God say about your situation?
2. How can we build greater trust in the Lord so that we stop worrying?
3. Meditate on the verse we just read in 1 Peter 5:7 (NIV) and the fact that God cares for you.
4. Do you have a testimony to share about how you were seeking the Kingdom of God first and all these things were added to you? (See Matt. 6:33.)

SHARE AND DISCUSS WITH THE GROUP

SESSION 21

Trusting God through Difficulties and Challenges

IN THIS SESSION, WE WILL LEARN how we can trust God in every situation, even in difficulties and challenges. We live in an imperfect world with imperfect people and an enemy who tries his best *"to steal, and to kill, and to destroy"* (John 10:10). God has not promised us a life free of problems. We will meet difficulties and challenges. However, He never leaves us alone to fix things by ourselves. He has promised us that He will always be with us.

God Never Promised Us a Problem-Free Life

None of the believers we read about in the Bible lived problem-free lives; however, we can see that God was with them through it all. We have many examples.

When the people of Israel finally entered the promised land in Canaan after wandering forty years in the desert, they had to fight against many kings before they conquered the land. As long as they trusted God and were obedient, they won the wars (Book of Joshua). It is essential to understand that they were in the midst of God's plan, even though they faced all these challenges and difficulties. It is easy to start questioning God if you get into difficult situations; however, this might be the exact way God wants to show his greatness and power in your life through solving an impossible situation that cannot be resolved by you alone.

David was anointed to become king, but he had to live in the desert and was hunted by King Saul and his men for many years before he became king of Israel. In the Book of Psalms, he describes many of his struggles and how he trusts in the Lord through it all (see 1 Sam. 16 onwards).

Another example is Joseph, who was sold as a slave by his brothers, and later thrown into prison for twelve years even though he had the promises and dreams of God inside of him. He never turned his heart away from God but always made the best out of the circumstances. He used his gift for interpreting dreams in prison. Because of his gift and the plans and purposes of God for Joseph's life, he was taken out of jail when the time was right and became the ruler of Egypt next to Pharaoh! God was with him the entire time, and He had a plan and a purpose even though it took many years of waiting (see Gen. 37 onwards).

In the New Testament, we have the Apostle Paul, the great missionary, who went through so many difficulties in his ministry, but he never quit or gave up.

> *Five times I received from the Jews the forty lashes minus one. Three times I was beaten with rods, once I was pelted with stones, three times I was shipwrecked, I spent a night and a day in the open sea, I have been constantly on the move. I have been in danger from rivers, in danger from bandits, in danger from my fellow Jews, in danger from Gentiles; in danger in the city, in danger in the country, in danger at sea; and in danger from false believers. I have labored and toiled and have often gone without sleep; I have known hunger and thirst and have often gone without food; I have been cold and naked. Besides everything else, I face daily the pressure of my concern for all the churches. Who is weak, and I do not feel weak? Who is led into sin, and I do not inwardly burn? If I must boast, I will boast of the things that show my weakness. (2 Corinthians 11:24-30 NIV)*

In 2 Corinthians 12:8-10 (NIV), we see Paul speaking again:

> *Three times I pleaded with the Lord to take it away from me. But he said to me, "My grace is sufficient for you, for my power is made perfect in weakness." Therefore I will boast all the more gladly about my weaknesses, so that Christ's power may rest on me. That is why, for Christ's sake, I delight in weaknesses, in insults, in hardships, in persecutions, in difficulties. For when I am weak, then I am strong.*

The Apostle Paul went through all these things in his passion and eagerness to bring forth the Gospel. He was very courageous and was willing to face whatever necessary to spread the Word. The Holy Spirit was with Paul the entire time. When he preached the Word, it was confirmed by mighty signs and wonders that followed. When Paul was stoned to death, the Holy Spirit raised him up. He was given strength to cope with what he faced, and he was led by the Spirit. The result was that he brought the Gospel to all the leading cities of the world at that time; hence, the price he paid was all worth it.

My point is that God has not promised us a comfortable, problem-free life with only sunshine and no clouds. He has a plan for our lives and a destiny for us to fulfill, and this plan is too big for us to work out on our own. We WILL have to walk by faith and trust God to open doors miraculously. We WILL need to depend on the Holy Spirit to lead us and strengthen us. It is not comfortable to have no control and to trust God when things are not going the way we planned or when we are waiting for a long time, but when we walk in faith and trust Him, we will see God's faithfulness and help in every situation.

God Has Promised to Make a Way through the Problem

Let us read from Isaiah in the Old Testament, which is full of prophecy concerning the coming of Jesus Christ and full of promises to us:

> *"Do not fear, for I have redeemed you;*
> *I have summoned you by name; you are mine.*
> *When you pass through the waters,*
> *I will be with you;*
> *and when you pass through the rivers,*
> *they will not sweep over you.*
> *When you walk through the fire,*
> *you will not be burned;*
> *the flames will not set you ablaze." (Isaiah 43:1b-2 NIV)*

In this passage, I want you to take notice of three things:

1. It says WHEN you pass through the waters, rivers and fire—it does not say IF but WHEN. This does not necessarily mean that we will go through actual water and fire, but it symbolizes situations that feel like overwhelming rivers where we think we are drowning or pressure that feels like fire.

2. When this happens, God will be with us. That is His promise.
3. It says PASS THROUGH the waters, the rivers and the fire, which means we are <u>going through it</u>. We are <u>not staying</u> in the river or the fire; we are passing through and getting over to the other side, and as we are passing through, God is with us.

Let us also look at Isaiah 43:16:

> *Thus says the Lord, who <u>makes a way</u> in the sea. And a path through the mighty waters,*

Here God is reminding the people of their exit from Egypt after their 400 years of captivity as slaves, when God led them towards the Red Sea. The Egyptian army was following them, regretting the fact that they had let them go. God could have led the Israelites another way, but He led them to the Red Sea so that they would be totally dependent on His miracle. There was no human solution. Then God told Moses to lift His staff towards the Red Sea, and God separated the sea so that the people of Israel could walk through it on dry land. When the Egyptian army followed, they drowned as the ocean came back upon them (see Ex. 13:17, 14:31).

The situation was impossible but, still, as we see in Isaiah 43:16, God made a way when it seemed impossible! He is still a God who MAKES A WAY for us when everything seems chaotic.

Our job is to trust in the Lord and listen to the voice of the Holy Spirit who wants to lead us and tell us what to do. God has a solution when we see no way out.

In Isaiah 41:10, God comforts us by saying:

> *Fear not, for I am with you;*
> *Be not dismayed, for I am your God.*
> *I will strengthen you,*
> *Yes, I will help you,*
> *I will uphold you with My righteous right hand.'*

We already talked about David and his life. In Psalm 23, David´s focus is on God´s goodness and faithfulness. He only mentions in verse 4:

> *Yea, though I walk through the valley of the shadow of death, I will fear no evil; For You are with me; Your rod and Your staff, they comfort me.*

Notice that David WALKS THROUGH the valley of death; he does not stay there (just as we read in Isaiah 43:1-2). He fears no evil because he knows that the Lord is with Him.

Psalms 91 is another great proclamation of God's promise to protect us through everything. You can read it in your own Bible. We can take refuge in God and trust in Him always and in all things.

God is not behind our troubles and problems; however, whatever happens, God can turn it around and make something good out of it.

> *And we know that all things work together for good to those who love God, to those who are the called according to His purpose. (Romans 8:28)*

If you are in a dark place in your life and find that you have camped there in "the valley of death," it is time to get up and trust God for deliverance. He has promised that you are to pass through, not stay there. If you are in a difficult situation, know that it is not your destination—you are just passing through on your way to victory. Trust in God and His promises and let Him take you over to the other side.

FOR SELF REFLECTION AND GROUP DISCUSSION

1. How do you practice trusting in the Lord through difficulties in your own life?
2. Please share with the others in the group how you overcame a difficult situation by trusting in the Lord.
3. Find Scriptures that can help you get through the challenges you are facing right now.

SHARE AND DISCUSS WITH THE GROUP

SESSION 22

Renewing of the Mind

Why Do You Need to Renew Your Mind?

WHEN YOU RECEIVED JESUS as your Lord and Savior, you became a new creation in Christ Jesus. The old man died, and the new man was born—in you (see 2 Cor. 5:17).

So, why can you still struggle with different issues when you are a new creation in Christ Jesus? Well, it was your spirit that was born again, not your mind. Your will, thoughts and emotions were not born again; they need to be renewed. When you make Jesus the Lord of your life, you will start submitting to His will in His Word. This will begin a life-long process of the renewing of your mind.

When you were born again, you were empowered to live a new life in Christ Jesus. In Romans 6:14, we read that "*sin shall not have dominion over you, for you are not under law but under grace*." You were freed from your sinful nature when you were born again. You are now free to live the new life with Jesus and empowered to say no to sin. The Bible tells you to put off the old man and put on the new man in Christ (see Eph. 4:20-24).

When you let God's thoughts influence your mindset, it enables you to connect to the purposes of God for your life. Your mindset and thinking will determine your living, which is why it needs to be renewed and aligned with God´s thoughts for you.

> *For as [a man] thinks in his heart, so is he. (Proverbs 23:7 AMPC)*

How Do You Renew Your Mind?

What you focus on will determine what you do and how you live. So, what are you continually thinking about, listening to and looking at? You cannot change your thinking if you are always hearing the wrong messages. You need to see and listen to the right thing. Your eyes and ears are gateways to your heart, and what they receive will create a mindset that affects your actions and direction—your whole life. This is why we must be careful with what we listen to even when it comes from Christian resources. If we continually feed on wrong Christian doctrines (doctrines based on Old Covenant Law and works), we can develop wrong mindsets. We need to be feeding on good news—the New Covenant message of grace and the Spirit. If the message brings you closer to Jesus, it is good news. If it focuses on you and what you need to do in your own strength, it is not good news.

By continually focusing on the Word of God, you can get hold of His heart and His will for your life—His thoughts for you. God's thoughts are so much higher than our thoughts. His Word is full of wisdom, promises and also instructions on how to live our lives. Jesus' way of life is an example of the way we should live.

> *Don't copy the behavior and customs of this world, but let God transform you into a new person by changing the way you think. Then you will learn to know God's will for you, which is good and pleasing and perfect. (Romans 12:2 NLT)*

"Transform" in this verse is the Greek word *metamorphoses*,[14] which means "a total transformation with no trace of the old"—like a butterfly's transformation. This happens when you open up your heart and allow the Holy Spirit to work in you and you start filling yourself with the Word of God. God breathes into His Word, so He and His Word are one. Read your Bible, speak the promises of God and keep them in front of you. It is also good to go to a Bible study, listen to teaching and preaching in church and online (podcasts, etc.), play worship music in your home and read good, grace-based, Spirit-filled, Christian books. As you do this, over time your old thinking will change, and you will start thinking the way God thinks.

> *And all of us, as with unveiled face, [because we] continued to behold [in the Word of God] as in a mirror the glory of the Lord, are constantly being transfigured into His very own image in ever increasing splendor and from*

one degree of glory to another; [for this comes] from the Lord [Who is] the Spirit. (2 Corinthians 3:18 AMPC)

You might be struggling with negative thoughts and wondering how to get rid of them. It takes a thought to heal a thought. It takes the right belief to replace the wrong idea. You cannot shake off a bad impression, but you must replace it with a good thought instead.

As you meditate on the Word of God, it will burn a new path in your mind. You see, thoughts burn trails into your brain physically.[15] When you start concentrating on a thought over and over again, it sticks to your brain and becomes a "truth" in your mind, even though it might be a lie. It becomes a path in your mind, a thought pattern and then a stronghold. A stronghold is a bunch of thought patterns that are piled up into a fortress in your mind. Your thoughts automatically follow that path, and this wrong way of thinking begins to rule your life. This might be negative thoughts about yourself, the way you think God sees you, your preconceived ideas about the character of God, wrong ideas about who you are in Christ, false beliefs about what other people are thinking of you, false ideas about what you are capable of doing, etc. So, to get rid of the wrong thoughts, replace them. The old path will gradually disappear—grass will grow over it until the old path is completely covered.[15]

Another example of this process is putting a glass of dirty water under running, clear water; gradually the running water will flush the dirty water out, and the water in the glass will become clear. Keep "your glass" (your mind) under the running water (the living Word of God), and it will flush out all of the negative things that come into your head. Even though you cannot prevent a bird from flying over your head, you can stop the bird from building a nest in your head.

Finally, brethren, whatever things are true, whatever things are noble, whatever things are just, whatever things are pure, whatever things are lovely, whatever things are of good report, if there is any virtue and if there is anything praiseworthy—meditate on these things. (Philippians 4:8)

In the Amplified Bible, instead of "*meditate on these things,*" it says, "*think on and weigh and take account of these things [fix your minds on them].*"

The Result of Renewing Your Mind

When you keep the Word of God in front of you and make it a lifestyle to do what I have described above, over time you will wash the wrong thoughts out of your mind. As you develop the right thought patterns, over time you will find yourself responding differently to situations. For example, in the past when you were faced with an unexpected and unfortunate situation, you may have reacted negatively with fear, anxiety or discouragement. However, as your mind is renewed with God´s thoughts, you will find yourself responding by trusting the Lord and expecting His help. You know that you are His favored one and that He will never leave you nor forsake you. You know that He will always provide what you need.

Protecting Your Mind against the Enemy

To keep your thoughts right does, however, take some determination because we have an enemy who will always try to speak lies into our mind. Our mind is a constant battlefield. This is why it is so important that we know the truth about who we are in Christ and what Christ has done for us at the cross. We need to stand firm in our salvation and our righteousness, say no to condemnation, guilt and shame and stay bold and firm "in grace," proclaiming the truth out loud against the enemy. Do not let him steal your joy, put guilt on you or make you feel like less than royalty in the Kingdom of God. Stand firm in Christ—using the "sword of the Spirit" (see Eph. 6:17) and putting on the whole armor of God (see Eph. 6:10-18). We do not fight our battles in the flesh but in the Spirit.

> *For the weapons of our warfare are not carnal but mighty in God for pulling down strongholds, casting down arguments and every high thing that exalts itself against the knowledge of God, bringing every thought into captivity to the obedience of Christ, and being ready to punish all disobedience when your obedience is fulfilled. (2 Corinthians 10:4-6)*

Take note that this verse says we are to bring every thought into captivity to the obedience <u>of</u> Christ, not the obedience <u>to</u> Christ. The obedience <u>of</u> Christ is what He has done for us at the cross. We are to bring every thought captive, submitting it to Christ's finished work.

> *And being found in appearance as a man, He humbled Himself and became obedient to the point of death, even the death of the cross. (Philippians 2:8)*

Before Jesus died, He cried, *"It is finished"* (John 19:30)—our job is to stand firm in His finished work. This is how we conquer the enemy—through what Jesus did for us on the cross. He atoned for our sin, crushed the enemy's power and gave us authority as sons and daughters of God. The place where Jesus was crucified is called Golgotha. This means *"the place of the skull."* Your breakthrough starts with your mind!

> *Since you have been raised to new life with Christ, set your sights on the realities of heaven, where Christ sits in the place of honor at God's right hand. Think about the things of heaven, not the things of earth. For you died to this life, and your real life is hidden with Christ in God. And when Christ, who is your life, is revealed to the whole world, you will share in all his glory. (Colossians 3:1-4 NLT)*

You are seated with Christ in the heavenly places (see Eph. 2:6), so think from this high place. When you complain about a situation, you remain in the situation. Instead, give thanks in every circumstance, and God will get you through. Think out of His supply and not out of the circumstances. Jesus was not limited by what He had, because He had a supply from the highest place. This is your position as well. So, begin to thank the Lord that He provides for all your needs. When your head starts spinning with worry and fear, remember this verse:

> *Do not fret or have any anxiety about anything, but in every circumstance and in everything, by prayer and petition (definite requests), with thanksgiving, continue to make your wants known to God. And God's peace [shall be yours, that tranquil state of a soul assured of its salvation through Christ, and so fearing nothing from God and being content with its earthly lot of whatever sort that is, that peace] which transcends all understanding shall garrison and mount guard over your hearts and minds in Christ Jesus. (Philippians 4:6-8 AMPC)*

In the next session, we will learn how to manage our thinking as well as our emotions.

FOR SELF REFLECTION AND GROUP DISCUSSION

1. In what areas do you need to change your thinking?
2. Are your thought patterns keeping you stuck in a place or taking you in the wrong direction?

3. How do you stop false thoughts from being planted in your head?
4. When you look back at your walk with Jesus so far, how have your thoughts changed over time?

SHARE AND DISCUSS WITH THE GROUP

SESSION 23

The Joy of the Lord Is Our Strength

SOMETIMES GOD'S SOLUTIONS to our problems don't make sense to us. In the natural, we want to react to whatever happens to us and let it rule our thoughts and emotions. However, the Word of the Lord says, "*Rejoice in the Lord always. Again I will say, rejoice!*" (Philippians 4:4). There is nothing wrong with emotions. God created emotions. God Himself has emotions. Emotions mean we are in touch with our hearts and feelings, which is a good thing. However, they can become our enemy if we don't control them. Worry and fear can bring us into a downward spiral of negative thinking if we are not careful. This is not the will of God for us.

How to Manage Your Thoughts and Emotions

Our emotions are a result of our thinking, so we need to learn to manage our thinking first. We are not to be ruled by our feelings. We cannot let them take the steering wheels of our lives. However, we should not stuff them in the trunk either.

So, what do you do when you are in a really tough situation and you feel you are really down emotionally and mentally? What do you do when depression is knocking at the door and you feel you are hanging above a big black hole, or you are already in the black hole? There are times we need to seek medical help, and there are times when we need professional counsel to find out what the root of our feelings and mental state is. The emotions can be symptoms of something we need to work on, something missing in our lives or other unresolved issues from our past. However, if we know it is not a severe medical condition, but rather a negative thought pattern that is developing, we need to make a choice to rejoice in spite of our feelings and emotions. We need to stand up against it and shout, "Stop it!"

As mentioned, our emotions are a result of our thoughts, so thought management is essential. We need to learn to recognize when our thoughts are going in a wrong and destructive direction, so we can arrest them. I just heard a great sermon,[16] where the preacher said she had learned to "switch the channel" when her thoughts started to spin in a negative direction. She forced herself to think about something else. She talked about how we, through negative thinking, can paint a black and hopeless picture of our future—which is a future where we forget to count on God's grace, goodness, faithfulness and provision. This future will not happen, so why not instead visualize a future that is bright and prosperous, filled with hope and good things? Why not rather believe for something good to happen?

We need to discern when we should just tell ourselves to "stop it" and when we need to take our emotions seriously and find out the roots of the feelings. In every circumstance, we can choose to rejoice, and we can count all our troubles for joy (see James 1:2). This is really hard, but it is still what God asks us to do.

To rejoice, thank and worship God in all circumstances are spiritual disciplines. You start worshiping, praising Him and rejoicing when you don't feel like it because of the Word of God and His promises related to it. Then, as a result, the joy of the Lord will be released in your life, giving you strength.

The Battle of Your Mind

It is a battle in our mind, and this battle is not always a natural battle.

> *For we do not wrestle against flesh and blood, but against principalities, against powers, against the rulers of the darkness of this age, against spiritual hosts of wickedness in the heavenly places. (Ephesians 6:12)*

Even though we are Christians, we can be under attack from the enemy in our thought life. The enemy can copy our own voice in our thoughts, so we think it is us thinking the negative things, but it is the enemy who plants these thoughts there; he whispers it in our ear, and we believe it is us. There can be spirits of depression, rejection, suicide, hopelessness and many other "monsters" oppressing us. In this case, it is important to discern that this is the enemy messing with us; it is not ourselves or our "flesh" we are fighting against.[17] We need to stand up against these spirits and command them to leave in the name of Jesus. We also need to proclaim the truth.

We have authority in the name of Jesus. Jesus took back all authority when He defeated the devil at the cross. We are to use His authority. The enemy still has some power, but he has no authority. We are given power above his power and all the authority in Jesus' name (see Eph. 1:19.23 and Eph. 2:4-7).

Rejoice before You Receive the Answer

In Isaiah 54:1 (MSG), a barren woman is asked to sing while she is still waiting to become pregnant:

> *"Sing, barren woman, who has never had a baby.*
> *Fill the air with song, you who've never experienced childbirth!*
> *You're ending up with far more children*
> *than all those childbearing women."*

Rejoice in the Lord before you have received it—while you are still "barren." Rejoicing and thanking Him for the answer before we receive it creates faith and expectation. We reach out to God, and as we rejoice and worship, we enter into the atmosphere of Heaven where we are open to receive from God promises to hold on to, faith and strength.

Let us go to the book of Nehemiah. The walls of the city of Jerusalem had miraculously been rebuilt within fifty-two days under the leadership of Nehemiah. In Chapter 8, all the people were gathered, and the priest read the Law of Moses to them. They wept as they understood the Word and that they had not lived up to the standards of God (see Neh. 8:9). But what did God ask them to do? Were they asked to be ashamed and get to work to improve themselves? No, they were actually told to do the opposite! Let us go to Nehemiah 8:9-12:

> *"This day is holy to the Lord your God; do not mourn nor weep." For all the people wept, when they heard the words of the Law.*
>
> *Then he said to them, "Go your way, eat the fat, drink the sweet, and send portions to those for whom nothing is prepared; for this day is holy to our Lord. Do not sorrow, for <u>the joy of the Lord is your strength."</u>*

> *So the Levites quieted all the people, saying, "Be still, for the day is holy; do not be grieved." And all the people went their way to eat and drink, to send portions and rejoice greatly because they understood the words that were declared to them.*

So, the Lord told them to feast, rejoice and worship because they had understood the Word. They were sad that they were not where they should be, but the Lord did not say that they should work to get things right first, then rejoice when everything was in order. No, they should celebrate first because the joy of the Lord was where they would find their strength. This is the grace of God that enables us and empowers us to do the work. (Even in the Old Testament, we see God's enabling grace.)

Also today, we are to rejoice and worship first. Also today, the joy of the Lord is our strength.

> *A happy heart is good medicine, and a cheerful mind works healing, but a broken spirit dries up the bones. (Proverbs 17:22 AMPC)*

How to Protect Your Joy

We need to protect our joy. There are some practical steps we can take to help us do that:

1. As the Lord told the people in Nehemiah to have a feast, eat, drink and be happy, so should we schedule and plan these feasts in our lives (breaks, holidays, date nights, dinners, girls' nights, etc....). Don't let it be only "everyday life." We see in the Old Testament that the Lord had ordained many feasts during the year for the people of Israel. We too need to feast and celebrate. We need to have something to look forward to.
2. If we are in a vulnerable place emotionally, we should be careful what songs we listen to. Don't put on sad, sentimental music when you are already down. It will not help you at all. We should also be aware of what movies and shows we watch. Watch something that makes you laugh and lifts you up.
3. If you are struggling with your joy already, be with people who can lift you up. Stay away from negative people that you know will drag you down.

4. Play worship music, fill yourself with the promises of God, worship and praise Him and give all your worries to God in prayer.
5. Practice gratefulness for everything God has done already! Meditate on the good things like we read in Philippians 4:8: "*Finally, brethren, whatever things are true, whatever things are noble, whatever things are just, whatever things are pure, whatever things are lovely, whatever things are of good report, if there is any virtue and if there is anything praiseworthy—meditate on these things.*"
6. Be aware of the enemy (the thief). Discover his dirty plans and stand up against them!

What God asks us to do is not easy. When unfavorable circumstances hunt us down and we feel rejected, hurt, depressed and discouraged, we want to do anything but rejoice, praise and worship. However, this is the solution God gives us to get us out of our problems. By doing this, combined with prayer and thanksgiving, we give it all over to Him. We offer our burdens to Him. We acknowledge His ability to help us and take charge of our situation. We give up our control to Him. Since He loves and cares for us more than we care for ourselves, we can know that our case is in good hands and peace and strength will be given to us so that we can manage to get through to the other side...

So, from now on remind yourself always that the JOY OF THE LORD IS YOUR STRENGTH!

FOR SELF REFLECTION AND GROUP DISCUSSION

1. Do you let your thoughts and emotions take control of your life or do you try to control them?
2. Have you experienced that the joy of the Lord—through worship, praise and expressed gratefulness—is your strength? Have you experienced it strengthening your faith and helping you to stand through a tough situation?
3. Review the list of practical steps to protect your joy. Which of these steps would be helpful to apply in your life to preserve and increase your joy? Be specific and write it down.

SHARE AND DISCUSS WITH THE GROUP

SESSION 24

Speak the Word of God – Speak Life

Death and life are in the power of the tongue, And those who love it will eat its fruit. (Proverbs 18:21)

SOMETIMES WE TEND TO SPEAK negative things over ourselves, our family and our circumstances, especially when we are frustrated and in a negative place. However, the Bible tells us that *"life and death are in the power of our tongue."* This means that we should be more concerned about what we say. Proverbs 18:21 even tells us we will *"eat its fruit"*—the fruit of what we say with our tongue! That is serious stuff! Therefore, let us choose to speak LIFE.

Spoken Words Have Power

We have all experienced how words spoken to us can affect us positively or negatively. Negative words can go like arrows into our hearts and hurt us deeply. Some people can struggle their whole lives due to negative words spoken over them when they were kids, especially by their parents. On the contrary, positive, encouraging words can bring courage, life, future and hope.

We need to be more conscious about what we speak to others but also over ourselves. Make it a habit of speaking positive words over yourself and to others! Encourage and compliment yourself when you look in the mirror. By doing this, you speak life.

The Word of God is our greatest life-giving source. God created the universe by His spoken Word (see Gen. 1). He spoke, and it came to pass. He did not just think it in His head. He spoke it out loud, and it happened. In the same way, the

Word of God is mighty to us when it is spoken out over our lives and circumstances.

We speak out the general Word of God since it is full of promises and truths we can use for our lives. However, when we are facing particularly difficult circumstances, or we are believing for something for our future, we should pray for a specific word from the Lord for that situation—a promise to hold on to. A word from God does what it is sent for.

> *So shall My word be that goes forth out of My mouth: it shall not return to Me void [without producing any effect, useless], but it shall accomplish that which I please and purpose, and it shall prosper in the thing for which I sent it. (Isaiah 55:11 AMPC)*

We speak LIFE over situations and proclaim the truth over it, which is the Word of God and His promises.

> *God, who gives life to the dead and calls those things which do not exist as though they did; (Romans 4:17b)*

Make God´s Word Your Word

For both the general Word of God and specific words given to us for a situation, we should meditate on these words until they become "our own." The Word needs to "melt together with faith in our hearts" for it to benefit us.

> *For indeed the gospel was preached to us as well as to them; but the word which they heard did not profit them, not being mixed with faith in those who heard it. (Hebrews 4:2)*

When we meditate on the Word and keep hearing it, it will create faith in us. When the Word has melted together with our faith and becomes a part of us, we can boldly proclaim it over our situations.

When we speak the Word of God, angels listen and get to work.

> *Bless the Lord, you His angels, Who excel in strength, who do His word, Heeding the voice of His word. (Psalms 103:20)*

> *Are they not all ministering spirits sent forth to minister for those who will inherit salvation? (Hebrews 1:14)*

Angels do not respond to our complaining, but they respond when we speak the Word of God.

The Word of God is powerful in our circumstances but also in our inner world—for our thoughts and mind. When we read the Word and speak the Word, it will do a work in us. It is a living Word. When we get the Word of God on the inside of us, the Holy Spirit can remind us of different Scriptures when we need them. (This comes back to meditating on the Word.) We can speak these Scriptures out loud to ourselves, and they help us in the particular situation we are facing. They can bring encouragement, wisdom or guidance. They can transform the way we see things.

> *For the word of God is living and powerful, and sharper than any two-edged sword, piercing even to the division of soul and spirit, and of joints and marrow, and is a discerner of the thoughts and intents of the heart. (Hebrews 4:12)*

Let us now look at Psalm 91—the Psalm where we learn to take refuge in the Lord in the midst of all kinds of tragedies that can happen. In verse 2, it says, *"I will say of the Lord, 'He is my refuge and my fortress, my God in Him I will trust.'"* This verse emphasizes that we actively "SAY of the Lord" (and, of course, not only say it but also trust and surrender the heart and will as well, which results in us saying it).

We also see how the angels are sent to work to protect us and help us: *"For He shall give His angels charge over you, To keep you in all your ways. In their hands they shall bear you up, Lest you dash your foot against a stone."* (Psalm 91:11-12)

Take this lesson as a reminder to be conscious of what you say out loud and what you speak over your family, yourself and your circumstances. Speak LIFE—speak the Word of God, which is the TRUTH. Speak to your "mountains." I can guarantee you that this will produce better results in your life than complaining and speaking negative things. Just try and see!

FOR SELF REFLECTION AND GROUP DISCUSSION

1. How was this session an eye-opener to you when it comes to what you allow yourself to speak out loud?

2. How have you seen or experienced the effect of the truth in this verse (things spoken over you or others) in your own life—both positive and negative?

   Death and life are in the power of the tongue, And those who love it will eat its fruit. (Proverbs 18:21)

3. Are there any bad patterns you need to change when it comes to what you speak over yourself and others? Be specific.

4. We have now learned both to manage our thoughts (and emotions) as well as what and how we speak. How do you see this influencing and changing your life for the better?

   SHARE AND DISCUSS WITH THE GROUP

SESSION 25

An Introduction to Spiritual Warfare

Know Your Enemy

IT IS CRUCIAL TO UNDERSTAND spiritual realities. We know that we belong to Jesus and that He won the victory for us at the cross, but we still have an enemy who is working hard to *"kill, steal and destroy."* We do not want to give him more attention than necessary, but we need to be aware of how he works.

> *The thief does not come except to steal, and to kill, and to destroy. I have come that they may have life, and that they may have it more abundantly. (John 10:10)*

We see that the devil is called a thief. He knows he is conquered, but he wants to steal as many people as he can away from God. If he cannot keep us away from the Kingdom of God, he works overtime to steal our joy and boldness and give us shame, guilt and condemnation. He tries to accuse us and sow poisonous thoughts and lies into our minds, to create misunderstandings between people and make us dwell on offenses until it turns into bitterness and unforgiveness, stealing our health, marriage, friendships etc.... He has many dirty schemes, and we need to be able to discern what they are to be able to resist him.

> *Stay alert! Watch out for your great enemy, the devil. He prowls around like a roaring lion, looking for someone to devour. Stand firm against him, and be strong in your faith. (1 Peter 5:8-9a NLT)*

Here we see that the devil prowls around LIKE a roaring lion. He is not a lion, but he acts like one. (Jesus is the real lion! See Rev. 5:5.) He wants to make us scared and fill us with fear. The Bible repeatedly says, "*Do not fear, do not be afraid, do not worry.*" This is because fear is a gateway for the enemy into your life—similar to faith being a gateway for God. As we see in 1 Peter 5:9, we need to resist and stand firm against the enemy, strong in our faith. We see a similar verse in James:

> *Therefore submit to God. Resist the devil and he will flee from you. (James 4:7)*

Where Do Satan and Demons Come From?

Let us stop for a minute to look at who exactly the devil and his army of demons are. In the ancient days before the Earth was created, the devil was a very beautiful archangel in Heaven called Lucifer. He became jealous and prideful and wanted to be praised and sit on a throne just like God. He rebelled against God together with one-third of the angels, and God threw them out of Heaven into darkness. Lucifer became Satan, our enemy, and the fallen angels became demons. They were all created by God for good, but they were given a free will, which they used to rebel against God.

> *And He said to them, "I saw Satan fall like lightning from heaven." (Luke 10:18)*

> *"How you are fallen from heaven,*
> *O Lucifer, son of the morning!*
> *How you are cut down to the ground,*
> *You who weakened the nations!*
> *For you have said in your heart:*
> *'I will ascend into heaven,*
> *I will exalt my throne above the stars of God;*
> *I will also sit on the mount of the congregation*
> *On the farthest sides of the north;*
> *I will ascend above the heights of the clouds,*
> *I will be like the Most High.'*
> *Yet you shall be brought down to Sheol,*
> *To the lowest depths of the Pit". (Isaiah 14:12-15)*

The devil hates human beings since we are created in God's image. The devil cannot read your thoughts; he has to wait until you speak to know what is going on in your mind. He does not know God's plan for your future. He tries his best to distract you, speak lies to you and accuse you, hoping you will listen to him.

Know Your Spiritual Position and Authority

To be able to resist and stand against the enemy, we need to know what Jesus did for us at the cross and what our position is in Christ. When we received Christ, we went from darkness to light (see 1 Peter 2:9) and became children of God and part of the Kingdom of God. When Jesus died at the cross and rose from the dead, He defeated all principalities and powers. He took away all our sin and gave us His righteousness, so the enemy cannot accuse us anymore, and sin has no control over us anymore if we submit to Christ. Our fight against the enemy is done based on the victory Jesus has <u>already</u> won at the cross.

> *Having disarmed principalities and powers, He made a public spectacle of them, triumphing over them in it [at the cross]. (Colossians 2:15)*

<u>This is the position we fight from—the victory of Christ</u>. It is only in Christ—because of our salvation and the protection we have through the blood of Jesus—that we can stand against the devil with authority. <u>Our authority and protection are in the name of Jesus</u>. We carry His name. His name belongs to us who have received Him as our Lord and Savior.

> *And Jesus came and spoke to them, saying, "All authority has been given to Me in heaven and on earth. Go therefore and make disciples of all the nations," (Matthew 28:18-19a)*

> *And these signs will follow those who believe: <u>In My name</u> they will cast out demons. (Mark 16:17a)*

Our authority as believers and our position in Christ is described clearly in Ephesians 1 and 2:

> *And what is the exceeding greatness of His power toward us who believe, according to the working of His mighty power, which He worked in Christ when He raised Him from the dead and seated Him at His right hand in the heavenly places, far above all principality and power and might and dominion, and every name that is named, not only in this age but also in that which is to come. And He put all things under His feet and gave Him to be head over all things to the church, which is His body, the fullness of Him who fills all in all. (Ephesians 1:19-23)*

> *But God... made us alive together with Christ (by grace you have been saved), and raised us up together, and made us sit together in the heavenly places in Christ Jesus, (Ephesians 2:4-6)*

I pray that you will get a strong revelation of your position in Christ! It says that Christ is seated in the heavenly places far above ALL principality and power, might and dominion. When it comes to our spiritual position, we are seated with Christ in the heavenly places. He is the Head of the body which is the church—we are part of that body! This means that ALL principality and power, might and dominion are under our feet as well! This is our position of authority in Christ! From this position, we fight against the enemy.

We need to know the ways the enemy works so that we can unveil his dirty schemes. The worst battlefield is our mind. If we start receiving lies from the enemy, those lies can create strongholds in our minds. This will negatively affect our lives since we know that "*as [a man] thinks in his heart, so is he*" (Proverbs 23:7 AMPC).

> *For though we walk in the flesh, we do not war according to the flesh. For the weapons of our warfare are not carnal but mighty in God for pulling down strongholds, casting down arguments and every high thing that exalts itself against the knowledge of God, bringing every thought into captivity to the obedience of Christ, (2 Corinthians 10:3-5)*

The weapons referred to here can be the Word of God (see Heb. 4:12-13), the blood of Jesus (see Rev. 12:11) and the name of Jesus (see Mark 16:17). The arguments that need to be cast down are arrogant and rebellious ideas and attitudes. When a negative thought enters your head, take it captive immediately and do not start dwelling on it. Just say, "No, this is not right; I don't want this thought, the truth is——" (you can proclaim a Scripture for the situation). (See also Sessions 22 and 23 for more on this.)

Put on the Full Armor of God

We need to know how to fight against the enemy. In Ephesians 6, we see that we are to put on the full armor of God:

> *Finally, be strong in the Lord and in his mighty power. Put on the full armor of God, so that you can take your stand against the devil's schemes. For our struggle is not against flesh and blood, but against the rulers, against the*

authorities, against the powers of this dark world and against the spiritual forces of evil in the heavenly realms. Therefore put on the full armor of God, so that when the day of evil comes, you may be able to stand your ground, and after you have done everything, to stand. Stand firm then, with the belt of truth buckled around your waist, with the breastplate of righteousness in place, and with your feet fitted with the readiness that comes from the gospel of peace. In addition to all this, take up the shield of faith, with which you can extinguish all the flaming arrows of the evil one. Take the helmet of salvation and the sword of the Spirit, which is the word of God. And pray in the Spirit on all occasions with all kinds of prayers and requests. With this in mind, be alert and always keep on praying for all the Lord's people. (Ephesians 6:10-18 NIV)

Let us look at this full armor of God:

For Defence

BELT OF TRUTH - Know God's truth in the Word and know what the truth is about you in Christ. Concerning your character, walk in the light, walk in truth, keep your conscience clean and don't stay in sin when Christ has set you free from it!

BREASTPLATE OF RIGHTEOUSNESS - Christ is your righteousness—it is a gift. When the enemy accuses you, you can point to Jesus who already took away all your sin and gave you His righteousness (see 2 Cor. 5:21). You know very well that you are not perfect, but through Jesus, you are totally accepted by God just as you are. By His grace, you are saved!

ON THE FEET - The readiness that comes from the Gospel of peace: You are ready to obey and be led by the Holy Spirit.

SHIELD OF FAITH - It stops all the flaming arrows of the evil one. Whatever happens, stand firm in faith in God, His Word and His promises and know that God is with you. He will never leave you nor forsake you.

THE HELMET OF SALVATION - Your mind and thoughts are protected by holding on to the truth, not accepting the enemy's lies.

For Attack

SWORD OF THE SPIRIT - The Word of God—one of our mighty weapons! We fight back, proclaiming the Word of God and speaking out the truth and God's promises to us. We do this in prayer. This is why we need to know the Word. Whatever you have deposited into your heart from the Word is a treasure chest you can draw from in times of need! Whatever revelation you have from the Word helps you to stand firm in faith (hold up the shield of faith) and fight back with the sword of the Spirit.

Let us look specifically at Ephesians 6:18 in the Amplified Bible:

> *Pray at all times (on every occasion, in every season) in the Spirit, with all [manner of] prayer and entreaty. To that end keep alert and watch with strong purpose and perseverance, interceding in behalf of all the saints (God's consecrated people)*

As part of using the sword of the Spirit, we are urged to pray in the Spirit. This can be prayer in tongues or Spirit-led prayer in a natural language. Prayer/intercession is very important to empower our sisters and brothers to stand firm in their faith and to help them in their situation. When we pray (led by the Holy Spirit), we will pray exactly what people need. We let the Holy Spirit pray through us.

There is a lot more to say about spiritual warfare, the full armor of God and Spirit-led prayer, so let this be just an introduction and inspiration to study more. This is a critical topic since we do not want to be deceived and tricked by the enemy. Let the passage from Ephesians 6:10-18 in the Message Bible sum it up:

> *And that about wraps it up. God is strong, and he wants you strong. So take everything the Master has set out for you, well-made weapons of the best materials. And put them to use so you will be able to stand up to everything the Devil throws your way. This is no afternoon athletic contest that we'll walk away from and forget about in a couple of hours. This is for keeps, a life-or-death fight to the finish against the Devil and all his angels.*
>
> *Be prepared. You're up against far more than you can handle on your own. Take all the help you can get, every weapon God has issued, so that when it's all over but the shouting you'll still be on your feet. Truth, righteousness, peace, faith, and salvation are more than words. Learn how to apply them. You'll need them throughout your life. God's Word is an indispensa-*

ble weapon. In the same way, prayer is essential in this ongoing warfare. Pray hard and long. Pray for your brothers and sisters. Keep your eyes open. Keep each other's spirits up so that no one falls behind or drops out.

FOR SELF REFLECTION AND GROUP DISCUSSION

1. We learned in this lesson how the devil wants to "*steal, kill and destroy.*" In what areas of your life have you experienced such attacks by the enemy? Did you realize at the time that it was the enemy messing with you? How did you deal with it?
2. God gives us three weapons for our spiritual warfare: the Word of God, the name of Jesus and the Blood of Jesus. From what position and with what authority do we use these weapons?
3. Do you experience a battle in your mind, with thoughts that are not from God? Have you let negative thoughts create strongholds/negative thought patterns that are hard to get rid of?
4. It is essential to understand that "*our fight is not against flesh and blood, but against principalities and powers.*" Are there problems you are facing that you should handle in prayer rather than in the natural?
5. What did you learn in this lesson that can help you fight your battles differently from now on?

SHARE AND DISCUSS WITH THE GROUP

SESSION 26

Redemption and Protection by the Blood of Jesus

IN THE PREVIOUS SESSION, we talked about spiritual warfare. The blood of Jesus is very central to that topic because it is through His blood that we are redeemed and protected. The enemy has no right to accuse us anymore because we are totally forgiven by God. However, we need to know this truth and how to apply it in our lives so that we can stand against the enemy—our accuser.

In the Bible, we read a lot about blood. It plays a very central role in cleansing and covering sin in the Old Testament. In the New Testament, we read a lot about the blood of Jesus. All this talk about blood can be strange to a new believer in Christ. Let me help you to understand it better.

Redemption and Salvation through the Blood of Jesus

Understanding the significance of blood is vital to understanding salvation and redemption in Jesus Christ. In the New Testament, we find these verses about our salvation through the blood of Jesus:

> *And since we have been made right in God's sight by the blood of Christ, he will certainly save us from God's condemnation. (Romans 5:9 NLT)*
>
> *In Him we have redemption through His blood, the forgiveness of sins, according to the riches of His grace (Ephesians 1:7)*

> *But now in Christ Jesus you who once were far off have been brought near by the blood of Christ. (Ephesians 2:13)*
>
> *He has delivered us from the power of darkness and conveyed us into the kingdom of the Son of His love, in whom we have redemption through His blood, the forgiveness of sins. (Colossians 1:13-14)*
>
> *But if we walk in the light as He is in the light, we have fellowship with one another, and the blood of Jesus Christ His Son cleanses us from all sin. (1 John 1:7)*
>
> *Knowing that you were not redeemed with corruptible things, like silver or gold, from your aimless conduct received by tradition from your fathers, but with the precious blood of Christ, as of a lamb without blemish and without spot. (1 Peter 1:18-19)*

We see that all these verses talk about the blood of Jesus—that His blood saves us.

When Jesus died on the cross, He shed His blood for us. Why is this important? Why doesn't the Bible just say that "He died"? Let us look into the Old Testament to see how God views blood:

> *'For the life of the flesh is in the blood, and I have given it to you upon the altar to make atonement for your souls; for it is the blood that makes atonement for the soul.' (Leviticus 17:11)*
>
> *For it is the life of all flesh. Its blood sustains its life. (Leviticus 17:14a)*

The blood represents the life-source of the living soul.

In Hebrews 9:22, it says that *"without shedding of blood there is no remission."* This word "remission" (in Greek *aphesis*) signifies a "release from bondage, dismissal, sending away and forgiveness, with the added quality of canceling out all judgment, punishment, obligation or debt."[18]

Throughout all of the Old Testament, animals and their blood were used as sacrifices to God to cover the sins of the people. In the tabernacle and the temple, the Jewish High Priest went into the Most Holy Place once a year to sacrifice. This sacrifice could only cover the sins of the people, never take it away, and it had to be done repeatedly every year.

The priests regularly entered the first room as they performed their religious duties. However, only the high priest ever entered the Most Holy Place, and only once a year. And he always offered blood for his own sins and for the sins the people had committed in ignorance. By these regulations the Holy Spirit revealed that the entrance to the Most Holy Place was not freely open as long as the Tabernacle and the system it represented were still in use. (Hebrews 9:6-8 NLT)

This was a foreshadowing of what would be the final sacrifice—Jesus Christ. When Jesus shed His blood at the cross, He became the perfect sacrifice that could take away our sins forever.

So Christ has now become the High Priest over all the good things that have come. He has entered that greater, more perfect Tabernacle in heaven, which was not made by human hands and is not part of this created world. With his own blood—not the blood of goats and calves—he entered the Most Holy Place once for all time and secured our redemption forever.

Under the old system, the blood of goats and bulls and the ashes of a heifer could cleanse people's bodies from ceremonial impurity. Just think how much more the blood of Christ will purify our consciences from sinful deeds so that we can worship the living God. For by the power of the eternal Spirit, Christ offered himself to God as a perfect sacrifice for our sins. (Hebrews 9:11-14 NLT)

And so, dear brothers and sisters, we can boldly enter heaven's Most Holy Place because of the blood of Jesus. By his death, Jesus opened a new and life-giving way through the curtain into the Most Holy Place. And since we have a great High Priest who rules over God's house, let us go right into the presence of God with sincere hearts fully trusting him. For our guilty consciences have been sprinkled with Christ's blood to make us clean, and our bodies have been washed with pure water. (Hebrews 10:19-22 NLT)

The curtain referred to in the verse above is the thick veil or curtain that was covering the entrance to the Most Holy Place in the temple. In the Most Holy Place was the Ark of the Covenant, where God´s presence dwelled on Earth in the Old Covenant. It was only the High Priest who could enter into the Most Holy Place and only once a year. When Jesus died on the cross, this thick veil was torn by the power of God from top to bottom. This was to show us that the entrance to the Most Holy Place is now open to all of us. Now, the Most Holy

Place is the presence of God in Heaven. That is why it says that *"we can boldly enter heaven's Most Holy Place because of the blood of Jesus. By his death, Jesus opened a new and life-giving way through the curtain into the Most Holy Place"* (Hebrews 10:19-20 NLT).

We understand that the blood of Jesus is very powerful. It made us 100 percent righteous before God. We need to stand firm in this position of righteousness, so guilt, shame and condemnation will not steal our boldness to come to God´s throne of grace.

In the Book of Revelation, we see that the blood of Jesus has made us kings and priests to God:

> *To Him who loved us and washed us from our sins in His own blood, and has made us kings and priests to His God and Father, to Him be glory and dominion forever and ever. Amen. (Revelation 1:5-6)*

> *"You are worthy to take the scroll,*
> *And to open its seals;*
> *For You were slain,*
> *And have redeemed us to God by Your blood*
> *Out of every tribe and tongue and people and nation,*
> *And have made us kings and priests to our God;*
> *And we shall reign on the earth." (Revelation 5:9-10)*

Protection by the Blood of Jesus

In Hebrews 12:22-24, we read that His blood speaks:

> *But you have come to Mount Zion and to the city of the living God... to Jesus the Mediator of the new covenant, and to the blood of sprinkling that speaks better things than that of Abel.*

To understand this, we need to go back to Genesis to read about Abel. Cain and Abel were the first two sons of Adam and Eve. Cain got so angry that he killed his brother, Abel. This is the first time "blood" is mentioned in the Bible.

> *And He [God] said, "What have you done? The voice of your brother's blood cries out to Me from the ground. (Genesis 4:10)*

We see that the blood has a voice. It speaks! Abel's blood had a voice of vengeance, while the blood of Jesus has a voice of forgiveness. The blood of Jesus still has a voice today.

Often, we pray for protection by the blood of Jesus. To understand why, let us look at how the blood protected the people of Israel when they were in captivity in Egypt. The people of Israel had been slaves in Egypt for 400 years, and God had chosen Moses to deliver them. Moses had made many appeals to Pharaoh to let God's people go, but Pharaoh had resisted every time, which caused plagues to come over Egypt. The last plague was about to begin. Every firstborn son in Egypt would die if Pharaoh continued to resist. So, the Lord got ready to release the plague over Egypt, but He wanted to save His people. We read about this in Exodus 12. It is called the Passover. The Lord told Moses to instruct the people to take a lamb without blemish (v.5) and kill it at twilight (v.6) (a symbol of Christ). Then they were to take the blood and put it on the two doorposts and on the lintel of the houses where they were eating (v.7).

We read in Exodus 12:13: *"Now the blood shall be a sign for you on the houses where you are. And when I see the blood, I will pass over you; and the plague shall not be on you to destroy you when I strike the land of Egypt."*

In Exodus 12:23, it says that *"when He sees the blood on the lintel and on the two doorposts, the Lord will pass over the door and not allow the destroyer to come into your houses to strike you."*

The blood here is a symbol of the blood of Christ, which is our final redemption and protection. Be aware that not only was the lamb going to be slaughtered, but they also had to apply the blood.

> *And you shall take a bunch of hyssop, dip it in the blood that is in the basin, and strike the lintel and the two doorposts with the blood that is in the basin. And none of you shall go out of the door of his house until morning. (Exodus 12:22)*

Hyssop was a small plant used as a brush. What does this mean for us? For us today, our tongue is what we use as hyssop to strike the blood of Jesus on "the doorposts of our lives." We proclaim the protection of the blood of Jesus over our lives, our loved ones' lives and our circumstances. Not only did Jesus, the perfect Lamb, die and shed His blood, but we also use our tongue to speak it out. The blood spoken over us has a voice not only to God but also to the enemy. As it says in Exodus 12: 23: The destroyer cannot come into our houses to strike us; however, we need to "stay inside the house" (v.22). Stay covered by the blood.

> *Then I heard a loud voice saying in heaven, "Now salvation, and strength, and the kingdom of our God, and the power of His Christ have come, for the accuser of our brethren, who accused them before our God day and night, has been cast down. And they overcame him by the blood of the Lamb and by the word of their testimony, and they did not love their lives to the death." (Revelation 12:10-11)*

The Blood in the Holy Communion

In the Holy Communion, we drink the wine/juice that symbolizes the blood of Jesus and we eat the bread that symbolizes His body, which was broken. Jesus commanded His disciples to take communion in remembrance of His finished work at the cross.

It is quite powerful to think about this in light of what we learned at the beginning of the lesson from Leviticus 17:11: *"For the life of the flesh is in the blood, and I have given it to you upon the altar to make atonement for your souls; for it is the blood that makes atonement for the soul."* Also, in Leviticus 17:14: *"For it is the life of all flesh. Its blood sustains its life."*

The life of Jesus is also in His blood. By taking the Holy Communion, we partake of His life and we also make our stand in the finished work of Jesus through His blood at the cross.

To sum it up, this lesson touched the core of what happened at the cross and how it applies to us today; however, there is a lot more revelation from God to be received in this area. I encourage you to pray and study the Bible in order to get more revelation on the power of the blood of Jesus in your life. From what we have learned today, we now understand how important it is for our salvation, redemption and protection.

FOR SELF REFLECTION AND GROUP DISCUSSION

1. In the Passover, they used a small brush called hyssop to apply the blood of the lamb to the doorposts for their protection. How do we apply the blood of Jesus for our protection today?

2. How does the taking of the Holy Communion proclaim Jesus' victory at the cross?

3. Your salvation, forgiveness and righteousness are based on the shedding of the blood of Jesus at the cross. Go back and read the Scriptures at the beginning of this session and meditate on them. Thank Jesus in prayer for what He did for us.

SHARE AND DISCUSS WITH THE GROUP

SESSION 27

Called into God´s Plan and Purpose

Called to be productive

WE KNOW THAT OUR SALVATION and righteousness are gifts from God and that our works cannot save us or add to our righteousness. We know that we are saved by grace alone. However, then comes the question: Even though works and good deeds are not saving us, and God loves us no matter what—does that mean that we should stay passive and do nothing? Of course not. From the very beginning, God planned for us to be fruitful. We can see this in the book of Genesis 1:27-28:

> *"So God created man in His own image; in the image of God He created him; male and female He created them. Then God blessed them, and God said to them, "Be fruitful and multiply; fill the earth and subdue it; have dominion over the fish of the sea, over the birds of the air, and over every living thing that moves on the earth." (Genesis 1:27-28)*

We were created in God's image, and He is the Creator of all things. He is very creative and productive, indeed, and He has a purpose for everything He does. After He had created Adam and Eve, He blessed them and told them to be fruitful, which means to be productive.

He wants us to live fruitful and productive lives as well—a life that matters and a life with a purpose. He has put seeds of greatness inside of us. He has created us as unique persons with a unique combination of gifts. These gifts are for us to discover and develop. He also has a calling upon our lives—a plan and a purpose. Our callings are all different, but we all have a part to play in God's big plan for this planet. This is so exciting!

> *'For I know the plans I have for you,' declares the Lord, 'plans to prosper you and not to harm you, plans to give you hope and a future.' (Jeremiah 29:11 NIV)*

We see throughout the whole Bible how God called people. God had a purpose and a plan for each person's life. In the New Testament, we see the Apostle Paul speaking to his dear son in the Lord, Timothy:

> *God, who has saved us and called us with a holy calling, not according to our works, but according to His own purpose and grace which was given to us in Christ Jesus before time began, (2 Timothy 1:8b-9)*

> *For the gifts and the calling of God are irrevocable. (Romans 11:29)*

This means that even though you have messed up and have been away from the Lord, He is still there waiting for you. It is not too late. Just as a GPS recalculates the route when you make a wrong turn with your car, God can recalculate your journey to get you back on the right track.

There are several places in the New Testament where we can read about the gifts of the Spirit and the ministry gifts. (We will study this topic thoroughly in the next sessions.) It is so exciting to learn that the Holy Spirit has supernatural gifts for us as well as a calling and plan for our lives. God wants to take us on an adventure with Him, inviting us to discover what is in His heart and what He wants to do on this planet.

Called to Abide in God

However, to get to know His heart and His will, we need to know HIM! God wants us to know Him intimately. He wants to have fellowship with us—a relationship—which means we walk with Him in our everyday life. This is the most important thing. Jesus wants to have priority in your life. The most important place in your life with Christ is in His presence— "at His feet." If you want your life to be fruitful for Christ, this is the place to be. All true calling and ministry are born out of this secret place in Him.

Let us read in the Gospel of John. This is Jesus Himself speaking to His disciples.

> *"I am the true vine, and My Father is the vinedresser. Every branch in Me that does not bear fruit He takes away; and every branch that bears fruit He prunes, that it may bear more fruit. You are already clean because of the word which I have spoken to you. Abide in Me, and I in you. As the branch cannot bear fruit of itself, unless it abides in the vine, neither can you, unless you abide in Me. I am the vine, you are the branches. He who abides in Me, and I in him, bears much fruit; for without Me you can do nothing.... You did not choose Me, but I chose you and appointed you that you should go and bear fruit, and that your fruit should remain, that whatever you ask the Father in My name He may give you." (John 15:1-5, 16)*

We will read again the most central verses here: John 15:4-5 (this time in the Amplified Bible).

> *Dwell in Me, and I will dwell in you. [Live in Me, and I will live in you.] Just as no branch can bear fruit of itself without abiding in (being vitally united to) the vine, neither can you bear fruit unless you abide in Me. I am the Vine; you are the branches. Whoever lives in Me and I in him bears much (abundant) fruit. However, apart from Me [cut off from vital union with Me] you can do nothing.*

Let us read verse 5 in The Message Bible:

> *"I am the Vine, you are the branches. When you're joined with me and I with you, the relation intimate and organic, the harvest is sure to be abundant. Separated, you can't produce a thing."*

You abide in Christ and are part of the vine when you are saved. As a new creation and a child of God, you already have the divine nature of God inside of you. You are filled with the Holy Spirit, and He will always be at work in you to help you, lead you and equip you. However, you also need to spend quality time with the Lord in His presence. Sing worship songs to Him. Sit and soak in His love. Thank Him for everything He has done for you. Thank Him for everything He says about you in His Word—who you are in Him. Praise Him. Tell Him how wonderful He is and what He means to you. Tell Him how grateful you are for Jesus and for all that He has done in your life. Thank Him for all of the promises in His Word for you and speak them out over your life. Our whole life springs out of our relationship with the Lord and our fellowship with Him—out of abiding in Him.

Give Him all your concerns and prayer requests and know that He hears you.

> *Do not be anxious about anything, but in every situation, by prayer and petition, with thanksgiving, present your requests to God. And the peace of God, which transcends all understanding, will guard your hearts and your minds in Christ Jesus. (Philippians 4:6-7 NIV)*

As you spend time with the Lord as described above, you might feel His tangible presence. He is there through His Holy Spirit to minister to you. As you read the Word in this atmosphere, the Word will be alive to you and speak to you. You might also hear the Lord talk to you in other ways: a still inner voice, an urge to do something, a reminder to read something in the Word and a reminder to pray for someone or contact them to give them encouraging words. In this atmosphere of His presence and His Word, He is at work in you.

God Is at Work in You

> *Being confident of this, that he who began a good work in you will carry it on to completion until the day of Christ Jesus. (Philippians 1:6 NIV)*

When we live in an intimate relationship with the Lord, He will put His dreams in our hearts, so His dreams become our dreams. We will get a strong desire to follow His will and plan.

> *For it is God who works in you to will and to act to fulfill his good purpose. (Philippians 2:13 NIV)*

When the Word has transformed us, His will has become our will and our desires are His desires.

> *If you abide in Me, and My words abide in you, you will ask what you desire, and it shall be done for you. (John 15:7)*

This is the same promise as we see in Psalm 37:4: *"Delight yourself also in the Lord, And He shall give you the desires of your heart."*

God will show us what to do through the leading of the Holy Spirit. He will open doors for us, and He will be with us. We will walk in the plan that He has already prepared for us. We will bear fruit! Just like a vine does not have to struggle to produce grapes, we don't have to struggle to bear fruit. Fruit comes naturally from a healthy vine. In the same way, the fruit of the Spirit will be produced in our lives as we abide in Him. Our union with Christ will affect our character.

But the fruit of the Spirit is love, joy, peace, longsuffering, kindness, goodness, faithfulness, (Galatians 5:22)

God´s Ultimate Plan and Desire

When we get to know the Lord, He will show us His heart for the people of this Earth. His heart's greatest desire is that all people will hear the Gospel so that they can be saved and enter into a relationship with Him. The Lord's plan for your life will be linked to His great plan and desire in some way, depending on your gifting and calling. Let us read the Great Commission in Matthew 28:18-20 (NIV):

Then Jesus came to them and said, "All authority in heaven and on earth has been given to me. Therefore go and make disciples of all nations, baptizing them in the name of the Father and of the Son and of the Holy Spirit, and teaching them to obey everything I have commanded you. And surely I am with you always, to the very end of the age."

After our fellowship with Him, our highest calling is the ministry of reconciliation (see 2 Cor. 5:18-20), which means telling people that God has already reconciled the world to Himself. We tell them to come to the Father, just as they are, and receive their gift of salvation...

If the Lord Calls You, He Also Equips You

We can trust that when the Lord calls us, He also equips us. He will never ask us to do anything that He has not equipped us for.

The Prophet Jeremiah got a specific calling when he was very young. We can read about this in Jeremiah 1:4-9:

Then the word of the Lord came to me, saying:
"Before I formed you in the womb I knew you;
Before you were born I sanctified you;
I ordained you a prophet to the nations."
Then said I:
"Ah, Lord God!
Behold, I cannot speak, for I am a youth."
But the Lord said to me:
"Do not say, 'I am a youth,'

> *For you shall go to all to whom I send you,*
> *And whatever I command you, you shall speak.*
> *Do not be afraid of their faces,*
> *For I am with you to deliver you," says the Lord.*
> *Then the Lord put forth His hand and touched my mouth, and the Lord said to me: "Behold, I have put My words in your mouth."*

We see that Jeremiah got a very specific calling from the Lord. He looked at his lack of ability, but the Lord put His words in Jeremiah's mouth. If you continue to read, you will see that the Lord asked him to "*prepare [himself] and arise*" (Jeremiah 1:17), which means he needed to accept the calling and step into it.

When we receive God's abundance of grace for our lives and realize how much He loves us and how He has sent the Holy Spirit to help us in every situation, we have the confidence to step out into what we believe He has put in our hearts. We do not need to be afraid of failing, because His grace is there to pick us up whenever we fall. If we go astray, He will find us and help us back on track.

As you spend time with Him and His Word and you let Him be the center of your life, you will find your God-given purpose. You can choose to use your gifts and talents for your own plan and purpose, but how much more significant to get into God's plan and surrender your life and your gifts and talents to Him. This way, you will make an eternal impact! That does not mean you need to be in full-time ministry in a church setting, but God will put you in the place where He wants you, which is your place in His big puzzle. By the grace of God, this will be a place that is aligned with the God-given dreams in your heart and the way you are equipped with gifts, talents and personality. How great is our God!

FOR SELF REFLECTION AND GROUP DISCUSSION

1. What does it look like in your life to abide in Jesus and to be connected to the vine as we read in John 15?
2. In John 15:2, Jesus says that if you bear fruit, He will prune you so that you will bear even more fruit. What do you think this means? Have you ever experienced God asking you to give something up so that you can be more fruitful in other areas? Can it be that Jesus prunes you by making you change how you spend your time and energy, your financial re-

sources and your focus? Perhaps even your perspective and attitude need to be pruned for Him to prosper you further into His plan?

3. Have you experienced that your desires, plans and purposes have changed as you have been "abiding in Him" and letting "His Word abide in you"? If yes, please explain.
4. Do you feel you have received a calling from God or that you are being led in a specific direction? Explain.

SHARE AND DISCUSS WITH THE GROUP

SESSION 28

Discover Your Spiritual Gifts Part 1

GOD HAS A BEAUTIFUL PLAN AND PURPOSE for each one of us. When we are in that right place, we will flourish and feel so fulfilled in life. God has given us spiritual gifts that equip us for His plans and purposes. The spiritual gifts give us anointing in certain areas to do the work we are called to do. They give us supernatural revelation, ability and power to do the work Jesus did on planet Earth. The Amplified Bible calls the spiritual gifts "*special endowments of supernatural energy*" (see 1 Cor. 12:1). We are very much encouraged to desire these gifts.

> *Now concerning spiritual gifts, brethren, I do not want you to be ignorant: (1 Corinthians 12:1)*

> *Pursue love, and desire spiritual gifts, but especially that you may prophesy. (1 Corinthians 14:1)*

Spiritual Gifts and the Body of Christ

Just like Jesus ministered by the Holy Spirit, He calls His church to do the same thing. When Jesus went to Heaven and sent the Holy Spirit, we—the church—became the body of Christ on planet Earth. The miracles and work are supposed to continue through us—the church—by the Holy Spirit.

There are three major passages on spiritual gifts in the Bible: Romans 12:1-8, 1 Corinthians 12 and Ephesians 4. It is interesting to see that in all of these passages, the Apostle Paul talks about the spiritual gifts in connection to the body of Christ.

> *For as we have many members in one body, but all the members do not have the same function, so we, being many, are one body in Christ, and individually members of one another. (Romans 12:4-5)*
>
> *But now God has set the members, each one of them, in the body just as He pleased. (1 Corinthians 12:18)*
>
> *For his "body" has been formed in his image and is closely joined together and constantly connected as one. And every member has been given divine gifts to contribute to the growth of all; and as these gifts operate effectively throughout the whole body, we are built up and made perfect in love. (Ephesians 4:16 TPT)*

We see from these verses that God has designed the church as a living organism (a body), and He has determined what the function of each of the individual members should be. Each one of us is given spiritual gifts to minister to other members of the body of Christ (the church) and people outside of the church as well. We are given different gifts to function in different ways and different areas, just as the body parts in the human body have various functions. <u>For our gifts to function at their full potential, it is crucial to get connected to the right parts (people) in the body</u>; for instance, if you are a thumb, then you need to connect to the palm and the other fingers to make a whole hand. Then you can do amazing things together, but as a lonely thumb, you can't do much.

Each One Has One or More Spiritual Gifts

Spiritual gifts are given to each one of us and are provided for ministry. In 1 Peter 4:10, we read, *"As each one has received a gift, minister it to one another, as good stewards of the manifold grace of God."*

Our gifts are connected to God's plan for our lives. He will not call us to do anything that He has not gifted us for, and He will not gift us if there is no way for us to use the gifts. God has designed each one of us in a unique way—just the way He wants us. He will lead our steps into His plan and calling. Ephesians 2:10

says it so beautifully: *"For we are His workmanship, created in Christ Jesus for good works, which God prepared beforehand that we should walk in them."*

Different Kinds of Spiritual Gifts

The Father, Son and Holy Spirit are all involved in giving us spiritual gifts, and each one in the Trinity has a distinct interest and does a different work in us to provide for our unique purpose and fulfillment![19] However, we need to understand the difference between these gifts, their purpose and how they work.

The Nine Gifts of the Holy Spirit

The nine gifts described in 1 Corinthians 12 are the gifts of the Holy Spirit. These gifts cause the believer to move in divine knowledge, revelation and power in ministry. These are gifts flowing as the Spirit wills through believers. You cannot use them whenever you want, but they are available for every believer as the Holy Spirit distributes them, and He is more than willing to do so. The gifts of the Spirit are given as tools for effective ministry, both within the church and to unbelievers. (When Jesus was on Earth, He was ministering through all of these gifts.)

> *There are diversities of gifts, but the same Spirit. There are differences of ministries, but the same Lord. And there are diversities of activities, but it is the same God who works all in all. But the manifestation of the Spirit is given to each one for the profit of all: for to one is given the word of wisdom through the Spirit, to another the word of knowledge through the same Spirit, to another faith by the same Spirit, to another gifts of healings by the same Spirit, to another the working of miracles, to another prophecy, to another discerning of spirits, to another different kinds of tongues, to another the interpretation of tongues. But one and the same Spirit works all these things, distributing to each one individually as He wills. (1 Corinthians 12:4-11)*

LET US TAKE A CLOSER LOOK AT THE NINE GIFTS OF THE HOLY SPIRIT:

1. *WORD OF WISDOM* - divine wisdom to handle situations, solve problems, make the right choices and give the right advice.
2. *WORD OF KNOWLEDGE* - divine knowledge regarding a person´s situation; for instance, their pain or sickness. When you release the word of knowledge to the person, he or she can be healed, set free or will open

up for what God wants to say through a prophetic message that may follow the word of knowledge.

3. *FAITH* - supernatural faith that will produce great results. It suddenly rises on the inside.
4. *GIFTS OF HEALINGS* - special gifts of delivering healing to people, which is in addition to the authority that all believers have as we are all told to lay hands on the sick and they will recover.
5. *WORKING OF MIRACLES* - display of power giving the ability to go beyond the natural; for example, turning water into wine, feeding 5000 people with two fish and five loaves of bread, etc.
6. *PROPHECY* - "*The gift of interpreting the divine will and purpose*" (1 Corinthians 12:10 AMPC). Prophesy does not have to be "so says the Lord." It can be simple, inspired words from the Lord to another person given verbally or in writing. 1 Corinthians 14:3 gives us some clear instructions about what prophecy is in the New Covenant: *"But he who prophesies speaks edification and exhortation and comfort to men."* Prophesy must always be based on grace and love. You do not prophesy judgment in the New Covenant! You call forth gifts you see in people and build them up.[20]
7. *DISCERNING OF SPIRITS* - can sense if a spirit is from God or the enemy; supernatural power to detect the realm of the spirits and their activity; supernatural insight and revelation of the plans and purposes of the enemy and his forces.
8. *TONGUES* - a message to the church spoken in a language never learned (different than tongues as prayer language). This should be interpreted; it can be an actual language or a heavenly language.
9. *INTERPRETATION OF TONGUES* - you get the interpretation of the message you or someone else spoke in tongues to the church; you don't understand what is spoken, but supernaturally sense the meaning of it.

Let us sum this up.[21] In 1 Corinthians 12:4-11 there are:

THREE VOCAL GIFTS (GIFTS THAT SAY SOMETHING): Tongues, Interpretation of Tongues and Prophesy

THREE KNOWING GIFTS (SUPERNATURAL KNOWLEDGE): Word of Wisdom, Word of Knowledge and Discerning of Spirits

THREE POWER GIFTS (GIFTS THAT DO SOMETHING): Gifts of Faith, Gifts of Healings and Working of Miracles

You might flow regularly in some of the gifts as the Holy Spirit prompts you and as you step out in faith and obedience. As you do this, you grow in faith and experience using the particular gift and the Holy Spirit can use you more in the same area. The gifts of the Spirit must always be exercised with humility and in love.

Please take notice that the gifts of the Spirit are not earned in any way; they are not merits or medals, but gifts given by grace alone. The gifts are not for your possession, but tools for the job God calls you to do. You flow in the particular gift of the Spirit that you need to get the ministry job done efficiently and to the glory of God.

The Gifts of God the Father

The gifts described in Romans 12 are given (or activated) by God the Father when you are born again. This is an anointing that will flow in certain areas of your life. The big difference between these gifts and the gifts of the Holy Spirit is that these are gifts you can use all the time. You can at any given time "step into the anointing" and flow in them. These gifts are not the same as your natural talents, but they can be closely related, since God designed you perfectly to fit into His great plan and into the body of Christ. The New Spirit Filled Life Bible puts it like this[22]: *"These gifts seem to be characterized by basic 'motivations' that is inherent tendencies that characterize each different person by reason of the Creator's unique workmanship in their initial gifting."*

> *Having then gifts differing according to the grace that is given to us, let us use them: if prophecy, let us prophesy in proportion to our faith; or ministry, let us use it in our ministering; he who teaches, in teaching; he who exhorts, in exhortation; he who gives, with liberality; he who leads, with diligence; he who shows mercy, with cheerfulness. (Romans 12:6-8)*

We see a similar passage in 1 Corinthians 12:28: *"And God has appointed these in the church: first apostles, second prophets, third teachers, after that miracles, then gifts of healings, helps, administrations, varieties of tongues."* (This passage includes gifts from all three categories.)

The gifts mentioned in these Scriptures are not all there is in the body of Christ. We can see these gifts related to ministry in Scripture too:

- Missionary (Ephesians 3:6-8)
- Hospitality (1 Peter 4:9)
- Speech (1 Peter 4:11)
- Deliverance (Mark 16:17)

We find other gifts in action as well, like worship leaders, musicians and intercessors who are anointed to do their ministry.

In the Old Testament, we see that the Spirit of God gave gifts for artistic work:

> *And He has filled him with the Spirit of God, in wisdom and understanding, in knowledge and all manner of workmanship, to design artistic works, to work in gold and silver and bronze, in cutting jewels for setting, in carving wood, and to work in all manner of artistic workmanship. (Exodus 35:31-33)*

I think God is giving the same gifts in the artistic area still today, although it is not specified in the New Testament. Let us sum this up:

THE GIFTS OF THE FATHER/MOTIVATIONAL GIFTS INCLUDE:

1. *SERVICE (MINISTRY)* - practical work in the church (ushers, traffic marshals, sound technicians, etc.)
2. *TEACHING* - supernatural ability to explain and apply the truths from the Word of God for the church
3. *EXHORTATION* - stimulating faith; encouraging; instructing
4. *GIVING* - contributing; giving out of a spirit of generosity; sharing your resources
5. *LEADERSHIP* - vision and ability to lead people in a particular direction
6. *MERCY* - to feel sympathy with the misery of others; comfort to the sorrowing; to show kindness
7. *HELPS* - helping and supporting others so they can be effective in their ministry

8. *ADMINISTRATION* - government; getting others to work together; putting plans into action and through to fulfillment
9. *MISSIONARY* - (Ephesians 3:6-8); someone going out to preach the Gospel to people groups in other nations
10. *EVANGELISTIC GIFT* - a person with a special anointing to preach in such a way that people come to Christ
11. *SHEPHERD* - shepherd for a "flock" in the church (e.g. a small group)
12. *HOSPITALITY* - (1 Peter 4:9); meaning to love; to do and to do with pleasure[20]; In NT it was utilized to care for believers and workers who visited to worship, work and become involved in the body of Christ.
13. *SPEECH* - (1 Peter 4:11)
14. *DELIVERANCE* - special gift to cast out demons and evil spirits[21]; (Mark 16:17)
15. *INTERCESSION* - a heart and motivation to "stand in the gap" and lift up people, situations, churches, nations, etc. in prayer
16. *LEADING WORSHIP (music)* - This gift is about bringing the congregation into the presence of God, and a special anointing is needed. Just being a good singer is not in any way sufficient!
17. *ARTISTIC WORK* - inspired/empowered by the Holy Spirit

This list is not complete as God will give gifts needed for every time and season in the lives of human beings.

The Gifts of the Son

In Ephesians 4:11, we see a third category of gifts: the "five-fold ministry gifts" that Jesus Himself gave the church with the purpose to make sure that the two previous types of gifts are functioning in the church.

> *And He Himself gave some to be apostles, some prophets, some evangelists, and some pastors and teachers, for the equipping of the saints for the work of ministry, for the edifying of the body of Christ, (Ephesians 4:11-12)*

1. *APOSTLE* - by definition a special messenger, a delegate, one commissioned for a particular task or role, sent forth with a message[23]; Often,

the apostle plants and overseas churches and functions in the ministry with signs, wonders and miracles.[24]

2. *PROPHET* - one who holds the office of a prophet
3. *EVANGELIST* - a person with an office of an evangelist with a special anointing to preach in such a way that people come to Christ
4. *PASTOR* - shepherd for the "flock" in the church
5. *TEACHER* - holds the office of a teacher in the church

The five-fold ministers themselves are the gifts. They do not only have a gift, but they are the gift to the church.[20] The "five-fold ministry" is a specific calling from Jesus, which means that you do not hold the office of a prophet, a teacher or an evangelist just because you flow in gifts of the prophetic, teaching, evangelism, leadership, etc.

The "five-fold ministry gifts" are found in the leadership of the local church as well as in the universal body of Christ. Their purpose is to edify the church so that we are all equipped for our ministry.[19] They are often called offices rather than gifts. However, they are gifts which become an office.[21] As mentioned, Jesus is the One who calls someone to be an apostle, a prophet, a teacher, an evangelist or a pastor. The person will flow in a particular gift with a high level of anointing. He or she is then recognized publicly by the leaders in the church for his or her gift and calling and is commissioned into the office of one of the five-fold ministry gifts (gifted, called, anointed, acknowledged by the church and commissioned). This is why we can find some of the gifts both under the category of the gifts of the Father and the gifts of the Son (five-fold ministry gifts). You can have a teaching gift, an evangelistic gift, the anointing of a "shepherd" or a prophetic gift without having an office of a teacher, a prophet, an evangelist or a pastor.

If a local church does not have all of the five-fold ministry gifts "in the house," the church should invite trusted ministers to "fill the gap" for the congregation to be equipped in every area of gifting and ministry. The specific impartation and equipping for an area of ministry (for instance, evangelism or the prophetic) come from that particular "five-fold minister"; in this case, the evangelist and the prophet.

What Are Your Spiritual Gifts?

So, what are your spiritual gifts? Most likely God has a mix of gifts for you—A GIFT MIX, which gives you a unique spiritual personality.[21] Wow! Moreover, this will fit with the plan God has for your life. Some of the gifts might be more dominant than others, and some might be stronger in certain seasons of your life. We all get to discover, develop and use the particular gifts God has given us.

We need to distinguish between the motivational gifts (the gifts of the Father), which you are equipped with all the time, and the gifts of the Holy Spirit, which are added to the gifts of the Father and given as the Spirit wills in different situations.

Many of the gifts are quite commonly paired up together.[21] Evangelists often work in miracles, words of knowledge, healings etc. Pastors would often have gifts of teaching and exhortation. A missionary would need all kinds of gifts... You can also have one major gift and another one that is not as strong.

In this session, you got a good overview of the spiritual gifts, and you have learned the difference between the gifts of the Holy Spirit, the motivational gifts from the Father and the "five-fold" ministry gifts given to equip the church. In the next session, we will continue learning about how to discover our spiritual gifts, how to use them and how to stir them up.

FOR SELF REFLECTION AND GROUP DISCUSSION

1. What are your motivational gifts? In what areas do you have a flow and anointing? Let each person in the group share and give feedback on the gifts they see in the other group members.
2. Have you experienced functioning in any of the gifts of the Holy Spirit? Have you been pursuing and desiring to flow in these gifts as we read in 1 Corinthians 14:1: *"Pursue love, and desire spiritual gifts, but especially that you may prophesy"?* If yes, please share with the group. If no, share what is stopping you from pursuing them.
3. Now that you know the gifts, it will be easier to start pursuing and desiring them. Pray for a release of the gifts of the Holy Spirit to begin functioning in the group. Practice on each other in a safe environment—especially the gift of prophecy (as encouraged in 1 Cor. 14:1). However,

be reminded of the guidelines of prophecy in the New Covenant: "*But he who prophesies speaks edification and exhortation and comfort to men*" (1 Corinthians 14:3). Let this be a common part of ministering to each other as you pray with and for each other in the group.

SESSION 29

Discover Your Spiritual Gifts Part 2

TO DISCOVER AND USE OUR SPIRITUAL GIFTS, we need knowledge. We also need to learn how to be good stewards of our gifts and keep the gifts alive when we have received them.

How to Discover Your Spiritual Gifts

How do we discover our spiritual gifts (gifts of the Father/ motivational gifts)? One good way is to get involved in church and Christian ministry and test whether you have gifts in different areas. As you do this, you will find out what gifts you do not have as well.[21] This is just as important since many times you might feel that you are expected to serve in a particular ministry (e.g., sing in the choir or do children's ministry), but perhaps, in reality, you don't have a beautiful voice, or you do not even like kids. Pay attention to what you feel good doing and also your desires.

Delight yourself also in the Lord, and He shall give you the desires of your heart. (Psalm 37:4)

For it is God who works in you both to will and to do for His good pleasure. (Philippians 2:13)

If your heart is entirely with Him and your desire is to do His will, He will put the longing in your heart to do what He wants you to do. His desires become your desires. His will becomes your will. However, there is always some pain involved when we step out of our comfort zone into new things, and this can, of course, affect our will to step out. Be aware of that fact and be willing to increase your capacity.

God gives gifts that match your personality, so it is normal to feel excited about your work for Him.[21] However, if you are a quiet person, God can still ask you to speak. We need to step out and trust that we are able in Him. The power and anointing of the Holy Spirit kick in when we step into what God asks us to do. With experience, our comfort zone is enlarged, and our faith grows. However, then God will be there with new and more significant challenges, so we must always rely on Him.

An excellent way to check if you have a gift is to see whether the task you are trying to accomplish, is actually achieved. You should be effective in what you are doing,[21] experiencing a flow. When true gifts are in operation, then whatever is supposed to happen through them will happen. For instance, if you have an evangelistic gift, people should be drawn to Jesus and saved when you preach and share. If you have a gift as a worship leader, the congregation should feel the anointing and the presence of God when you are singing. If you have a special gift of hospitality, people should feel especially welcome and taken care of by you. If you have a gift of exhortation, people should feel very encouraged when they speak to you! Seek confirmation from others on your gifts as well. There is also growth in the functioning of our gifts. We need to learn how to flow in our gift and be good stewards of the gift. We grow with experience and through learning about how the gifts work.

Do Not Confuse Spiritual Gifts With...

We should not confuse spiritual gifts with natural talents.[21] All people have natural talents, including those who are not Christians. However, sometimes your spiritual gift can be added to your natural abilities. This is only sometimes the case. Several well-known preachers could not even speak without stuttering before they received the spiritual gift of an evangelist or teacher.

We should not confuse the spiritual gifts with the fruit of the Spirit that is found in Galatians 5:22-23: love, joy, peace, longsuffering, kindness, goodness, faithfulness, gentleness and self-control.[21] The fruit is not discovered; it is developed through your walk with God and your yielding to the Holy Spirit. However, you do need the fruit of the Spirit to function in the gifts in the right way. All ministry and use of spiritual gifts must be done in love, kindness, goodness and humility. When you meet trials, challenges and pressure along the way, you need joy, peace, longsuffering and faithfulness to not give up. Self-control will sustain you through temptation. The enemy knows your weak spots. Your character is what will carry your ministry and spiritual gifts in the long term. The Apostle Paul corrected the church in Corinth for functioning like crazy in the gifts but forgetting about the fruit. However, the result of this correction is the beautiful passage about love in 1 Corinthians 13, which talks about how everything is worth nothing if you do not have love.

We should not confuse the spiritual gifts with the general things you are doing as a believer.[21] As a believer, you are supposed to help in the church or some ministry, have faith, give to the church, be hospitable and generous, lay hands on the sick and pray for them, have a prayer life and so on. These are not spiritual gifts, as we are talking about in this session, but general motivations we all have as Christians as we obey the Word.

God has a plan and purpose for your life, and He has gifted you to fit perfectly into it. This is not about doing things for God but about being everything God has created you to be and finding your place where you will have the most joy in serving and ministering. This place is where you will feel fulfilled and discover the purpose of life. God wants to bless others through your gifts and your life.

It is not difficult to find the plan and purpose of God. He is more than willing to speak to you and to lead you if you seek Him. He has perfectly designed you with all the gifts you need and has already prepared the good works you are supposed to walk in... So, be excited and go after God and everything He has for you!

How and at What Level Do We Use the Gifts?

When you have discovered your gifts, you need to take into consideration that it differs how, where and to what extent we are called to use our gifts. This is described in 1 Corinthians 12:4-6 as different gifts, ministries and activities. Where is the gift performed and at what scale? [25] As an evangelist, are you preaching to 200 people in the Philippines or 200,000 people in Africa?

In addition to geography and scale, also consider if you are called to a certain demographic group.[25] This can be an ethnic group or a specific age group like youth, kids, adults, women or senior citizens. You can also be called to minister to a particular interest group in a society such as business people or politicians. Your gift will flow the most in the place and with the people you are called to, so pray and follow the leading of the Holy Spirit so that you can find your "sweet spot."

As we become aware of our calling, gifts and place in the body of Christ, we are content and don't compare ourselves with others. We know that the gifts are given by grace alone and are not deserved in any way. So, there is no reason to brag or be proud. Your gift is not more valuable than other gifts, nor is it worth less. God looks at our faithfulness in how we use our gifts, not how great the gift is.

Stirring Up Your Spiritual Gifts through the Gift of Praying in Tongues

When we have received or discovered our spiritual gifts, we are called to be good stewards of the gifts and not let circumstances or discouragement cause us to bury them. Let us take a closer look at one gift you can use whenever you want that can stir up all the gifts of the Spirit[26]—the gift of speaking in tongues as a prayer language (which is different from the gift of tongues that needs interpretation). This gift has a lot of benefits.

When Jesus was about to ascend to Heaven, He asked the disciples to WAIT in the city until they had received POWER from above. He told them they would be *"baptized with the Holy Spirit not many days from now"'* (Acts 1:5). This power they were going to receive was the DUNAMIS power that Jesus was using as He did His miracles. Wow! We learned in Session 13 how the Holy Spirit came like a mighty wind on the Day of Pentecost, and the disciples were all baptized with the Holy Spirit, and they started to speak in other tongues (see Acts 1 and 2). Speaking in tongues was a sign that they had been baptized with the Holy Spirit. This is still available to all true believers in Jesus Christ today.

The prayer language of speaking in tongues to God can be very strange when we are not familiar with it, but we need to get used to the thought that this is a good gift from God, given for a purpose and with many benefits. We pray the <u>perfect prayer</u> when we pray in the Spirit (in tongues). It says in Romans 8:26-27:

Likewise the Spirit also helps in our weaknesses. For we do not know what we should pray for as we ought, but the Spirit Himself makes intercession for us with groanings which cannot be uttered. Now He who searches the hearts knows what the mind of the Spirit is, because He makes intercession for the saints according to the will of God.

It is interesting that the next verse says, "*And we know that all things work together for good to those who love God, to those who are the called according to His purpose*" (Romans 8:28). The order of these verses can be interpreted to mean that it is the Holy Spirit who helps us to pray the perfect prayer with the result that all things work together for good in our lives.

When we pray in tongues, we edify ourselves—spirit, mind and body (see 1 Cor. 14:4). When we look at the word "edifies" in the original language, it means "to build your house, to repair your house." [27] This shows us that praying in tongues not only builds up our spirits but also our souls and our bodies—our entire lives, since the Holy Spirit will pray perfect prayers through us, covering all the needs in our lives and families. That is awesome!

By building ourselves up, we can build up others next. This is another purpose of the gift of praying in tongues. It stirs up the other gifts God has given you, which are given to minister to others.

Therefore I remind you to stir up the gift of God which is in you through the laying on of my hands. (2 Timothy 1:6)

The meaning of "stir up" is actually "rekindle the embers of, fan to flame and keep burning." [28] You add wind to the embers/ashes to make it into a fire or a flame.

That is why I would remind you to stir up (rekindle the embers of, fan the flame of, and keep burning) the [gracious] gift of God, [the inner fire] that is in you by means of the laying on of my hands [with those of the elders at your ordination]. (2 Timothy 1:6 AMPC)

The Greek word used for "gift of God" in this verse is *charisma*,[29] which refers to the nine gifts of the Holy Spirit. This means that Timothy was reminded to stir up the "*charisma* gift" he had been given. (See Session 28 for the nine gifts of the Holy Spirit.)

When we "fan to flame" this gift of praying in tongues, we will also "fan to flame" the *charisma* gifts in 1 Corinthians 12:7-11 (the nine gifts of the Holy Spirit).[26]

I encourage you to study the two sessions on spiritual gifts (Sessions 28 and 29) carefully and do as Scripture says— "*desire*" and "*pursue*" the gifts of the Spirit. When it comes to your motivational gifts (gifts of the Father), they need to be discovered and developed as they often come in "seed" form, which means they need to grow forth in your life. Your spiritual gifts will help you find God's will and purpose for your life. As you become aware of and start flowing in your spiritual gifts, you will be an even greater blessing at your church, your workplace and in your ministry—you will be efficient in your calling.

FOR SELF REFLECTION AND GROUP DISCUSSION

1. Do you feel a calling to a particular nation, ethnic group, age group or interest group as described in this session? How do you see yourself using your gifts in this place or to these people?
2. Why is the "fruit of the Spirit" (love, joy, peace, longsuffering, kindness, goodness, faithfulness, gentleness and self-control) important in our lives in order for us to use our spiritual gifts in the right way? Why is it your developed character that will carry your ministry and spiritual gifts in the long term? Read 1 Corinthians 13 to see how important love is. Our gifts are worth nothing if we don´t have love.
3. How can you see that the gift of praying in tongues can benefit you in your life? Have you received the gift of speaking/praying in tongues? If not, you can obtain it by faith through the laying on of hands by a Spirit-filled believer in your group or church. You can also ask God for it yourself. He is more than willing to give you this useful gift. (Read Luke 11:11-13.)

SHARE AND DISCUSS WITH THE GROUP

SESSION 30

How to Be Led by the Holy Spirit

WE KNOW THAT THE HOLY SPIRIT IS A PERSON in the Trinity together with the Father and the Son. When Jesus died and was resurrected, He appeared to the disciples and others for forty days before He went to Heaven to be with His Father. Jesus told the disciples that it was to their benefit that He went away because if He stayed, He could be in only one place at a time. If He went away, He would come back by the Holy Spirit and live inside every believer on planet Earth! He would do greater things through us than He did Himself on Earth! So, if you are a believer, know that He lives within you. We need to be aware of His presence and lean towards the Spirit to hear His voice and be led by Him in everyday life.

John 16:7 calls the Holy Spirit a *HELPER*. The Amplified Bible expounds on what the original language meant by the word "Helper":

> *However, I am telling you nothing but the truth when I say it is profitable (good, expedient, advantageous) for you that I go away. Because if I do not go away, the Comforter (Counselor, Helper, Advocate, Intercessor, Strengthener, Standby) will not come to you [into close fellowship with you]; but if I go away, I will send Him to you [to be in close fellowship with you]*

So, we understand that the Holy Spirit is here to help us in every possible way. Today, we will look more closely into HOW the Holy Spirit will lead you in your walk with God.[30] We will also look into how He will NOT lead you.[30]

The Word of God is the Will of God

• *The Holy Spirit Inspired the Word*

The Scripture itself was written inspired by the Holy Spirit, so He will lead us and speak to us as we read the Word.

> *All Scripture is given by inspiration of God (AMPC: God-breathed) and is profitable for doctrine, for reproof, for correction, for instruction in righteousness, (2 Timothy 3:16)*

• *The Word is a Lamp to Your Feet*

> *Your word is a lamp to my feet and a light to my path. (Psalm 119:105)*

The Word of God will lead you step by step on your path. It is interesting to note that a lamp only lights up the area right in front of you—not a mile down the road. This means that the Holy Spirit will most likely lead you only one step at a time. Sometimes you don't understand what is going on. You just need to take the small steps He is showing you and trust that He has the steps further down the road under control.

• *The Holy Spirit Will Use Scripture that is Deposited in Your Heart*

> *But the Helper, the Holy Spirit, whom the Father will send in My name, He will teach you all things, and bring to your remembrance all things that I said to you. (John 14:26)*

I encourage you to fill yourself with the Word of God and learn Scriptures by heart so that the Holy Spirit can bring them to your remembrance when you need them the most! Very often, the Holy Spirit will lead you in a decision or confirm the leading of your heart with Scriptures.

It is difficult to be led astray if you know the Word. Anything you hear can be judged by the Word of God. The Word and the Spirit will never disagree.

How the Holy Spirit Leads

• *The Inner Witness – God's Still, Small Voice*

The inner witness is a still, small voice on the inside of you. It is the leading of your own spirit, which is filled with the Holy Spirit. It could be described as a compass, a green light or a "seems good" voice. You may hear it as a passing thought, a sudden impression or an internal sense of something God is saying.

• *The Voice of Your Spirit*

The voice of your spirit is your *conscience*. At the fall, the Law of Conscience came into effect. Unless altered by continual disobedience or culture, people instinctively know right from wrong. Every human being has a conscience, but if one is not born again, the conscience is not always a good guide. As a believer, your spirit is in constant communion with the Holy Spirit and He will speak His mind to you. If you do something wrong, you will feel it in your conscience! The Holy Spirit will convince you to get things right.

• *The Holy Spirit Can Speak in an Authoritative Voice*

> *Then the Spirit said to Philip, "Go near and overtake this chariot." (Acts 8:29)*
>
> *While Peter thought about the vision, the Spirit said to him, "Behold, three men are seeking you. Arise therefore, go down and go with them, doubting nothing; for I have sent them." (Acts 10:19-20)*

The voice of the Holy Spirit is clear and may even seem audible. Moses heard that voice at the burning bush. The Holy Spirit usually only speaks to us audibly if we are not listening to our spirit, if we need correction or warning or if it is critical that we know God has spoken.

• *Dreams*

> *'And it shall come to pass in the last days, says God, That I will pour out of My Spirit on all flesh; Your sons and your daughters shall prophesy, Your young men shall see visions, Your old men shall dream dreams.' (Acts 2:17)*

Not all dreams are from God, but God can speak to you through dreams. If a dream is from God, you will usually remember it clearly when you wake up and the Holy Spirit can give you the interpretation of the dream if you ask Him.

• *Visions*

> *And a vision appeared to Paul in the night. A man of Macedonia stood and pleaded with him, saying, "Come over to Macedonia and help us." Now after he had seen the vision, immediately we sought to go to Macedonia,*

concluding that the Lord had called us to preach the gospel to them. (Acts 16:9-10)

There are two types of visions. The first is the vision of the mind, in which the Lord projects images and pictures onto the "screen" of our mind. This can be called a "sanctified imagination" or an imagination that is under the influence of the Holy Spirit. The second type of vision is an open vision. This is an image that you see with your natural eyes.

• *Trance*

This can be compared to visions, except that if you are in a trance, you are entirely unaware of your surroundings. You are "out of your mind." You are taken out of your own mind and into God's mind.

In Acts 10:9-11, Peter falls into a trance.

The next day, as they went on their journey and drew near the city, Peter went up on the housetop to pray, about the sixth hour. Then he became very hungry and wanted to eat; but while they made ready, he fell into a trance and saw heaven opened and an object like a great sheet bound at the four corners, descending to him and let down to the earth.

• *Angelic Visitation*

Angels are another voice from the heavenly realm. Throughout the New Testament, angels visited and spoke to people concerning what they should do.

Now an angel of the Lord spoke to Philip, saying, "Arise and go toward the south along the road which goes down from Jerusalem to Gaza." (Acts 8:26)

For there stood by me this night and angel of the God to whom I belong and whom I serve, saying, 'Do not be afraid, Paul; you must be brought before Caesar; and indeed God has granted you all those who sail with you.' (Acts 27:23-24)

• *Peace or Lack of Peace*

And let the peace (soul harmony which comes) from Christ rule (act as umpire continually) in your hearts [deciding and settling with finality all questions that arise in your minds, (Colossians 3:15a AMPC)

The Holy Spirit can lead you by giving you peace in your heart and mind if you are making the right decision in a situation, and lack of peace if you are about to make the wrong choice.

How the Holy Spirit Does Not Lead

Let us now look at how the Holy Spirit does <u>not</u> lead in the New Covenant:

• *Fleeces*

In Judges 6:36-40, Gideon put out a woolen "fleece" to determine what God was saying to him. This means that he asked God for a physical sign. (Read the story in your own Bible.) In the New Covenant, you have the Holy Spirit living in you, and so you are led from the inside, not from outside "fleeces."

> *For as many as are led by the Spirit of God, these are sons of God. (Romans 8:14)*

> *For we walk by faith, not by sight. (2 Corinthians 5:7)*

This means that you should not tell the Lord that if this is His will, then this and that must happen. By doing this, you might be led in the wrong direction since this is not the Lord's way of leading us in the New Covenant.

• *Open Doors*

Just because a door is open, does not mean that we are supposed to walk through it. We should always pray about it. There are so many opportunities and open doors in our workplace, church and in our free time. If we think that all open doors are from the Holy Spirit, we will get very busy and we will be doing a lot of things God never intended for us to do! We will get out of focus. So, pray about every open door and opportunity to find out whether it is from the Lord or not.

We see that Paul had open doors for the Gospel, but the Holy Spirit stopped Him:

> *Now when they had gone through Phrygia and the region of Galatia, they were forbidden by the Holy Spirit to preach the word in Asia. After they had come to Mysia, they tried to go into Bithynia, but the Spirit did not permit them. (Acts 16:6-7)*

However, an open door <u>can be</u> from the Lord, of course. We see in Revelation 3:8:

> *"I know your works. See, I have set before you an open door, and no one can shut it; for you have a little strength, have kept My word, and have not denied My name."*

This is why we have to pray and ask the Holy Spirit to guide us.

• *Circumstances*

God can direct our circumstances; however, we should not automatically take circumstances as a sign of leading from the Holy Spirit. For instance, we might face many challenges in our situation, but this does not necessarily mean that we are in the wrong place. The devil will always try his best to stop us from what we are doing for God. We need to stay in faith and trust the Lord to bring us through the challenges.

Sometimes, as Christians, we have to face challenges just for our testimony of Christ. Let us see how Paul experienced this:

> *And see, now I go bound in the spirit to Jerusalem, not knowing the things that will happen to me there, except that the Holy Spirit testifies in every city, saying that chains and tribulations await me. But none of these things move me: nor do I count my life dear to myself, so that I may finish my race with joy, and the ministry which I received from the Lord Jesus, to testify to the gospel of the grace of God. (Acts 20:22-24)*

Many people were advising Paul not to go to Jerusalem based on the circumstances (danger, fear and persecution), but Paul was "bound in the spirit." He knew he was supposed to go. It was following this leading that later opened up the door for him to take the Gospel message to the Romans.

When the Lord leads us into difficult circumstances, we must trust Him.

> *Trust in the Lord with all your heart, And lean not on your own understanding; (Proverbs 3:5)*

• *Personal Prophecy*

We love the gifts of the Spirit to work in the church, and God can speak to us through prophecy. It is a beautiful way to receive God´s intimate and specific words for our situation. However, there have been times when prophecy has been misused and not correctly judged, creating a lot of chaos and confusion for people. We need knowledge about the prophetic in order to both give and receive prophesy in the right way.

Romans 8:14 does not say, "For as many as are led by prophets, they are the sons of God," but *"For as many are led by the Spirit of God, these are sons of God."*

> *Let two or three prophets speak, and let the others judge. (1 Corinthians 14:29)*

Prophecy should be judged by the following[25]:

1. *THE WORD OF GOD* - Is the prophetic word in alignment with the Word of God? If it contradicts Scripture, throw it out.
2. *THE INNER WITNESS* - Does it confirm something you already have in your heart? If yes, take it as a confirmation and thank God! If the prophecy does not bear witness with the inner witness, "put it on the shelf," meaning, set it aside for now.

Do not receive prophetic words of judgment over you either. Judgment has no place in New Covenant prophecy.[20]

> *But the one who prophesies speaks to people for their strengthening, encouraging and comfort. (1 Corinthians 14:3 NIV)*

Prophecy should never be used to judge people or to tell them what is wrong with them. Most people already know what is wrong with them.[31] Prophetic words should encourage others, reveal "gold and precious stones" in the midst of their "dirt and mess," call forth a future and hope in them and comfort them.[20] So, we see that the Holy Spirit can lead through prophecy if it is appropriately used and tested to determine if it is a genuine message from the Lord.

In closing, it is not hard to be led by the Holy Spirit. Now that you know how He leads, it will be easier for you to step out in confidence on His guidance. We read in John 10:27 that *"My sheep hear My voice."* You are His sheep, which means that you will recognize His voice. Let us be aware of the presence of the Holy Spirit in our lives. When we are born again, we know that we are online with the Holy Spirit. Our spirit is connected to the Holy Spirit. We can tune in to Him like we turn on a radio and tune in to the right channel. The Holy Spirit is there for us to lead us, help us and guide us every day. What a privilege!

Let Us Pray

Dear Heavenly Father, thank you so much for sending the Holy Spirit to us. Holy Spirit, we want to be led by You every day of our lives. We pray that we will get a greater awareness of who You are and how You want to guide us. Help us to understand what You are saying to us and what You want us to do. We want to live in the midst of Your will for our lives, and we want nothing more than to be led by You every step of the way. Help us to trust You and be obedient as we hear Your voice. Let it be our greatest joy to follow You! We know that You want our very best and that You have a great plan and purpose for our lives. Only by walking in the Spirit and being led by You, can we be in the midst of God's plan. AMEN.

FOR SELF REFLECTION AND GROUP DISCUSSION

1. How do we know that it is the Holy Spirit that is leading us or if it is just our own thoughts or good ideas?
2. How do you judge a personal prophecy given to you?
3. Share stories with each other about how you have been led by the Holy Spirit.

SHARE AND DISCUSS WITH THE GROUP

SESSION 31

Vision, Purpose and Preparation

How to Receive a Vision?

VISION IS ESSENTIAL TO HAVE DIRECTION IN LIFE. According to the Bible, vision is something supernaturally given to you by God. It is not something you come up with yourself. A vision from God is born out of the Word and in prayer and fellowship with Him. We want to align our dreams with God's will and dreams for us. We want to live in His plan for our lives and fulfill His purpose. Godly vision will direct us towards His plans and intentions for our lives.

In Philippians 2:13 (AMPC), we read, *"For it is God Who is all the while effectually at work in you [energizing and creating in you the power and desire], both to will and to work for His good pleasure and satisfaction and delight."*

If we have given our lives to Jesus and we seek Him with all our heart to know His ways for our lives, we can trust that the Holy Spirit will work in our hearts to give us direction. His desire becomes our desire.

There is power in writing down what you have in your heart and what you want to see happen. This is the first step of faith and will cause you to start moving towards it.

> *Write the vision*
> *And make it plain on tablets,*
> *That he may run who reads it.*
> *For the vision is yet for an appointed time;*
> *But at the end it will speak, and it will not lie.*

Though it tarries, wait for it;
Because it will surely come,
It will not tarry.
Behold the proud,
His soul is not upright in him;
But the just shall live by his faith. (Habakkuk 2:2-4)

Even though a vision can be supernaturally given by God, don´t be afraid of writing something down because you are uncertain that it is from God. Feel free to dream and put down whatever is in your heart. Our good Father wants to bless us, and He wants to give us the desires of our hearts. See what it says in Psalm 37:3-5:

Trust in the Lord, and do good; Dwell in the land, and feed on His faithfulness.

Delight yourself also in the Lord, And He shall give you the desires of your heart. Commit your way to the Lord, Trust also in Him, And He shall bring it to pass.

First, we give our lives to Him, and then we delight ourselves in Him and in what He has done for us. When He has us in this place of surrender, He will give us the desires of our hearts.

We might desire nice material things. God does not mind us having this, as long as we are not bound by materialism and greed. When material things do not own us—and we consider them minor things compared to knowing God—then He can give them to us.

Our good Father wants us to live our lives with purpose and direction. He has gifted us with a unique combination of gifts and talents, and He has a plan and a purpose for our lives. In Jeremiah 29:11 (NIV), He says, "*'For I know the plans I have for you,' declares the Lord, 'plans to prosper you and not to harm you, plans to give you hope and a future."*

Our purpose will in some way be connected to His big mission for His church and for the people of this planet: <u>to know Him and to make Him known.</u>

He wants us to get to know Him more and more and live our lives in such a way that whatever we do, we do for His glory. Whether you are a nurse or an investment banker, you can do your job to His glory. He also wants all the people of this Earth to hear about His great love and salvation.

In Jeremiah Chapter 1, God calls Jeremiah to become a prophet. It is, however, interesting to see how God challenges Jeremiah in verse 11 and 12:

> *Moreover the word of the Lord came to me, saying, "Jeremiah, what do you see?"*
>
> *And I said, "I see a branch of an almond tree."*
>
> *Then the Lord said to me, "You have seen well, for I am ready to perform My word." (Jeremiah 1:11-12)*

We can see that the Lord wanted Jeremiah to see the vision (the branch of an almond tree). And when he sees it, God says He is ready to perform His word. Take notice of what God says later in the chapter:

> *"Therefore prepare yourself and arise, And speak to them all that I command you." (Jeremiah 1:17)*

God wanted Jeremiah to prepare himself for what he was about to step into. God wanted Jeremiah to "arise"—to rise up and step out into what he had been called to do. I think this applies to us as well: PREPARE AND ARISE!

Have the confidence to step out into what God has already shown you and use your God-given gifts and talents. You don't always need specific guidance for every small step if God has already given you the direction. Listen to the Holy Spirit, but don't be afraid to act on the revelation you already have.

Two Practical Steps to Write Your Vision Down

1. *KEEP A JOURNAL* - Write down what you have in your heart and what you want "to see." Some things only God can do, and you need to wait and pray for His fulfillment of the vision. Other things you can turn into a plan with practical steps to make it happen within a timeframe and with milestones.

   In order to turn your vision into reality, there are decisions you need to make. You need the determination to see it come to pass. You also need to prepare, set goals with time frames and have steps of action—all of it led by the Holy Spirit and in God´s timing. This kind of planning can be done in faith. The solutions don´t have to come from you, but you rely on God´s answers. The important thing is that you are moving forward. Just don´t run ahead of God. His timing is always the best timing.

2. *MAKE A VISION BOARD* - Find images of the things you want to see come true in your life. Put these images on a big piece of cardboard or in a book (you may include letters cut out from magazines, newspapers, etc.) You can also draw and write on your vision board. Keep it in a place where you can see it every day.

   When you have written your vision down, you will start acting and moving towards the fulfillment of it without even knowing it.

My testimony

I can testify that there is great power in writing your vision down. One day in 2006, I was dreaming with God while I was on my computer and I started to type out my dreams. At that time, I was taking my Master´s degree with a major in finance, and I had no idea what was going to happen when I was finished. What I wrote down was this:

> When I am done with my Master´s degree, what if I could work full-time with our privately-owned investment company (work from home)? What if we could live and work abroad for a while? What if we could buy the farm, where I grew up, from my parents so that it can stay within our family? What if I could start an import business from Asia where I could use the barn at the farm as storage for the inventory?

For years, my husband and I also had a dream about having a summer cabin by the ocean in the area where my husband grew up and where our extended family lived. To own a place like that was so far above our financial ability at that time; it was a utopia (this was in 1999). However, I had faith, and I wrote my vision down, just in a different format. I made a "faith box" where I put all the blue things we had in our apartment—coffee mugs, candle holders, teapots, wall decors, etc. (We like to have a blue maritime theme for the decor of our summer cottages in Norway.) On this box I wrote "FOR THE CABIN," and then we put it in storage in the attic.

So, what happened? When I finished my Master´s degree in 2007, I started working full-time for our own company, which was my first vision statement. Then in 2008, my husband got a job offer in the Philippines, which we accepted, so our whole family moved to Manila, where we stayed for three years. After four years back in Norway, we moved back to Manila again and have now lived there for another four years—another vision statement "ticked off." In 2009, we were able to buy the farm from my parents, and in 2011, I started the import business and used the barn as storage for the inventory. The last two things on the list were "ticked off!"

The most amazing thing was that we were able to buy the cabin by the ocean. We had been saving as much money as we could to get equity. In 2010, we found our little dream place by the sea and were able to buy it (with help from the bank). It was a big day when I could unpack the "faith box" and put the blue things in our cabin. Eleven years of faith and waiting were not wasted!

FOR SELF REFLECTION AND GROUP DISCUSSION

1. Do you have a vision or a dream you want to see fulfilled? What steps have you taken to see it come to pass?
2. "Prepare yourself and arise." In what way can you prepare yourself and increase your capacity to fulfill your vision?
3. Share your vision with the group. You can also receive prayer from the others about your vision coming to pass.

   SHARE AND DISCUSS WITH THE GROUP

SESSION 32

Called to Be Light and Salt in the Workplace

GOD HAS NOT ONLY CALLED US TO Christian ministry or church but also to the workplace.

In Genesis 1:28 (NIV), God said to Adam and Eve, *"'Be fruitful and increase in number; fill the earth and subdue it. Rule over the fish in the sea and the birds in the sky and over every living creature that moves on the ground.'"*

We see the same principle in the Book of Psalms:

> *You made them rulers over the works of your hands; you put everything under their feet: all flocks and herds, and the animals of the wild, the birds in the sky, and the fish in the sea, all that swim the paths of the seas. Lord, our Lord, how majestic is your name in all the earth! (Psalm 8:6-9 NIV)*

As human beings, we have been given the responsibility to manage the Earth, take care of the planet and develop it for the benefit of human beings. We are to take part in forming society. As Christians, we need to rise up and ask God what our role is to play. We can't just leave "ruling the world" to unbelievers.

Serving God in the Workplace

In many Christian circles, the thinking has been that the only way to serve God and make Him happy is to be in full-time ministry in the church, or the only thing that is important to God is what we do in Christian ministry outside the workplace. Because of this kind of thinking, many Christians who are really passionate about serving God, neglect getting higher education because they do not perceive it as necessary. Many people have been led to believe that the only thing that matters is getting out on the streets to evangelize or having a Christian ministry. However, God needs us in all parts of society! He needs us to play an active role in shaping laws, in businesses, the cultural arena, politics, media, the entertainment industry, the education system, in hospitals and clinics... God really needs the best and brightest believers out there in the world where the people are, where culture and attitudes are shaped and where significant decisions for our society are made.

Many Christians throughout history have felt bad because they chose to become a lawyer, teacher, investment banker, actor and so on—as if they let God down by choosing a secular job instead of wanting to be in full-time ministry. This is a big misconception. God is the One who told human beings from the very beginning that we should work and take responsibility. He is the One who has gifted us in so many different ways. God wants us to take care of and develop society and the world according to His Kingdom principles.

God has placed His destiny inside of you. Start dreaming with God. Ask Him what He wants for you. He will probably ask back, "What do YOU want? What do YOU have in your heart to do? What do YOU see in society that needs to change? What is it that you do that makes you happy? In what areas do you find your natural 'workflow' and gifting?" He does not want to overrule you, but He wants you to partner with Him. As you submit your life to Him, your will and His will are being aligned as the Holy Spirit works in you.

> *For it is God who works in you to will and to act to fulfill his good purpose. (Philippians 2:13 NIV)*

This is by the grace of God, so you can do His will with pleasure.

When you get a direction in your heart, start praying about it. Ask God to show you what steps to take, be patient and do not run ahead of God. Wait for Him to show you and lead you to the right decisions and open the right doors at the right time. Mixing your dream with determination and patience is essential. There will be some waiting time before the dream comes to pass. Take it as a time of prayer and preparation. Gain knowledge and skills, do research, get prepared or perhaps even go back to college to get a certain education if that is required in the area you want to enter into.

Perhaps you do have a calling into ministry or the church, which is good since we need great people in the church and in ministry. However, it is only good for the ones who are actually called to be there. So, let's say God is calling you to the workplace—into business, politics, health care, into the education system, etc. How can you serve God in this place? After all, you will be doing a lot of work and tasks that do not seem spiritual at all.

1. *GOD CREATED US FOR WORK AND TO BE FRUITFUL AND PRODUCTIVE. WORK IS GOOD IN ITSELF.* Using your gifts and feeling that you contribute help make you content and happy. We are encouraged as we see fruitfulness coming out of our lives and as we see an increase in what God has given us to steward.
2. *WE ARE CALLED TO BE LIGHT AND SALT IN THE WORLD.* Light makes darkness flee. We don't ask darkness to leave; we just light a lamp. Salt is used for preservation. Many years ago, before people had fridges and freezers, they would cover their meat with salt to preserve it. Surrounded by salt, the meat stayed fresh. The same is true for the children of God in the workplace. We are there to stop the world from becoming rotten. We are there to influence the world, not be affected by it.

If the world is a dark and rotten place, could this be because the Christians who are light and salt have been absent? Is the world so dark because Christians have isolated themselves from the world because they think it is sinful and wicked? God loves the world and wants us to be <u>in</u> the world as light and salt. Going back to the example of salt being used for preservation: If the meat juice soaks into the salt, the salt becomes useless as a preserving agent. The same is true with us: We are <u>in</u> the world, but not <u>of</u> the world. We are to influence the world, not the other way around.

How Can We Make a Difference in the Workplace?

We bring something different to the workplace: a different culture, a different spirit, a different atmosphere. We bring love to our colleagues, and we encourage others and help them reach their goals instead of seeking our own selfish ambitions. We go the extra mile; we are positive and bring solutions inspired by God to our workplace.

God cares about our colleagues. He wants them to get to know Him; however, we cannot walk around as evangelists in the workplace, preaching about Jesus all the time. Instead, we need to build relationships and be there at the right time when a colleague needs to talk or is going through a life crisis. They will start asking why we are so different. There will be openings to talk about Jesus, but we need to know our role and timing. You are God's "secret agent" with a mission to bring love and life.

God is there to support you every step of the way. He will also help you to be the best teacher, lawyer, salesperson, banker, environmentalist, etc. possible. He wants you to flourish in your gifting and be a positive influence.

Finding Your Place

We are all created differently with different gifts, interests and talents. This is because all parts of society need to be taken care of and managed. The garbage being taken care of is just as important as the kids getting an education. Even the most straightforward job is important to God. Everybody is just as valuable and necessary. Whatever we do, we do it as to the Lord. When you use your gifts for the Lord and to serve other people, God can use you wherever you are. Imagine that you are a barista at a coffee shop. How can God use you there? Well, you can be an encouragement and give a smile to hundreds of people every day while serving coffee and chatting with them over the counter. You can provide all these customers with an excellent start to their day. You just need to be aware that you matter and know that you can be a light in your world.

Perhaps you have already found your place and are flourishing. Great! Trust God to enlarge your dreams and visions so that He can take you further than you would ever be able to go in your own strength and ability.

> *Never doubt God's mighty power to work in you and accomplish all this. He will achieve infinitely more than your greatest request, your most unbelievable dream, and exceed your wildest imagination! He will outdo them all, for his miraculous power constantly energizes you. (Ephesians 3:20 TPT)*

If you are in the "waiting room," keep praying so that you are ready to step out at the right time. Wait for God's guidance. However, don't be afraid to step out because you are afraid of doing something against God's will. We can get too passive because we are scared of failure. You are created in the image of God to dream, to step out, to take responsibility, to engage yourself, to use your gifts and to be light and salt in the world. You are unique and have incredible value to God. He has bought you at a high price. He wants to partner with you and be with you every step of the way. Don't be afraid of failure. Get back on your feet if you fall, learn and try again. Don't stay in discouragement. Shake it off and keep going. God is waiting for us to rise up and be the people He has created us to be and to enter into all that He has planned for us. He wants His light to shine so that all people can see it, not only the people in the church.

This teaching is meant to wake us up and challenge the idea that Christians only serve God in ministry and not at the workplace, which is a big misconception. We serve God and bring light, positive change and influence wherever we are. Some are called to ministry in the church; however, most people are called to be in the workplace.

You might be in a situation where you cannot go into the workplace. Your culture or personal situation might restrict you in that area. You might also have a disability, a sickness, etc. that hinders you. God knows all of this, and it is not the work that gives you value; it is who you are! God loves you no matter what. We are not to feel bad about ourselves because we cannot work, as it might not even be our choice, but wherever we are in life and whatever season we are in, we can ask God how we can serve Him, the people around us and the society. We can get involved in one way or another. Let God show you how. What you can bring to the table is essential! Raising children at home is one of these crucial tasks we are called to do. There are seasons for everything. However, the point of this teaching is to encourage those who feel drawn into the workplace. This is an important place to be. God cares about society, and as Christians, we are to influence the direction society is going. The ones in the workplace are just as important in the Kingdom of God as those working in the church or in Christian ministry. However, know why you are there and be the light and salt you are called to be.

FOR SELF REFLECTION AND GROUP DISCUSSION

1. What has been your thoughts on the calling of God until now? Did you think God only called people into ministry in the church? Were you surprised to hear in this teaching that God calls people into the workplace? Have you ever felt bad about working an ordinary job because you thought you had to be in full-time ministry to be a good Christian and a part of God's plan?

2. What problems do you see within the society in which you live that could be solved if Christians got involved and brought in wisdom and solutions from God? Is there any area in society where you could contribute and bring in the light of God?

   SHARE AND DISCUSS WITH THE GROUP

SESSION 33

God´s Principles for Prosperity and Personal Finance - Part 1

DOES THE BIBLE HAVE ANYTHING TO SAY about money? It sure does. In the next two sessions, we will look at God´s principles in the areas of prosperity and personal finance. In some churches, there has been unbalanced and, to some extent, extreme teachings on this topic. In one "ditch," we have some TV preachers promising people that God will make them super rich if only they give to their ministry. In the other "ditch," we find traditional churches who embrace a poverty mentality and think that keeping people in poverty is the best way to keep them humble and away from temptation and sin. They consider money in itself as evil (even though their own churches might be filled with gold and riches). Let me present to you a balanced picture of what the Bible says about this topic.

A God of Abundance

God shows us throughout the Bible that He wants us to be blessed and prosperous, which includes material blessings and prosperity. In Psalm 35:27, we read that *"[He] has pleasure in the prosperity of His servants."* God wants us to have more than enough so that our lives reflect who He is: A God of abundance. When we look at creation, we can clearly see the abundance of God. If God was a God of "just enough," He would have created only the fundamental and practical things needed on this planet. Instead, He chose to fill the Earth with beautiful nature, animals, birds and fish of all kinds, with the most beautiful colors, shapes and patterns. (I am a scuba diver, and I am always amazed when I go underwater. In deep waters, you see the most beautiful landscapes of corals and the most fantastic fish!) When it comes to nutrition, God could have chosen to give us some powder or roots to eat each day just to survive but, instead, He chose to provide us with taste buds, which allow us to taste a broad spectrum of flavors so that we can enjoy many kinds of foods. We could go on and on, pointing out God´s abundance in creation. So, why am I saying all of this? I want you to grasp how rich and generous God is.

In Philippians 4:19, we see that *"God shall supply all your need according to His riches in glory by Christ Jesus."* It is according to HIS RICHES that He will provide, not according to our situation. And He is a rich God! Hallelujah!

Blessed to Be a Blessing

When it comes to material things and money, why does God want us to have more than enough? Why not just enough? When you think about it, it is kind of selfish to wish for just enough for you and your family. You see, your blessing has a purpose: God wants you to be blessed so that you have enough for your family and you can be a blessing to others. You are blessed to be a blessing. When someone has a big need, you are able to help! You are able to help pay for a new sound system in the church; you are able to feed the poor; you are able to support missionaries; you are able to help in any situation. If God calls you to do something, you have the resources to do it! This is where God wants you to be in your finances. This principle was revealed when God made a promise to our father of faith, Abraham: *"I will make you a great nation; I will bless you, And make your name great; And you shall be a blessing"* (Genesis 12:2).

God wants you to have a generous spirit. Generosity is in the character of God. He gave us everything—even His only Son to come and die on a cross for our sins. As children of God, we have His DNA and we are generous too. Generosity is an attitude of the heart that will manifest in every area of your life. There are great promises given to the generous.

> *There is one who scatters, yet increases more; And there is one who withholds more than is right, But it leads to poverty. The generous soul will be made rich, And he who waters will also be watered himself. (Proverbs 11:24-25)*

Poverty is not the will of God. Throughout church history, poverty has been perceived as holy and wanted by God to keep us humble. This is a great misunderstanding. God does not want you to be poor!

In 2 Corinthians 8:9, we read, *"For you know the grace of our Lord Jesus Christ, that though He was rich, yet for your sakes He became poor, that you through His poverty might become rich."*

But isn´t money the root of all evil? No, this is not what the Bible says. See what it says in 1 Timothy 6:10: *"For the love of money is a root of all kinds of evil, for which some have strayed from the faith in their greediness, and pierced themselves through with many sorrows."*

Our focus should never be on money itself. This can create greed that leads to destruction. We should not focus on building an empire for ourselves and forget about others. We must understand that we are blessed to be a blessing. We should not put our trust in money either; we should always put our trust in God. Our money can be gone in an instant, but the Kingdom of God lasts forever.

> *Command those who are rich in this present world not to be arrogant nor to put their hope in wealth, which is so uncertain, but to put their hope in God, who richly provides us with everything for our enjoyment. Command them to do good, to be rich in good deeds, and to be generous and willing to share. In this way they will lay up treasure for themselves as a firm foundation for the coming age, so that they may take hold of the life that is truly life. (1 Timothy 6:17-19 NIV)*

We see in this passage that God richly provides everything for our enjoyment, but we should never become arrogant or put our hope in our wealth. We should always be ready to give and share with others.

Responsible Stewardship

Responsible stewardship is an important concept in the Bible.[32] God will test if you are a good steward of what He has already given you. He will put you in charge of little first to check if you are responsible and capable of stewarding what you have in a diligent manner. This includes your tithing and giving, paying your bills on time, keeping a budget, having your paperwork in order, not borrowing money from others without paying them back, paying your taxes, not bribing anyone, looking after your investments, planning for your future, maintaining your property, car and other things you own etc. (See some practical steps you can take to become a better steward at the end of this session.)

If you pass the test with what you have, God can give you more. The Bible even says that if you are diligent in the stewardship of money, God can entrust you with the true riches in His Kingdom.

> *Whoever can be trusted with very little can also be trusted with much, and whoever is dishonest with very little will also be dishonest with much. So if you have not been trustworthy in handling worldly wealth, who will trust you with true riches? And if you have not been honest with someone else´s property, who will give you ownership of your own? (Luke 16:10-12 NIV)*

Prosperity in All Areas of Life

God is concerned about your heart and your relationship with Him. He wants you to enjoy a good life in the midst of His will. He does not want you to live stressed out, only focusing on your business or career and neglecting your family, your church and your health. There needs to be balance in your life.

In 3 John 2:2, we read, *"Beloved, I pray that you may prosper in all things and be in health, just as your soul prospers."* God wants us to prosper in ALL areas of our lives, not only in the area of finances.

In Proverbs 10:22, we read, *"The blessing of the Lord makes one rich, And He adds no sorrow with it."* Let me repeat: He adds no sorrow to it! This means that when we do it God´s way, we can prosper in all areas of our lives without sacrificing our family, church life and health on the altar. It is the blessing of the Lord that makes us rich.

Seeking His Kingdom First

God wants us to seek His Kingdom first, and when we do so, He has promised to give us all the other things we need, like food, clothes and a place to live. He knows that we need these things.

> *"And do not seek what you should eat or what you should drink, nor have an anxious mind. For all these things the nations of the world seek after, and your Father knows that you need these things. But seek the kingdom of God, and all these things shall be added to you." (Luke 12:29-31)*

What does it mean to seek God´s Kingdom first? It has a lot to do with our priorities. Where is our focus, our hearts, our motivation? *"For where your treasure is, there your heart will be also"* (Luke 12:34). Is it in your heart to serve the Lord and live for Him? Or is it to serve yourself and gain as much wealth as possible for your own benefit? The Bible says you cannot serve two masters. You cannot serve both God and mammon (money). This does not mean it is wrong to gain wealth. We have already learned how God wants us to be blessed so that we can be a blessing, but money cannot be your ruler; you must be ruler over it.

To seek the Kingdom first also means that we seek God first in prayer and trust in His promises for our provision. But what is the next step after praying? Should we just sit and wait for God to do something? Some Christians use the phrase "God will provide" as an excuse for not working. This is not how it should be. We are created to be productive and do our part for our provision—of course with the blessing and favor of the Lord in our work. In special situations, the Lord will absolutely provide for us supernaturally.

An excellent example of this is how God provided for the people of Israel when they wandered around in the wilderness for forty years. Every day, the Lord gave them manna to eat from Heaven, but they only had enough for one day. This was not God´s perfect plan for them. His perfect will for them was to be in the promised land where He had a better way of providing for them—through them being good stewards of the land, working and being productive.

Provision in the Promised Land

When they entered into the promised land, the manna stopped. They were then supposed to eat from the produce of the land. They had to work, and not only work but work smart. They had to learn how to be farmers and how to grow things. They had to sow and reap. This was a place where they could prosper and build up reserves for their future. There, they did not only have enough for the day, but they could store up to have more than enough to help others too. This is where they could live in the abundance God wanted for them.

> *Trust in the Lord, and do good; Dwell in the land, and feed on His faithfulness. (Psalm 37:3)*
>
> *I have come that they may have life, and that they may have it more abundantly. (John 10:10b)*

Pray that the Lord will show you what your promised land is. Don´t stay in the "wilderness" if there is a "promised land" where there is provision for you. Wherever you are right now, you can trust that the Lord is your Provider, but it is also important for you to do your part. He might give you a job opportunity or a business idea that might be the promised land for you, but you need to step into it. You need to learn new skills, read, study, be diligent, increase your capacity... As a child of God, we do all of these things by His grace and with His empowerment. We see in the next verse that God is the One who gives you the power to get wealth. The power He is presenting here is the ability and capability.[33]

> *"And you shall remember the Lord your God, for it is He who gives you power to get wealth," (Deuteronomy 8:18)*

For those who are called to be pastors and in full-time ministry, God might choose other ways to provide for you. Pastors should be paid a salary through their church, but in church plantings and in small churches, there might not be room for this financially. In periods like these, pastors might have to take work outside of the church. This might also be the case for full-time ministers. Even the Apostle Paul worked as a tentmaker, while he was in full-time ministry, to provide for himself. However, another way is to receive monthly financial support from other churches, friends and family who want to partner with you in your ministry. The Holy Spirit will also tell people to give to you. The Lord is your Provider. Pray and ask Him what to do.

God has also given us some fundamental keys to help us prosper financially. We use these keys by faith. We will look into them in the next session.

FOR SELF REFLECTION AND GROUP DISCUSSION

1. Until now, have you seen God as a God of abundance or are you stuck in a poverty mentality, always afraid that you will not have enough?
2. How does your mentality towards money affect your generosity? Do you find it easy or hard to give and share with others?
3. In the situation you are in now financially, what is good stewardship? What are the areas that need improvement in your financial stewardship? (Get ideas from the list of "10 Simple Steps to Better Financial Stewardship" on the next page.)

4. Is there a "promised land" you have not stepped into yet? For example, skills you could use to create income, a business idea you have not tested out, a different location to live where the job market and salaries are better or natural talents/God-given gifts that you could develop further through training and education, which could provide you with a new income.

   SHARE AND DISCUSS WITH THE GROUP

10 Simple Steps to Better Financial Stewardship

1. Money Management in the Family

Usually, it works best if one person is in charge of money management. If you are married, let the person who is most organized and most capable with the money be the one responsible for money management. Traditionally, it is the husband who has been in charge of this even though they are not always the most capable. Husbands: Let your wife do it if she is better at it! However, as a married couple, you should both agree on how to steward your money—how much to spend, how much to save and give away. Both husband and wife should be fully informed about the financial situation of the family even though only one might be the breadwinner. Communication is the key.

2. Pay Your Bills on Time!

Let this be a character witness before the Lord. Also, pay back the money you have borrowed from others as you have promised.

3. Pay Off Your Credit Card Every Month!

If you use a credit card, pay it off in full every month. The interest rates are extremely high if you let credit card debt grow! If you don´t have the discipline to do this, cut up your credit card! Stay far away from consumer loans! Similar to credit cards, the interest rates are very high.

4. Keep Your Paperwork in Order

Keep a binder where you put all your budgets, invoices, receipts, bank statements, tax papers, insurance papers and other important papers related to your finances. Keep it all in one place and mark the binder with what year it is—e.g., "Personal finances 2019." Sometimes you need to find papers from years ago, and with this system, you can quickly find what you are looking for. Also, keep folders for your personal finances on your computer so you can easily find what you are looking for.

As you keep your paperwork in order, you will always know where to find your papers and documents, which will save you time, reduce your stress level and help you to be a good steward.

5. Make a Budget and Follow It

Make a budget and follow it! You might also want to make a simple "financial statement" at the end of the month to keep track of everything you spent.

6. Have Several Bank Accounts for Different Purposes

Have several bank accounts. Have one for daily use to pay for food, fuel, gifts and daily expenses. Then keep a separate bank account where you save money for payment of bills. Keep a third account, a savings account, where you always keep a buffer for unexpected expenses (your car or washing machine breaks down, you get a big medical bill, etc.). This account will also be for savings for your future and for the things you want to buy.

7. Monthly Money Management

Every month when you get your salaries, manage the money. Pay your tithes, pay your mortgage or rent, set aside money for the bills you know will come on the bills account (see next point), put the money you will need in the daily use accounts of the husband and wife and set aside money for savings and investments. Let the money have "an address and a name."

8. How to Get a Steady Monthly Cash Flow?

How do you get a steadier flow of money throughout the months of the year? Make a liquidity budget where you take expected bills that come twice a year or quarterly and divide the costs between each month of the year.

For instance, if your insurance bill comes twice a year and amounts to 1200 USD each time, the monthly cost is 1200/6 = 200 USD per month. Do this with all of your regular expenses and add them up per month. By doing this, you will find your total monthly expenses.

When you get your salary every month, put the amount of your monthly expenses in your bills account. When the bills come, you always have enough money to pay for your bills in the bills account! You can stay in peace, knowing that when several big bills come at the same time, you will still have money for food. If you live in a country where internet banking is not yet standard and you have a cash economy, you can do the same planning. Just set the cash aside and keep it in a safe place.

9. Live within Your Means

Don´t live in a house/apartment you cannot afford. If your rent or mortgage is so high that every month you are short of money, you are living far above your means. This hinders you from enjoying life because you are always stressed out due to a lack of funds. Wouldn´t it be better to buy/rent a smaller and cheaper place to live in and have enough money to enjoy life?

10. Buy Durable, High-Quality Goods on Sale

When investing in furniture, clothes, electronic devices and other durable goods, buy the best quality you can afford. Don´t buy the cheapest thing possible, which will probably break and have to be replaced within no time. Buy things out of season when they are on sale. Keep money in your savings account so that you are prepared to take advantage of the best offers. (However, don´t buy things that you don´t need just because they are on sale.)

SESSION 34

God´s Principles for Prosperity and Personal Finance - Part 2

WE HAVE LEARNED THAT our God is a God of abundance. He wants us to have more than enough so that we can have our own needs met and be a blessing to others.

> *And God will generously provide all you need. Then you will always have everything you need and plenty left over to share with others. (2 Corinthians 9:8 NLT)*

In this session, we will look at some essential keys and principles God has given us to prosper financially in His Kingdom. We use these keys by faith.

The First Key Is the Tithe

The first key is the tithe, which is giving one-tenth of your income to God. Is this something we must do? We don´t have to do anything in the Kingdom of God. That is not how it works. We don´t have to—we get to![34] When we give the first ten percent of our income to God, He will abundantly bless the ninety percent that is left and cause it to last longer than the original hundred percent would have lasted. It is like insurance for your income.[32] It is a way of telling God that you trust Him fully in this area of your life!

> *"Bring all the tithes into the storehouse, That there may be food in My house, And try Me now in this," Says the Lord of hosts, "If I will not open for*

> *you the windows of heaven And pour out for you such blessing. That there will not be room enough to receive it. And I will rebuke the devourer for your sakes, So that he will not destroy the fruit of your ground, Nor shall the vine fail to bear fruit for you in the field," Says the Lord of hosts; "And all nations will call you blessed, For you will be a delightful land," Says the Lord of hosts. (Malachi 3:10-12)*

God´s promises are great for those who give the tithe. The tithe is also God´s plan to finance the local church. When we say we give the tithe to God, we do this by giving to the local church (see Heb. 7:8).

Then you might ask the question: "Since this verse is from the Old Testament and is written under the Law, is the tithe still valid in the New Covenant?" The answer is yes. I really believe the tithe is still an important key for us as New Covenant believers. The tithe was there from the beginning with our father of faith, Abraham. Abraham lived long before the Law of Moses was given. We see in Genesis 14:18-20 that Abraham gave a tithe of everything to Melchizedek. Let us read:

> *Then Melchizedek king of Salem brought out bread and wine; he was the priest of God Most High. And he blessed him and said: "Blessed be Abram of God Most High, Possessor of heaven and earth; And blessed be God Most High, Who has delivered your enemies into your hand." And he gave him a tithe of all.*

We see in Hebrews 7:17 that Melchizedek is a foreshadow of Jesus Christ: "*For He testifies: 'You are a priest forever According to the order of Melchizedek.'*"

Jesus is our perfect High Priest, and He is a priest according to the order of Melchizedek *"who has come, not according to the law of a fleshly commandment, but according to the power of an endless life"* (Hebrews 7:16). When Abraham gave His tithe to Melchizedek, He was giving it to Christ. He did not do it because He <u>had to</u>, but because He <u>wanted to</u>. Abraham lived in a covenant with God, in which God had promised to bless him and make him a blessing. God prospered Abraham until he became a very wealthy man.

This promise was passed on to Abraham´s descendants. In Genesis 28:22, we see Abraham's grandson Jacob making a promise to God. Jacob said, "*And of all that you give me, I will surely give a tenth to you.*" Abraham and his descendants gave the tithe in faith, not by law. Abraham was made righteous by His faith in

God. We are children of Abraham in the sense that we are also made righteous by faith. Like Abraham, we also give our tithe in faith to God. We know that God has already blessed us, and we give back to Him in faith and gratefulness.

Jesus confirms that it is still right to give the tithe when He talks to the Pharisees.

> *"What sorrow awaits you Pharisees! For you are careful to tithe even the tiniest income from your herb gardens, but you ignore justice and the love of God. You should tithe, yes, but do not neglect the more important things." (Luke 11:42 NLT)*

Offerings – "Sowing and Reaping"

A second key in the area of personal finance in the Kingdom of God is "sowing and reaping." This principle was established from the very beginning of human history, just after the great flood.

> *"While the earth remains,*
> *Seedtime and harvest,*
> *Cold and heat,*
> *Winter and summer,*
> *And day and night,*
> *Shall not cease." (Genesis 8:22)*

We read in Luke 6:38: *"Give, and it will be given to you: good measure, pressed down, shaken together, and running over will be put into your bosom. For with the same measure that you use, it will be measured back to you."*

This comes back to the principle of generosity, but there is more to it than that. We need to understand the principle of the seed. A seed is small, but when sown into the right ground, it will bring forth a harvest after its own kind. Take, for example, an apple seed that grows up into an apple tree and produces a lot of apples. In every apple, there are many more seeds that can be planted. Besides that, the apple is food to eat. It takes some time before the seed becomes an apple tree that brings forth fruit, but if the seed has been planted, we know that the harvest is coming.

Giving an offering (sowing into the Kingdom of God) is in addition to the tithe.[32] To know where to sow, we need to follow the guidance of the Holy Spirit. We also need to know what part of our finances is seed to plant and what is for food to eat.

> *But this I say: He who sows sparingly will also reap sparingly, and he who sows bountifully will also reap bountifully. So let each one give as he purposes in his heart, not grudgingly or of necessity; for God loves a cheerful giver. And God is able to make all grace abound toward you, that you, always having all sufficiency in all things, may have an abundance for every good work. As it is written: "He has dispersed abroad, He has given to the poor; His righteousness endures forever." Now may He who supplies seed to the sower, and bread for food, supply and multiply the seed you have sown and increase the fruits of your righteousness, (2 Corinthians 9:6-10)*

First, we see that the harvest depends on how much seed you sow. This makes sense to all of us. In the next verse, we see that God wants us to give out of a joyful heart. We are not to be pressured or manipulated to give. We pray about it and give as the Holy Spirit leads.

Many times, I have experienced being led by the Holy Spirit to give specific amounts of money to certain people at particular times, and it happened to be just the amount they needed and what they had been praying for. It can be small amounts or significant amounts. The important thing is that we are obedient to the Holy Spirit. When He asks you to sow, it is because He has a harvest for you on the other end, and what a joy to be an answer to somebody´s prayers!

It also says in verse 7 that we are to give as we purpose in our hearts. You make a commitment to give regularly to a specific ministry, missionary, orphanage or something similar that you have in your heart. Personally, we are supporting missionaries monthly who bring the Gospel all over the world. By doing this, we enter into a God-given partnership and become partakers in the harvest of souls, together with the missionaries. There will surely be a harvest from the seed you sow into the most significant purpose on this planet, which is bringing the Gospel to all people, groups and nations (fulfilling the Great Commission of Matthew 28:18-20).

I love the promises in verse 8: *"And God is able to make all grace abound toward you, that you, always having all sufficiency in all things, may have an abundance for every good work."*

We sow into the Kingdom of God in faith. We believe in His promise that He is able to make sure we always have everything we need in all things, and on top of that, we have an abundance for every good work!

Ok, so now we understand that we need to sow, but how do we get seed? The answer is—by the grace of God! We see in verse 10 that *"now may He who supplies seed to the sower and bread for food, supply and multiply the seed you have sown and increase the fruits of your righteousness."*

The Lord supplies seed to sow. Our job is to plant the seed and eat the bread, not eat the seed. Neither shall we sow the bread He has given us for food. This is provided to you by the Lord for consumption for you and your family. The Holy Spirit is there to guide you so that you know what is seed and what is bread.

Sow into the Worldly Economy – Invest

It is not wise to consume everything you have left after you have sown. It is wise to keep some of it as savings, so you have reserves for the future. Secondly, it is smart to plant seeds into the world economy as well, which means to invest.[32] Before you make investments, you need to study and get the necessary knowledge and skills. When you make wise investments, you give the Lord something to bless.

In Matthew 25:14-30, we have the parable of the talents, where the Lord gives a certain amount of talents (money) to several servants for them to steward and increase. To the servants who increase His money, the Lord says, *"Well done you good and faithful servant."* However, the Lord is not happy with the one who hid his money in the ground, because he was either lazy or afraid of taking any risks. We see that the Lord wants us to dare to take risks and invest (however, we must do so wisely). He is not pleased if we just play it safe all the time.

Build Reserves for the Future – Don`t Borrow from Your Future

The Bible speaks about building a heritage. In Proverbs 13:22, we read that *"A good man leaves an inheritance to his children´s children."*

Scripture warns us of borrowing money. Proverbs 22:7 says, *"The rich rules over the poor, And the borrower is servant to the lender."* In Deuteronomy 28:12, where we see all of the blessings of the Lord, it says, *"You shall lend to many nations, but you shall not borrow."* We see a similar verse in Deuteronomy 15:6: *"For the Lord your God will bless you just as He promised you; you shall lend to many nations, but you shall not borrow; you shall reign over many nations, but they shall not reign over you."*

The Bible indicates that we should grow our values, not live on tomorrow´s earnings. Concerning loans, it is wise only to borrow money to buy a house or something that increases in value. It is not wise to borrow for consumption using credit cards, where the debt is growing month by month. This takes away your freedom and inner peace, and you are not building for the future but, rather, "stealing" from your future.

The Scriptures give promises that we are the ones who can lend to others. There is especially one verse that has a great promise: *"He who has pity on the poor lends to the Lord, And He will pay back what he has given"* (Proverbs 19:17). Lending to the Lord sounds like a terrific deal.

Let us sum this up. In these two sessions, we talked about entering the "promised land," where we will get provision from the place we are in. We talked about the tithe, which belongs to God and is like insurance for the other ninety percent. The ninety percent is for us to steward well and wisely. We put some aside for offerings, which is sowing into the Kingdom. We also keep some for savings and some for sowing into the worldly economy through investments. Then we talked about building wealth for the future, not living in advance by borrowing money unwisely. The Lord also wants us to care about the poor. When we give to the poor, we lend to Him and He will repay us. All of this is by the grace of God. We give because He gave first. We bless because He blessed us first. We love because He loved us first. He will enable us to be good stewards of our money. We do not give just because we want a harvest. We give because we love God and want to be part of what He is doing to expand His Kingdom on this planet.

Know that the Lord is your Provider and that He wants to take you into your "promised land." However, when you get there, you need to be prepared with the skills that you need to be a good steward and also be aware that conquering the promised land involves opposition and battles. The people of Israel had to fight a lot of battles after they entered the land, which could have made them think they had made a mistake—this could not be the promised land with so much opposition. But it was. However, God fought the battles with them, and they won. As long as their hearts were with God, He gave them victory in every situation and circumstance.

He will never leave you nor forsake you! Your future is in His hands! Trust in Him! He will guide you and lead you into your "promised land!" If you want to know what that can look like in your life, you can read Deuteronomy 28:1-14 yourself. All His promises are yes and amen in Christ Jesus!

FOR SELF REFLECTION AND GROUP DISCUSSION

1. What is the difference between the tithe and sowing seeds/giving a financial offering?
2. Are these concepts of the tithe and seed/offering new to you or is it something you are practicing already?
3. Do you have a testimony to share related to the tithe or sowing a financial seed and receiving a harvest?
4. Share testimonies with the group of how you have received provision as an answer to prayer. Also, share how you have been an answer to prayer to others in the area of financial provision.

SHARE AND DISCUSS WITH THE GROUP

SESSION 35

Receive Your Breakthrough

AT TIMES, WE FEEL STUCK in a situation in life. We might have unfulfilled promises from God, sickness or other things hindering us from moving forward. We are in desperate need of a breakthrough. In this session, we will study how to step into our breakthrough and victory.

In the New Covenant, we receive God´s promises by grace through faith. All God´s promises are yes and amen in Christ Jesus (see 2 Cor. 1:20). However, there are still some principles in the Kingdom of God we need to follow.

What Are You Declaring?

The first principle relates to what you are declaring over your life. Your confession is important, and it needs to be aligned with God´s promises. With your heart, you believe, and with your mouth, you confess. Get a word from God to "stand on" and proclaim.

> *So shall My word be that goes forth from My mouth; It shall not return to Me void, But it shall accomplish what I please, And it shall prosper in the thing for which I sent it. (Isaiah 55:11)*

We step into the promises by confessing and declaring His Word and what we are believing for. We claim God´s promises for us.

> *Death and life are in the power of the tongue, And those who love it will eat its fruit. (Proverbs 18:21)*

Be careful what you are saying. Speak the Word of God and blessing over yourself, your situations and the people around you. Do not complain and speak defeat over yourself (or others). Watch your tongue! Your words have power and authority. God created Heaven and Earth by speaking the Word. In Mark 11:23, Jesus talks about the power our words can have:

> *For assuredly, I say to you, whoever says to this mountain, 'Be removed and be cast into the sea,' and does not doubt in his heart, but believes that those things he says will be done, he will have whatever he says. (Mark 11:23)*

Make sure you don´t "cancel" the answer to your prayers by speaking the opposite of what you pray for.

In addition to declaring God´s promises, you need to align your lifestyle and actions to the Word and apply the principles and wisdom of God in your area in need of a breakthrough. You cooperate with God. He does His part, and by His grace, you will be led, motivated and empowered to do your part.

Don´t Give Up Until You Overcome the Resistance!

We don´t give up but press through the challenges and overcome the resistance. We must be determined! An excellent example from the Bible of someone with great determination is the woman with an issue of blood:

> *So Jesus went with him, and a great multitude followed Him and thronged Him. Now a certain woman had a flow of blood for twelve years and had suffered many things from many physicians. She had spent all that she had and was no better, but instead grew worse. When she heard about Jesus, she came behind Him in the crowd and touched His garment. For she said, "If only I may touch His clothes, I shall be made well."*
>
> *Immediately the fountain of her blood was dried up, and she felt in her body that she was healed of the affliction. And Jesus, immediately knowing in Himself that power had gone out of Him, turned around in the crowd and said, "Who touched My clothes?" But His disciples said to Him, "You see the multitude thronging You, and You say, 'Who touched Me?'" And He looked around to see her who had done this thing. But the woman, fearing and trembling, knowing what had happened to her, came and fell down before Him and told Him the whole truth. And He said to her, "Daughter, your faith has made you well. Go in peace, and be healed of your affliction." (Mark 5:24-34)*

This woman had faith for her miracle and expected it to happen. She just went forward through the crowd and took her miracle from Jesus. He did not even know who had touched Him; He just felt the power go out of Him. The woman knew Jesus had the power to heal, and so she just received it by faith.

Another example of great faith and not giving up in spite of challenges is found in Luke 5:18-20, 24b-26:

> *Then behold, men brought on a bed a man who was paralyzed, whom they sought to bring in and lay before Him. And when they could not find how they might bring him in, because of the crowd, they went up on the house-top and let him down with his bed through the tiling into the midst before Jesus. When He saw their faith, He said to him, "Man, your sins are forgiven you." ... "I say to you, arise, take up your bed, and go to your house." Immediately he rose up before them, took up what he had been lying on, and departed to his own house, glorifying God. And they were all amazed, and they glorified God and were filled with fear, saying, "We have seen strange things today!"*

The Bible does not even say that the man on the stretcher had faith, but his friends certainly did!

Faith and Expectation

Faith and expectation are essential ingredients needed to receive a miracle. Expectation is the breeding ground for the miraculous (ref. the woman with the issue of blood we just read about). Let´s take a look at what the Bible says about faith:

> *Now faith is the substance of things hoped for, the evidence of things not seen. (Hebrews 11:1)*

"Substance" means "realization or confidence."[35] Faith is the realization and confidence of things hoped for! "Faith" (*pistis* in Greek) means "the divinely implanted principle of inward confidence, assurance, trust, and reliance in God and all that He says."[36]

In Scripture when people approached Jesus with faith and expectation, they received their miracle. Let's look at an example where a whole crowd came to Jesus with expectation:

> *And He came down with them and stood on a level place with a crowd of His disciples and a great multitude of people from all Judea and Jerusalem, and from the seacoast of Tyre and Sidon, who <u>came to hear Him and be healed of their diseases</u>, as well as those who were tormented with unclean spirits. And they were healed. And the whole multitude sought to touch Him, for <u>power went out from Him and healed them all.</u> (Luke 6:17-20)*

In Matthew Chapter 8 and 9, we can also read many examples of people who came to Jesus with faith and expectation, and they all got what they came for! You can study this in your own Bible.

Do you remember the other crowd we read about earlier: the crowd that the woman with the issue of blood had to press through to get to Jesus? The power of Jesus was present to heal, but we only hear the record of this one woman receiving her miracle. Is it possible that the crowd the woman pressed through was just there to watch and see what was happening, not to hear and receive from Jesus? It seems that they did not come with faith and expectation to receive. From this, we can see that it is not enough to just be in the presence of Jesus; we need to expect to receive from Him and receive by faith.

How Do We Get This Faith?

> *So then faith comes by hearing and hearing by the word of God. (Romans 10:17)*

To grow your faith, keep listening to teaching and preaching, study Scriptures that reveal God's promises and the truth about your area in need of breakthrough and believe His Word for you. Trust that God is able and willing to attend to your need. He loves you so much, and He hears your prayers. Don´t focus on your circumstances but keep your eyes on Jesus who is "*the author and finisher of our faith*" (Hebrews 12:2). Our expectation is in Him alone.

> *My soul, wait silently for God alone, For my expectation is from Him. (Psalm 62:5)*

The more we hear about who Jesus is—about His goodness and faithfulness; Him healing all—the more faith grows. Great faith comes from seeing a great Jesus.

The woman with the issue of blood first believed something she had heard about Jesus before she could come with expectation to receive from Him. When there is no hearing about Jesus, there will be no expectation. If you are hearing the wrong thing, you will get false expectation. Hearing the truth about Him will create great expectation!

Faith is also strengthened through PRAISE AND WORSHIP. When you lift up the name of Jesus and proclaim who He is and what He has done, your faith will grow. See what happened to Abraham:

> *No unbelief or distrust made him waver (doubtingly question) concerning the promise of God, but he grew strong and was empowered by faith as he gave praise and glory to God, Fully satisfied and assured that God was able and mighty to keep His word and to do what He had promised. (Romans 4:20-21 AMPC)*

Pray and Obey

Pray and obey—take the steps you hear the Holy Spirit telling you to take. Every step leads to the next step that leads you on the path to your victory.

Position yourself and pray if there are any changes you need to make to be in the right place for your breakthrough. Maybe you need to change something in your life to see the breakthrough you need; it could be a geographical location or what church/denomination you are a part of (make sure you are in a place where you are fed, where your faith grows and where your gifts can flourish). Who do you allow to speak into your life? What friends do you hang out with? What are you listening to? What about your daily habits and lifestyle? Maybe you need to clean your house of idols that open the door for the enemy etc. There might also be some preparation you need to do for you to rise up into your destiny and breakthrough. Ask the Holy Spirit to show you if any of these are relevant to you.

Finally, let the anointing break the yoke and receive prayer from your brothers and sisters with the laying on of hands. Let the Holy Spirit do His job in you. There may also be a need to release forgiveness to other people and receive counsel from Godly counselors.

Pray with the group

Please focus on one person at a time in the group. Let the person tell the others in what area he/she needs a breakthrough. Then let the other members of the group lay hands on the person to pray and proclaim the promises of God over him/her. This is not the time for long explanations of situations, but for flowing in the breakthrough anointing and letting the Holy Spirit work. He knows everything.

FOR SELF REFLECTION AND GROUP DISCUSSION

1. In what areas of your life do you need a breakthrough? What are the promises of God concerning this particular area or situation in your life?
2. Pray and ask God what steps you need to take to receive your breakthrough.

   SHARE AND DISCUSS WITH THE GROUP

SESSION 36

What about Me, God?

THERE ARE MANY THINGS WE NEED TO BALANCE in our lives. We have so many demands on us from our family, our job, friends, school and the social arena. We can get exhausted. As Christians, we are called to lay down our lives to follow Christ and be servants. At the same time, we too have needs, and sometimes we can feel like we have nothing to give—like our battery is almost flat and our tank is running low on fuel. This can happen when we do not take time to take care of our own needs because we are busy doing all of the tasks we "feel" are expected of us.

In this situation, you need to ask yourself what you are actually called to do and what your priority should be. You cannot please everyone and do everything you are asked to do everywhere. Especially if you are a "yes-person," you will always be asked to do things because people know you will say "yes." We are supposed to be servants, but we also need to protect ourselves so that we have something to give in the arena we are actually called to. We need to protect our calling and be able to say "no." We also need to make sure we are there for the people who are most important to us, like our spouse and kids. If we are not living conscious of these things, we might burn out. God never intended for us to be the ones to save the world and be everything to everybody, but He wants us to be faithful and diligent in the area and to the people He has assigned to us.

"What about me, God?" is a very relevant question asked in the right context. We need to pay attention to our own needs to have something to give to others. How do we take care of ourselves properly without getting overly self-focused and selfish? What is the source we draw from to take care of ourselves? What areas of our lives need our attention for us to function properly so that we have something to give to others? Let us try to put these things in the right perspective and the right order.

Spirit, Soul and Body

As human beings, we consist of three parts: body, soul and spirit. We ARE a spirit, we HAVE a soul and we LIVE IN a body. To function properly, all these parts need attention. In church, we might focus mostly on the needs of the spirit, but not so much on the soul and the body. The spirit is very important. It is our spirit that connects with God who is our source of eternal and abundant life, and this abundant life and power are meant to flow over to our soul and body—bringing peace, healing, restoration and wholeness.

Taking Care of Your Spirit

> *I have come that they may have life and that they may have it more abundantly. (John 10:10b)*

When we were born again, it was our spirit that was born again, not our soul. We became a new creation in Christ Jesus, and the Holy Spirit filled our spirit and connected us to the spiritual well of the Father. This is a river of living water that never runs dry. This is the well we are to drink from. The most important thing we do to take care of ourselves is to come to this well to drink. Our source needs to be God.

> *'If anyone thirsts, let him come to Me and drink. He who believes in Me, as the Scripture has said, out of his heart will flow rivers of living water.' (John 7: 37b-38)*

How do we come to this well to drink?

1. *YOU ARE ALWAYS "ONLINE":* You have an ongoing relationship with Jesus 24/7. You are always online with Him and can talk to Him and pray in every situation during the day. You can always "drink from the well of the Holy Spirit" who lives inside of you. Make sure you are conscious of His presence in your everyday life.
2. *QUIET TIME WITH PRAYER, SCRIPTURE AND WORSHIP:* It is good to take time in the morning (or another time of the day) to spend time alone with God in worship and prayer, reading the Bible and just being in His presence. During this time, your spirit is filled up and strengthened, and

you are empowered and equipped for the day. Spending time alone with God is building a relationship with Him. You take time to talk and listen to Him. Here you can get direction and help to prioritize how to spend your time. When you give God your time first, the rest of your time will be more efficient. Even Jesus needed this. The Bible says that He often went off alone to pray and be with the Father. If Jesus—the Son of God—needed that, we need it too!

3. *BE PART OF A CHURCH AND A LIFE GROUP/CHRISTIAN FELLOWSHIP:* In this setting, you can hear teaching and preaching to gain knowledge and revelation and have fellowship with other Christians. We worship and pray together and receive prayer and counsel from others.

4. *OTHER CHRISTIAN RESOURCES:* There are a lot of excellent teaching, preaching and worship online that you can listen to "on the go" while exercising, getting ready, driving, cooking, cleaning, etc. Use every opportunity to be filled and equipped. A lot of great Christian books are available as well.

It takes some discipline to "feed on God" and meet your spiritual needs every day. Just know that it is something you get to do, not something you should feel guilty about if you did not do it. As your relationship with God grows, you will be looking forward to spending time with Him. What you receive from Him is your strength and nourishment for the rest of your day.

When we take care of ourselves properly, we don´t burn out. What God wants us to do, He gives us grace for. We will feel His favor and flow in what we are doing. We are allowed to say "no" to the things that we know are not what we are called to do, especially if it involves a commitment of our time. Of course, we help others and help in the church, but not to the extent that these things are stealing time and focus from our main calling. Hence, it is important to know what God wants you to make a priority in this season of your life so that you can focus on the right things. Jesus never meant walking with Him to be exhausting and hard. See what He says in this Scripture:

> *"Walk with me and work with me—watch how I do it. Learn the unforced rhythms of grace. I won't lay anything heavy or ill-fitting on you. Keep company with me, and you'll learn to live freely and lightly." (Matthew 11:29-30 MSG)*

What About the Soul?

Let us move on to the soul. Does God care about our soul? Of course, He does. He is the One who created us as spirit, soul and body. The Lord wants us to be proactive about taking care of our whole person. WE are the ones who have to do it. Nobody else will do it for us.

> *Beloved, I pray that you may prosper in all things and be in health, just as your soul prospers. (3 John 1:2)*

Prosperity in all things means that we become fully alive and fully ourselves, living as who we are created to be. This prosperity goes far beyond money. As we see in Scripture, it also includes health.

How can our soul prosper? In his book *Destined to Win,*[37] Kris Vallotton puts it like this, "We are all born with an intense need to feel significant, loved, valued and accepted. What water, food, air, sleep and sunlight are to our body; love, acceptance, attention, approval and significance are to our soul." We cannot ignore these things.

God´s love needs to be experienced. Head knowledge is not enough. In the presence of God, we can receive His love as we trust in Him. In Ephesians, it is described beautifully:

> *Then Christ will make his home in your hearts as you trust in him. Your roots will grow down into God's love and keep you strong. And may you have the power to understand, as all God's people should, how wide, how long, how high, and how deep his love is. May you experience the love of Christ, though it is too great to understand fully. Then you will be made complete with all the fullness of life and power that comes from God. (Ephesians 3:17-19 NLT)*

In Psalm 23, we see that the Lord is concerned about our needs. He prepares a place for us to rest. He restores our soul. He anoints us so our cup runs over. He obviously cares about our whole human being.

> *The Lord is my shepherd;*
> *I shall not want.*
> *He makes me to lie down in green pastures;*
> *He leads me beside the still waters.*
> *He restores my soul;*

He leads me in the paths of righteousness
For His name´s sake.
Yea, though I walk through the valley of the shadow of death,
I will fear no evil;
For You are with me;
Your rod and Your staff, they comfort me.
You prepare a table before me in the presence of my enemies;
You anoint my head with oil;
My cup runs over.
Surely goodness and mercy shall follow me
All the days of my life;
And I will dwell in the house of the Lord
Forever. (Psalm 23)

We see something similar in Matthew 11:28-30 (NLT): "*Then Jesus said, 'Come to me, all of you who are weary and carry heavy burdens, and I will give you rest. Take my yoke upon you. Let me teach you, because I am humble and gentle at heart, and you will find rest for your souls. For my yoke is easy to bear, and the burden I give you is light.'"*

When it comes to the balance between our spirit, soul and body, it is essential to understand that our spirit has unlimited resources as it is connected to God. It does not sleep. It is much stronger than our soul and body. Our soul and body, however, have limits that we need to pay attention to. For example, our soul and body are limited by time. We cannot overdraw time, because time is set. Therefore, we run out of time. We need to manage our time and commitments to maintain our soul and body. If we don´t do this, we might crash and get sick.

There are, however, situations where we will have to put our own needs aside and stretch our limits to reach out to people in need. God will give us grace and strength to do that. I am always touched by the story in Matthew 14 where Jesus had just received the message that John the Baptist (His cousin) had been beheaded by King Herod. Jesus was probably very upset and saddened by the news, so He went off to a remote place to be alone, but then the multitude came out after Him... Let us read the story from Matthew 14:13-23:

When Jesus heard it, <u>He departed from there by boat to a deserted place by Himself.</u> But when the multitudes heard it, they followed Him on foot from the cities. And <u>when Jesus went out He saw a great multitude; and He was</u>

> *moved with compassion for them and healed their sick. When it was evening, His disciples came to Him, saying, "This is a deserted place, and the hour is already late. Send the multitudes away, that they may go into the villages and buy themselves food." But Jesus said to them, "They do not need to go away. You give them something to eat." And they said to Him, "We have here only five loaves and two fish." He said, "Bring them here to Me." Then He commanded the multitudes to sit down on the grass. And He took the five loaves and the two fish, and looking up to heaven, He blessed and broke and gave the loaves to the disciples; and the disciples gave to the multitudes. So they all ate and were filled, and they took up twelve baskets full of the fragments that remained. Now those who had eaten were about five thousand men, besides women and children. Immediately Jesus made His disciples get into the boat and go before Him to the other side, while He sent the multitudes away. And when He had sent the multitudes away, He went up on the mountain by Himself to pray. Now when evening came, He was alone there.*

Jesus was moved with compassion for the people and tended to their needs, even when He was heartbroken and really needed time alone. He put His own needs on hold, but He knew He would attend to them later as we see at the end of the passage when He went up on a mountain by Himself to pray. It is also interesting to note that in this story, Jesus met the needs of the multitude physically, emotionally and spiritually. He saw them, loved on them, healed them AND He did a miracle so that they could all eat as well. We need to be prepared to put aside our own needs temporarily to help others and then tend to our needs later on, just as Jesus did.

Another key to soul health is being present in your current season and in the moment. Don´t overthink yesterday or tomorrow—be present with the people you are with in this moment. Don´t think about someone you want to be with when you are spending time with someone else. We are missing out on life when we are not present in the moment. The Lord has planned many encounters with people throughout the day, but we can miss out on these because we are not present—in our thoughts, we are somewhere else. (Social media and cell phones are big thieves in this matter.)

To sum up the section about the soul, we need to pay attention to our soul to be whole and healthy human beings. We need to have balance in our lives. If there are things that we are struggling with, we need to sort it out and get rid of those things that are hindering us from being everything God created us to be. There are also professional counselors who can help us and pray for us. We might just have to start setting boundaries for our lives and learn to manage our time and priorities better. We also need to surround ourselves with people who add to us, not drain us. We need a healthy soul to be able to minister to others. If we are exhausted or struggling with many things from the past, it will affect the way we relate to other people as well. To love our neighbor, we have to love ourselves.

Taking Care of the Body

Our body needs attention as well. It is the temple of the Holy Spirit, and it needs to be in good shape and health to carry us around, so we can do what we need to do. We need to maintain a healthy diet, exercise, get adequate sleep and sunlight and any other daily care our bodies need. When these things are neglected, we can feel miserable, weak and tired, which in turn affects our soul and spirit as well. I can recommend the book, *The Daniel Plan,* by Rick Warren if you need to rethink and adjust the way you take care of your body.

To Sum It Up...

This teaching is not meant to be an excuse to start living a self-centered, self-focused life. We are expected to be servants and lay our lives down for others. We are meant to go the extra mile. There will be grace to do these things. However, often we do much more than God asks us to do—things we don´t have the grace to do because we feel it is expected of us. Sometimes, we don´t realize that a season of our life is over, and we hold on to it for too long. This is when we get exhausted. God wants us to live balanced lives, and as we work, it is Christ who works in us and through us by His power and grace. We are equipped and empowered to do what we are supposed to do so that there is a natural flow. We will still get tired, but in a good way—fulfilled, instead of exhausted and burnt out. Let us take care of ourselves so that we can last and run our race to the finishing line.

FOR SELF REFLECTION AND GROUP DISCUSSION

1. Evaluate your current life situation, commitments and involvements. Are you doing more than you should do—things you don´t have grace for or joy doing?
2. How are you taking care of your spirit, soul and body? Are any of these lacking your attention and care?
3. How can you feed your spirit better?
4. Make a list of the needs of your soul. Evaluate what you can do to fill these needs.
5. Make the same kind of list for the needs of your physical body. Are there any adjustments that need to be made to your current habits?

SHARE AND DISCUSS WITH THE GROUP

SESSION 37

Be Bold, Strong and Courageous Part 1

IN SOME SEASONS OF OUR LIVES, we might be tempted just to give up. The challenges seem too big, or our confidence is too low. Situations we are facing make us fearful. We start thinking that we don't have what it takes. We are tempted just to go and hide somewhere to avoid facing our fears. We might even believe that these thoughts of withdrawing are humble thoughts. However, the humility God wants from us is not thinking less of ourselves or feeling wiped out and powerless. He wants us to embrace who He says we are, rise up and do what He says we can do.

If you have been feeling like what I just described, you have probably allowed the enemy to play around with your mind—without fighting him back. The enemy wants to destroy you and make you powerless. He wants to crush your sense of identity in Christ, which in turn will take away your boldness. He wants you to feel fearful and small so that you will not do any harm to his evil plans.

Don´t Miss the Plan of God

God has a good plan for us, but if we are always bowing down to our fears and low self-esteem, we might miss it. This happened to the people of Israel. They had been slaves under the Egyptians for 400 years. Moses was sent by God to tell Pharaoh to let the people go, and after some time of strong resistance and many plagues, Pharaoh finally released them. God did great miracles—He part-ed the Red Sea and took them through on dry land, while the Egyptian soldiers who followed them drowned. God fed them miraculously in the desert, and they saw His faithfulness and help every day. God had a great plan for them. He had prepared an awesome country for them where they could live life in abundance. However, there were giants in the promised land... (You can read the whole story in the book of Exodus.)

Twelve spies were sent into the promised land to check it out. Ten of them came back full of fear because of the giants. Only two spies, Joshua and Caleb, trusted the Lord and believed that they should enter the land. Unfortunately, all of the people of Israel listened to the ten fearful spies, which ruined their destiny They spent the next forty years wandering around in the desert instead of entering the promised land, and all of them, except Joshua and Caleb, died in the desert. Only their children (the new generation) entered the promised land led by Joshua later on.

It´s essential for us to see that when the ten spies came back from spying out the land, they said, “We were like grasshoppers in their sight.” The truth was that the people (and giants) that lived in the promised land were terrified of the people of Israel because they had heard about everything God had done for them when He delivered them from the Egyptians. The children of Israel based their decision on what they “thought” their enemy was thinking about them; however, the truth was very different.

What can we learn from this? We know that God has a plan and a good future for us just like He did for the children of Israel. However, this plan is too big for us to make it happen in our own strength. If we can do it without God, it is probably not God´s plan. This means that we will have to face situations that are impossible in the natural. We will meet hindrances that we can´t break through on our own. We will need God’s miraculous power and intervention. In these situations, let us not lose faith and trust in God. Let us not bow down to our fears or low self-esteem.

We see throughout the whole Bible that God’s people faced scary and impossible situations.

1. In the Old Testament, *the prophets* were challenged to rise up and say what the Lord told them to say. Many times, they risked their lives as they had to say things that the people did not want to hear. *Jeremiah* was one of them. It must have been terrifying.

2. In other places in the Bible, we read about enemies and armies different people had to face in battles of war. One of them was *Joshua* as he was the one to enter the promised land with the new generation of the people of Israel. There were many cities they had to conquer in the land.
3. *David* was faced with the giant Goliath but was so brave to stand up against him and kill him. Later David was at risk again as he was hunted in the wilderness by Saul for many years. David really had to face his fears.
4. *Esther* was positioned as the one who could save her people when they were in danger of being killed. She rose up and did what she had to do even though she knew she was risking her life (Esther Chapter 4).
5. *Daniel* was thrown to the lions because he prayed to God against the order of the king (Daniel 6:10–23).

There are many more examples of men and women in Scripture who refused to bow down to fear but, instead, rose up, trusted God and changed the course of history. God never promised us an easy life, but He did promise us that in every challenge we face, He will be right there with us. He does not leave us alone but is always there to help us through.

Arise!

Arise! Throughout the Old Testament, when God gave someone an assignment or calling, He told them to ARISE. Jeremiah was told to prepare himself and arise in Jeremiah 1:17. Joshua was told to *"arise"* and enter the promised land with the new generation. In Isaiah 60:1-3, we are told to *"arise and shine"*:

> *Arise, shine; For your light has come!*
> *And the glory of the Lord is risen upon you.*
> *For behold, the darkness shall cover the earth,*
> *And deep darkness the people;*
> *But the Lord will arise over you,*
> *And His glory will be seen upon you.*
> *The Gentiles shall come to your light,*
> *And kings to the brightness of your rising.*

We are told to arise and shine because Jesus, our Light, has already come. We arise into what He has prepared for us, into who He says we are and into our identity in Christ.

Be Courageous and Strong

Throughout the Bible, we see God speaking these words to His people to encourage them: "*Be strong and of good courage.*" Let's take a look at some of these instances:

> *After the death of Moses the servant of the Lord, it came to pass that the Lord spoke to Joshua the son of Nun, Moses´ assistant, saying: "Moses My servant is dead. Now, therefore, arise, go over this Jordan, you and all this people, to the land which I am giving to them—the children of Israel. Every place that the sole of your foot will tread upon I have given you, as I said to Moses. From the wilderness and this Lebanon as far as the great river, the River Euphrates, all the land of the Hittites, and to the Great Sea toward the going down of the sun, shall be your territory. No man shall be able to stand before you all the days of your life; as I was with Moses, so I will be with you. I will not leave you nor forsake you. Be strong and of good courage, for to this people you shall divide as an inheritance the land which I swore to their fathers to give them. Only be strong and very courageous, that you may observe to do according to all the law which Moses My servant commanded you; do not turn from it to the right hand or to the left, that you may prosper wherever you go. This Book of the Law shall not depart from your mouth, but you shall meditate in it day and night, that you may observe to do according to all that is written in it. For then you will make your way prosperous, and then you will have good success. Have I not commanded you? Be strong and of good courage; do not be afraid, nor be dismayed, for the Lord your God is with you wherever you go." (Joshua 1:1-9)*

In Joshua 1:18, these words are repeated to Joshua again: *"Only be strong and of good courage."*

In 2 Chronicles, we find a situation where the king of Assyria wants to make war against the tribe of Judah. King Hezekiah, the King of Judah, hears the rumor of war and speaks to the people:

> *"Be strong and courageous; do not be afraid nor dismayed before the king of Assyria, nor before all the multitude that is with him; for there are more with us than with him. With him is an arm of flesh; but with us is the Lord our God, to help us and to fight our battles." And the people were strengthened by the words of Hezekiah king of Judah. (2 Chronicles 32:7-8)*

When Joshua is to become the leader of Israel after Moses, this is what Moses says:

> *"Be strong and of good courage, do not fear nor be afraid of them; for the Lord your God, He is the One who goes with you. He will not leave you nor forsake you." Then Moses called Joshua and said to him in the sight of all Israel, "Be strong and of good courage, for you must go with this people to the land which the Lord has sworn to their fathers to give them, and you shall cause them to inherit it. And the Lord, He is the One who goes before you. He will be with you, He will not leave you nor forsake you; do not fear nor be dismayed." (Deuteronomy 31:6-8)*

When King David prepares his son Solomon to take over as king, he tells him: *"Be strong and of good courage, do not fear nor be dismayed"* (1 Chronicles 22:13). He repeats these words again in 1 Chronicles 28:20:

> *And David said to his son Solomon, "Be strong and of good courage, and do it; do not fear nor be dismayed, for the Lord God—my God—will be with you. He will not leave you nor forsake you until you have finished all the work for the service of the house of the Lord."*

We can see from these verses that the Lord wants us to be strong and courageous, not afraid or dismayed. Why? Because He has promised to always be with us to help us and fight our battles. He will never leave us nor forsake us. Why did these words need to be repeated over and over again? Because everybody faces fear. Everybody feels afraid when they are to face their giants, including us. That is why we need to embrace these verses.

Let us face our fears, arise and shine! Let us arise into our destiny with courage, strength, boldness and confidence in the Lord, knowing that He will always be with us to help us and fight our battles.

In the next session, we will look into the New Testament where a different term is used for strength and courage: BOLDNESS! As believers, we have the source of boldness inside of us—The Holy Spirit.

FOR SELF REFLECTION AND GROUP DISCUSSION

1. Do you have an area in your life where you know that you should step up—"arise and shine"—but fear is stopping you (fear of failing, fear of man, etc.)? Are you ready to decide to rise above your fears and be strong and courageous in the situation?
2. The Israelites listened to the ten fearful spies with a bad report and negative mindset, which cost them their destiny. What can we learn from this? How can we focus on the opportunities and potential positive outcomes in the situation, instead of the "bad reports," when we are making decisions?

SHARE AND DISCUSS WITH THE GROUP

SESSION 38

Be Bold, Strong and Courageous Part 2

IN THE PREVIOUS SESSION, we learned that the Lord wants us to be strong and courageous, not afraid or dismayed. We can do this when we know that He is always with us to help us and fight our battles. He will never leave us nor forsake us.

Until now, we have looked at Old Testament examples. What about the New Testament? In general, God uses different words in the New Testament, although He still wants us to be strong and courageous, as the Apostle Paul says in his letter:

Watch, stand fast in the faith, be brave, be strong. (1 Corinthians 16:13)

In the New Testament, the words BOLD and BOLDNESS are the ones most commonly used. Boldness is a result of being filled with the Holy Spirit. Our boldness and confidence are in Jesus, not in ourselves. We get bold in Jesus by the Holy Spirit.

In the Old Testament, the people were not filled with the Holy Spirit as we are. The Holy Spirit was with them to help them, but strength and courage did not come from the Holy Spirit within them. We have His power inside of us that makes us BOLD! Isn't that awesome?

When I am weak, He is strong in me! (see 2 Cor. 12:10). We are broken vessels, but the power and glory of God can shine through the cracks.

I can do all things through Christ who strengthens me. (Philippians 4:13)

Boldness Is a Result of Knowing God and Knowing Who We Are in Christ

The first step to boldness is knowing who God is and His character so that you can have the boldness to trust Him. You know He is always with you. He will never leave you nor forsake you. He is good, faithful and trustworthy.

Boldness is also a result of knowing who we are in Christ. Let us look at some examples:

> *(In Christ Jesus, our Lord,) in whom we have <u>boldness and access with confidence</u> through faith in Him. (Ephesians 3:12)*
>
> *Let us therefore come <u>boldly</u> to the throne of grace, that we may obtain mercy and find grace to help in time of need. (Hebrews 4:16)*
>
> *Therefore, brethren, having <u>boldness</u> to enter the Holiest by the blood of Jesus, by a new and living way which He consecrated for us, through the veil, that is, His flesh, (Hebrews 10:19-20)*

John calls it confidence:

> *Beloved, if our heart does not condemn us, we have <u>confidence</u> toward God. (1 John 3:21)*
>
> *Therefore do not cast away your <u>confidence</u>, which has great reward. For you have need of endurance, so that after you have done the will of God, you may receive the promise: (Hebrews 10:35-36)*

Boldness and confidence before God are very important. We must be bold in our relationship with God before we are bold before people. Our boldness and confidence towards God are based on us resting in His grace and love, and it comes when we understand that we are forgiven by God and made 100 percent righteous. He has set us free from all guilt, shame and condemnation. When we mess up, we know that we can shake it off, repent and receive the forgiveness that was already provided when Jesus died on the cross 2000 years ago. We can look unto Jesus and know that we are fully accepted and loved. Knowing we have this backing from God, who is <u>only good</u> and only <u>for us</u>, gives us confidence and boldness to face the challenges of this world.

Boldness Comes from the Holy Spirit

In the early church, the apostles were known for their courage. They spoke boldly and acted boldly. This all started after the Day of Pentecost when they were filled with the Holy Spirit.

> *Now when they saw the boldness of Peter and John and perceived that they were uneducated and untrained men, they marveled. And they realized that they had been with Jesus. (Acts 4:13)*

Boldness was also what they prayed for:

> *"Now, Lord, look on their threats, and grant to Your servants that with all boldness they may speak Your word, by stretching out Your hand to heal, and that signs and wonders may be done through the name of Your holy Servant Jesus." And when they had prayed, the place where they were assembled together was shaken; and they were all filled with the Holy Spirit, and they spoke the word of God with boldness. (Acts 4:29-31)*

The Apostle Paul was also known for speaking the Word of God with boldness, not fearing for his own life. He also asked for prayer for boldness. This was even what he asked for when he was in prison!

> *Praying always with all prayer and supplication in the Spirit, being watchful to this end with all perseverance and supplication for all the saints—and for me, that utterance may be given to me, that I may open my mouth boldly to make known the mystery of the gospel, for which I am an ambassador in chains; that in it I may speak boldly, as I ought to speak. (Ephesians 6:18-20)*

Wherever Paul went, he spoke and preached the Gospel boldly.

> *So he was with them at Jerusalem, coming in and going out. And he spoke boldly in the name of the Lord Jesus and disputed against the Hellenists, but they attempted to kill him. (Acts 9:28-29)*

> *Therefore they stayed there a long time, speaking boldly in the Lord, who was bearing witness to the word of His grace, granting signs and wonders to be done by their hands. (Acts 14:3)*

> *And he went into the synagogue and spoke boldly for three months, reasoning and persuading concerning the things of the kingdom of God. (Acts 19:8)*

Let´s sum this up. The first step to boldness is knowing who God is and His character so that you can have boldness in your faith in Him. Secondly, you need to know who you are in Christ. You need to know that you are righteous and forgiven so you can come boldly to the throne of grace in prayer. As you pray with your own words and in the Spirit, the Holy Spirit Himself will build you up, and boldness will rise up inside of you and empower you to speak what you need to speak and do the work of the Lord.

Even if you don't feel bold, it is not about your feelings. As you step out into what God is asking you to do, the Holy Spirit will back you up and give you the boldness you need in the situation. It is stepping out in faith. When you are weak, you are strong because the Holy Spirit is within you and gives you what you need in every situation.

FOR SELF REFLECTION AND GROUP DISCUSSION

1. Have you experienced the Holy Spirit making you bold to act and to speak?
2. How is your boldness and confidence towards God in prayer? Are you resting in His grace in full assurance that you are righteous and forgiven, loved and accepted?
3. Share with the group situations where you need boldness right now and pray for each other.

SHARE AND DISCUSS WITH THE GROUP

SESSION 39

Your Life Counts

You Are Noticed and Seen by God

I WANT TO ENCOURAGE YOU TODAY and tell you that your life counts. Your life matters! We might feel insignificant and invisible at times—like our effort is not noticed or appreciated or what we do is not important. Even though there can be times when you think that your life is small, I can assure you that your life matters. God sees you and takes notice of everything you do: every prayer you send up to Him and every kind word you say or thing you do for others. And He sees your heart. We are all playing our part in God's grand story orchestrated by Him through the Holy Spirit. We are all connected, and it matters that we play our role.

> *"For God is not unjust to forget your work and labor of love which you have shown toward His name, in that you have ministered to the saints, and do minister. And we desire that each one of you show the same diligence to the full assurance of hope until the end, that you do not become sluggish, but imitate those who through faith and patience inherit the promise." (Hebrews 6:10-12)*

We see from this verse that God sees all of your work and labor. You are noticed and seen by God. However, there is a warning not to become sluggish and indifferent and give up but to diligently keep "playing your part."

In Galatians 6:9-10, we see the same thing: *"And let us not grow weary while doing good, for in due season we shall reap if we do not lose heart. Therefore, as we have opportunity, let us do good to all, especially to those who are of the household of faith."*

If we know that God sees us and that what we do matters, it makes it easier not to give up.

The Part You Play Is Important in the Kingdom of God

Throughout the New Testament, the church is called "the body of Christ," and every one of us is a member of that body. The Bible talks about how every part of the body is equally necessary, and so we should not compare ourselves to others. What is a hand without a thumb? What is a foot without an ankle? What is a head without a neck? You can read about this in 1 Corinthians 12:12-27.

In Romans, we read about different functions and different gifts given to the different parts of the body.

> *For just as each of us has one body with many members, and these members do not all have the same function, so in Christ, we, though many, form one body, and each member belongs to all the others. We have different gifts, according to the grace given to each of us. If your gift is prophesying, then prophesy in accordance with your faith; if it is serving, then serve; if it is teaching, then teach; if it is to encourage, then give encouragement; if it is giving, then give generously; if it is to lead, do it diligently; if it is to show mercy, do it cheerfully. (Romans 12:4-8 NIV)*

These gifts are given by the Father. For your life to count the most, live close to the Holy Spirit and be led by Him in your everyday life. Then you will focus on doing the right things—the things God wants you to do. You will be sensitive to get in touch with the right people and be an answer to people´s prayers. You will feel whom you should be connected to who will help you prosper. You will not just run around doing anything and everything. The Holy Spirit will help you to zoom in on what exactly your part is to play and what your place is to fill.

So far, we have learned that we are noticed and seen by God. We have also discovered that we are made as a particular member of the body of Christ, and we are gifted and equipped to fill that place. This is all by the grace of God and the leading of the Holy Spirit. He wants us to use our gifts to serve His people. In the Kingdom of God, it is all about people. God loves people. Jesus came so He could help, serve, die for and redeem people. We are His hands, His mouth and His feet on the Earth today.

Who You Are Is Important to God and Others

However, it is not only what you do that matters but just as much that you are who you are. Just you being YOU is important. God created you just as you are because He wanted a son or a daughter just like you. He looks at you and smiles; He rejoices over you. He is so proud of you! See what it says in Zephaniah 3:17:

> *"The Lord your God in your midst, The Mighty One, will save;*
> *He will rejoice over you with gladness, He will quiet you with His love,*
> *He will rejoice over you with singing."*

The first "rejoice" in this verse is the word *sus* in Hebrew, which means "to be bright, i.e., cheerful: — be glad, rejoice greatly, joy, make mirth, rejoice."[38] The second "rejoice" in this verse is a different word, which means "to spin around (under the influence of any violent emotion)" and to "be glad, joy, be joyful, rejoice."[39] Wow! The Lord is so happy when He looks at you that He spins around!

The Lord is really so pleased with you and so glad that you are His daughter or son. He wants you to receive His great love for you and experience His delight in you so that you know that you are loved for who you are!

Your life also counts when it comes to the different roles you play in the lives of others. This could be your role as a friend, mother, father, wife, husband, mentor, colleague, etc. What you bring to other people, just by being in their lives, can be very important. Your support, encouragement and prayers can be "make it or break it" for others. More than anything, it matters what you bring into their lives when it comes to faith and discipleship. The spiritual seeds you sow into your kids, family and friends can change the lives of generations to come.

Let us look in 2 Timothy, which was written by the Apostle Paul when he was in prison and was soon going to be executed. When we read what he writes to Timothy in this first chapter, we understand how much Timothy means to Paul, what support he has been to him and how important it is for Paul that Timothy will continue the ministry when he is unable to do it himself.

> *I, Paul, am on special assignment for Christ, carrying out God´s plan laid out in the Message of Life by Jesus. I write this to you, Timothy, the son I*

> *love so much. All the best from our God and Christ be yours! Every time I say your name in prayer—which is practically all the time—I thank God for you, the God I worship with my whole life in the tradition of my ancestors. I miss you a lot, especially when I remember that last tearful good-bye, and I look forward to a joy-packed reunion. That precious memory triggers another: your honest faith—and what a rich faith it is, handed down from your grandmother Lois to your mother Eunice, and now to you! And the special gift of ministry you received when I laid hands on you and prayed—keep that ablaze! God doesn´t want us to be shy with his gifts, but bold and loving and sensible. (2 Timothy 1:1-7 MSG)*

I want you to take note of something significant said in this passage: Timothy´s faith was a result of the faith of his mother and grandmother. How important it was that these two mothers were faithful in their faith and faithful to raise their kids in the faith. Their lives really mattered! What if Timothy had not been there for Paul? Would Paul have been able to spread the Gospel in the same way? What we know is that Timothy was a great encouragement and support for the Apostle Paul. In the same way, you never know what plans God has for your kids, friends and the random people you meet. Be faithful and sow into them what you are led to. Regarding your kids—plant faith and Godly wisdom diligently over time. You never know what they will become.

Paul also reminds Timothy that he cannot give up on his gift. His ministry and gifts matter. He has an important part to play.

> *Therefore I remind you to stir up the gift of God which is in you through the laying on of my hands. For God has not given us a spirit of fear, but of power and of love and of a sound mind. (2 Timothy 1:6-7)*

Just like Timothy, we all need to stir up our gifts and keep our focus on where we are going and what we are doing. As we read in The Message version above about our gifts, *"Keep that ablaze! God doesn't want us to be shy with his gifts, but bold and loving and sensible."*

Let Us Sum Things Up:

- Our lives matter. We have a unique role to play, a special place to fill in God´s plan and unique gifts to serve others with. You have a special place in the Father´s heart as well that only you can fill.

- God sees everything you do, and He will reward you for it. However, be led by the Holy Spirit in what you do so that you are focused and aligned with the will of God for your life. Then you avoid doing a lot of things God never asked you to do, and you will not be worn out.
- Be awake and alert. Stay focused and motivated. Discouragement and a feeling of insignificance (that what you do doesn´t matter) can cause you to *"grow weary in doing good"* (see Eph. 6:9).
- Keep your gifts alive and in use. *"Keep it ablaze"* as it says in the Message Bible.
- Most of all, know that just YOU being YOU is crucial to so many people.
- You being YOU is even more important to God, who created you in His image to have fellowship with YOU! So, stay in close fellowship with Him.

Perhaps we will not see in this life how much our lives really mattered—only when we get to Heaven, will we know. Our lives then become a matter of faith, patience and endurance. Perhaps one of our great-grandchildren is the next Billy Graham? What we sow into our kids today, can produce a harvest generation down the line. Maybe a random person we have an encouraging word for cancels his suicide plans and, instead, becomes a Christian who leads many to Christ. What we do and say matters because it starts a chain reaction like rings in the water. We are all connected, and we are all dependent on each other, so be encouraged. Play your part, use your gifts and be the original YOU God created you to be, and one day you will see that your life matters more than you ever imagined

FOR SELF REFLECTION AND GROUP DISCUSSION

1. Are there things you are doing right now that you consider insignificant, but in God´s eyes they are not?
2. *"And let us not grow weary while doing good, for in due season we shall reap if we do not lose heart."* (Galatians 6:9)

   Think of your life from the perspective of eternity and how God can multiply the seeds you sow into people right now and produce a harvest for generations to come. Let this be an encouragement to keep going and not "grow weary in doing good" as we read above. Write about it in your journal and share your thoughts with the group.

3. In this lesson, we learned that the word "rejoice" means that God is so pleased with you that He is spinning around. Take some time to meditate on how delighted God is with you.

   The Lord your God in your midst, The Mighty One, will save; He will rejoice over you with gladness, He will quiet you with His love, He will rejoice over you with singing (Zephaniah 3:17)

   SHARE AND DISCUSS WITH THE GROUP

SESSION 40

Your Eternal Reward in Heaven

Living Life with Eternity in Mind

ONCE IN A WHILE, WE NEED TO STOP and ask ourselves: Do we live with temporary or eternal things in mind? Many people live to gather more and more expensive possessions, always wanting to buy an even nicer house and car. They might sacrifice relationships and marriage on the altar of their career goals. I heard one rich guy say to the other, "The one of us who has the most toys when he dies wins." I suppose he had actually seen the irony in the way he was living.

When you go to Heaven, you need to leave all material things behind. However, there are some things you bring with you:

1. The people that were touched and saved through your life—you will meet them in Heaven, together with all your sisters and brothers in the Lord from all different churches and nations who have received Jesus as their Savior.
2. What you gave into the Kingdom of God (money and other things)
3. Your relationship with God
4. Your revelation and knowledge of God
5. The REWARD for your work here on Earth, which is according to your calling and purpose (your faithfulness in doing what God asked you to do and what you allowed the Holy Spirit to do through you)
6. The REWARD for obeying God´s Word and the Spirit

How to Receive Your Full Reward in Heaven

The Bible talks about receiving your full reward in Heaven from Jesus (I will show you the Scriptures later on in the session). He will look in His book at what the purpose and plan for your life were and compare it to what you actually did. Your reward is a result of the way you lived your life here on Earth. That does not mean you are supposed to live stressed out and worried that you are not doing enough! No, the opposite is true: You walk in the works that God prepared for you to walk in from the beginning of time and as the Holy Spirit leads in everyday life. It is all by grace.

> *For we are His workmanship, created in Christ Jesus for good works, which God prepared beforehand that we should walk in them. (Ephesians 2:10)*

> *For we are God's masterpiece. He has created us anew in Christ Jesus so we can do the good things he planned for us long ago. (Ephesians 2:10 NLT)*

In the Book of Psalms, we see how all of our days were numbered and planned in His book ahead of time:

> *Like an open book, you watched me grow from conception to birth;*
> *all the stages of my life were spread out before you,*
> *The days of my life all prepared*
> *before I'd even lived one day.*
> *Your thoughts—how rare, how beautiful!*
> *God, I'll never comprehend them! (Psalm 139:16-17 MSG)*

Let us look at verse 16 in the New Living Translation:

> *You saw me before I was born. Every day of my life was recorded in your book. Every moment was laid out before a single day had passed.*

We are designed by God to fill a place in His Kingdom. We are called into His purpose. Isn´t it great to know that our lives have a higher meaning? Our lives count for eternity! We are not here by accident, and many people depend on our obedience. It is also great to hear that there is a reward waiting for us in Heaven.

It is essential to understand that we are <u>saved</u> by grace alone, not by works or good deeds. Our salvation is only based on what Jesus did at the cross, and we can do nothing to add to that. Ephesians 2:8-9 says, "*For by grace you have been saved through faith, and that not of yourselves; it is the gift of God, not of works, lest anyone should boast."*

Our salvation decides where we will spend eternity. However, the way we run our race and fulfill our purpose and calling will determine our reward in Heaven and how we will spend eternity. One day in Heaven, Jesus will judge believers. This judgment is NOT about our sins or salvation but about what we did with our lives: our calling, purpose and gifts. See what the Bible says about these things:

> *For we must all appear and be revealed as we are before the judgment seat of Christ, so that each one may receive [his pay] according to what he has done in the body, whether good or evil [considering what his purpose and motive have been, and what he has achieved, been busy with, and given himself and his attention to accomplishing]. (2 Corinthians 5:10 AMPC)*
>
> *For the Son of Man will come in the glory of His Father with His angels, and then He will reward each according to his works. (Matthew 16:27)*
>
> *And behold, I am coming quickly, and My reward is with Me, to give to every one according to his work. (Revelation 22:12)*

Please do not let this scare you but, rather, take it as an encouragement that all the effort you put in for the Kingdom of God will be greatly rewarded by Jesus.

So, does this mean that you are supposed to do as much as possible for God? No, that is not the case. Seek God to find out what He wants you to do, embrace it and start running with it. This could be staying at home looking after small kids, working in the marketplace or full-time ministry... Just make sure you are in the right place. It is just as wrong to try to be a pastor when God has meant for you to be a business person, as it is to stay in the workplace when you know you are called into ministry. Just follow the leading of the Holy Spirit and do what is in your heart.

God Will Make His Will Come to Pass in Your Life

God has equipped us and designed us with natural talents, spiritual gifts and personality to walk in His plan. When we are born again, He puts His divine purpose inside of us and He is the One to make it come to pass as long as we seek Him and let Him work in us. He has promised that He is with us and for us. He lives within us and works through us by the Holy Spirit. By His grace, He empowers us to do what He wants us to do.

The Lord will perfect that which concerns me; (Psalm 138:8 AMPC)

In this context, "to perfect" means "the completing, finishing and perfecting of God´s work in one´s life." [40]

The Lord will work out his plans for my life—for your faithful love, (Psalm 138:8 NLT)

I will cry to God Most High, Who performs on my behalf and rewards me [Who brings to pass His purposes for me and surely completes them]! (Psalm 57:2 AMPC)

And I am convinced and sure of this very thing, that He Who began a good work in you will continue until the day of Jesus Christ [right up to the time of His return], developing [that good work] and perfecting and bringing it to full completion in you. (Philippians 1:6 AMPC)

[Not in your own strength] for it is God Who is all the while effectually at work in you [energizing and creating in you the power and desire], both to will and to work for His good pleasure and satisfaction and delight. (Philippians 2:13 AMPC)

For God is working in you, giving you the desire and the power to do what pleases him. (Philippians 2:13 NLT)

Commit your way to the Lord, Trust also in Him, And He shall bring it to pass. (Psalm 37:5)

It is actually a matter of being obedient and humble and <u>submitting</u> to the purpose that God is already working in you and through you.

Don't you realize that in a race everyone runs, but only one person gets the prize? So <u>run to win</u>! All athletes are disciplined in their training. They do it to win a prize that will fade away, but we do it <u>for an eternal prize</u>. So <u>I run with purpose in every step</u>. I am not just shadowboxing. I discipline my body like an athlete, training it to do what it should. Otherwise, I fear that after preaching to others I myself might be disqualified. (1 Corinthians 9:24-27 NLT)

Let us see what Hebrews says about the race:

Therefore we also, since we are surrounded by so great a cloud of witnesses, let us lay aside every weight, and the sin which so easily ensnares us, and let us run with endurance the race that is set before us, looking unto Jesus, the author and finisher of our faith, who for the joy that was set before Him endured the cross, despising the shame, and has sat down at the right hand of the throne of God. (Hebrews 12:1-2)

We are to play our part in God´s great purpose and plan for the times we are living in. He has a race for us to run! He wants every one of us to seek Him and pay attention to the race He has for us individually. However, there is timing and there are seasons. What does God want you to focus on in this season of your life? Pay close attention to that and let that be your main focus.

People are waiting on the other end of our obedience. Many people depend on us to play our part. Be the piece in God´s puzzle that you are created to be. Be the unique you and do what you are called to do. The Holy Spirit is there to guide you every step of the way. Do not compare yourself to others. Each one of us has got an individual race to run, and our reward depends on our obedience to follow our own path.

Now he who plants and he who waters are one, and each one will receive his own reward according to his own labor. (1 Corinthians 3:8)

Don´t give up when you go through hard times. Make the tough choices. Look to your eternal reward like Moses did.

By faith Moses, when he became of age, refused to be called the son of Pharaoh's daughter, choosing to rather suffer affliction with the people of God than to enjoy the passing pleasures of sin, esteeming the reproach of Christ greater riches than the treasures in Egypt; for he looked to the reward. (Hebrews 11:24-26)

What Else Brings a Reward?

The Bible also talks about a reward we receive when we walk in the Spirit instead of the flesh, when we are persecuted for Christ´s sake and when we serve others. Let us look at some Scriptures:

"Blessed are you when they revile and persecute you and say all kinds of evil against you falsely for My sake. Rejoice and be exceedingly glad, for great is your reward in heaven, for so they persecuted the prophets who were before you." (Matthew 5:11-12)

> *Blessed are you when men hate you, And when they exclude you, And revile you, and cast out your name as evil, For the Son of Man´s sake. Rejoice in that day and leap for joy For indeed your reward is great in heaven, For in like manner their fathers did to the prophets. (Luke 6:22-23)*
>
> *But love your enemies, do good, and lend, hoping for nothing in return; and your reward will be great, and you will be sons of the Most High. For He is kind to the unthankful and evil. (Luke 6:35)*
>
> *If your enemy is hungry, give him bread to eat; And if he is thirsty, give him water to drink; For so you will heap coals of fire on his head, And the Lord will reward you. (Proverbs 25:21-22)*
>
> *"He who receives a prophet in the name of a prophet shall receive a prophet´s reward. And he who receives a righteous man in the name of a righteous man shall receive a righteous man´s reward. And whoever gives one of these little ones only a cup of cold water in the name of a disciple, assuredly, I say to you, he shall by no means lose his reward." (Matthew 10:41-42)*
>
> *For whoever gives you a cup of water to drink in My name, because you belong to Christ, assuredly, I say to you, he will by no means lose his reward. (Mark 9:41)*
>
> *And whatever you do, do it heartily, as to the Lord and not to men, knowing that from the Lord you will receive the reward of the inheritance; for you serve the Lord Christ. (Colossians 3:23-24)*

Even though we are now aware of the great reward waiting for us, our motivation cannot be the reward alone. We do all of these things because we love Jesus and want to do what He asks us to do. We want to partner with Him and show His love to people. At the same time, when we keep the reality of our eternal reward in focus, we will live life with the right perspective and make the right choices. We will find it easier to handle tough situations. We will live not only for the temporary but for the eternal things of God.

FOR SELF REFLECTION AND GROUP DISCUSSION

1. We were reminded at the beginning of this session that it is good sometimes to stop and evaluate the way we are living from the perspective of eternity. Losing focus in our busy, everyday lives is natural. What is your main focus in life? Is it material/worldly things or eternal things?
2. Do you find it encouraging to know that you will receive a reward from Jesus in Heaven?

   Think about it: First God equips you and gives you gifts and talents. Then He puts His dreams inside of you so that they become your dreams as well. Then He helps you every step of the way to fulfill your destiny, and He works behind the scenes and prepares everything to make it happen for you. All you need to do is submit, obey and cooperate. It is all by the grace of God—and we still get the reward. That is pretty awesome!

   SHARE AND DISCUSS WITH THE GROUP

THANK YOU FOR BUYING MY BOOK

I really appreciate all your feedback and I love hearing what you have to say.

I need your input to make the next version better.

Please leave me a helpful review of Amazon letting me know what you thought of the book and how it has impacted your life.

Thank you so much!

Blessings from

Hilde Lundgaard Grimstad

Reference List

1. SOURCES FOR THE HISTORY OF THE BIBLE:

Fairchild, Mary (2018) History of the Bible –

Trace the History of Scripture from Creation to Current Day Translation,

https://www.thoughtco.com/history-of-the-bible-timeline-700157

Jeffcoat III, John L. (2018) English Bible History Article & Timeline,

https://www.greatsite.com/timeline-english-bible-history/#timeline

O´Neal Sam (2019) When Was the Bible Assembled? - The Old Testament Was Already Put Together by the Time of Jesus,

https://www.thoughtco.com/when-was-the-bible-assembled-363293

Hvalvik, Reidar/Stordalen Terje (1999) «Den store fortellingen.» Page 38-41.

https://en.wikipedia.org/wiki/Bible_translations

2. The Holy Bible, New King James Version (1982) Introduction to the Pentateuch
3. Felde, Mary (2014) Living the Better Covenant. Page 173, 191, 207.
4. Keener, Craig S. (2014, 2nd. Edition) The IVP Bible Background Commentary – New Testament.
5. Strong´s Dictionary: ref g5485. χάρις charis; from 5463; graciousness (as gratifying), of manner or act (abstract or concrete; literal, figurative or spiritual; especially the divine influence upon the heart, and its reflection in the life; including gratitude): — acceptable, benefit, favour, gift, grace(- ious), joy, liberality, pleasure, thank(-s, -worthy).Grace that which affords joy, pleasure, delight, sweetness, charm, loveliness: grace of speech, good will, loving-kindness, favour of the merciful kindness by which God, exerting his holy influence upon souls, turns them to Christ, keeps, strengthens, increases them in Christian faith, knowledge, affection, and kindles them to the exercise of the Christian virtues
6. Vallotton, Kris, Johnson Bill (2017) The Supernatural Ways of Royalty
7. Hayford Jack W. (2002) The New Spirit Filled Life Bible, page 3-4, 6

8. Munroe, Dr. Myles (Sermon October 27th, 2012) The Purpose of Prayer. https://www.youtube.com/watch?v=pTYG43i_mxM

9. The New Spirit Filled Life Bible (2002) Commentary on Matt. 11:23 on Hades, page 1310.

10. Hayford Jack W. (2002) The New Spirit Filled Life Bible, page 1409

11. The New Spirit Filled Life Bible (2002), commentary on Phil. 4:6-7, page 1665

12. Strong´s Dictionary ref. g1977 ἐπιρίπτω epiriptō; or ἐπιρρίπτω epirriptō; from 1909 and 4496; to throw upon (literally or figuratively): — throw, or cast upon.

13. Strong´s Dictionary ref. g3199. μέλω melō; a primary verb; to be of interest to, i.e. to concern

14. Strong´s Dictionary ref. g3339 μεταμορφόω metamorphoō; from 3326 and 3445; to transform (literally or figuratively, "metamorphose"): — change, transfigure, transform.

15. Dr. Kim & Dr. Hill (2010), Neural Plasticity: 4 steps to Change your Brain & Habits.

http://www.authenticityassociates.com

16. Stumvoll, Ami, (sermon 27th of September 2017) "How do we manage our emotions?" in Bethel Church, Redding, CA

17. Vallotton, Kris (Blogpost June 28th, 2018) "Prophetic Word for the Body of Christ, Your spiritual battle is for a purpose".

18. Strong´s Dictionary g0859. ἄφεσις aphesis; from 863; freedom; (figuratively) pardon: — deliverance, forgiveness, liberty, remission.

19. Walker, Paul (2002) The New Spirit Filled Life Bible, Article: Holy Spirit Gifts and Power, The Gifts of the Godhead, page 1854

20. Vallotton, Kris (2015) School of the Prophets, Chapter 2 & 3, page 114, 118, 124.

21. Wagner, Peter C. (2012) Discover Your Spiritual Gifts

22. Walker, Paul (2002) The New Spirit Filled Life Bible, Article: Holy Spirit Gifts and Power, The Gifts of the Son, page 1858

23. Strong´s Dictionary g0652. ἀπόστολος apostolos; from 649; a delegate; specially, an ambassador of the Gospel; officially a commissioner of Christ ("apostle") (with miraculous powers): — apostle, messenger, he that is sent.

24. The New Spirit Filled Life Bible (2002), commentary on 1. Cor.12:28, apostles page 1598.

25. Mc Collam, Dan (2017) The Good Fight, page 21, 22, 102 and 103

26. Prince, Joseph (2012) Spirit Led – Moving by Grace in the Holy Spirit´s Gifts. (DVD-series)

27. Strong´s Dictionary ref. g3618. οἰκοδομέω oikodomeō; from the same as 3619; to be a house-builder, i.e. construct or (figuratively) confirm: — (be in) build(-er, -ing, up), edify, embolden. To build a house, erect a building to build (up from the foundation) to restore by building, to rebuild, repair.

28. Strong´s Dictionary ref. g0329 ἀναζωπυρέω anazōpyreō; from 303 and a compound of the base of 2226 and 4442; to re-enkindle: — stir up.

29. Strong´s Dictionary ref. g5486. χάρισμα charisma; from 5483; a (divine) gratuity, i.e. deliverance (from danger or passion); (specially), a (spiritual) endowment, i.e. (subjectively) religious qualification, or (objectively) miraculous faculty: — (free) gift. Grace or gifts denoting extraordinary powers, distinguishing certain Christians and enabling them to serve the church of Christ, the reception of which is due to the power of divine grace operating on their souls by the Holy Spirit

30. New Life School of Ministry, "How to be led by the Holy Spirit" (teaching outline)

31. Vallotton, Kris (2014) Basic Training for the Prophetic Ministry, Chapter 1

32. Anderson, Dr. C. Thomas (2004) Becoming a Millionaire God´s Way, page 22, 40

33. Strong´s Dictionary ref. h3581. כֹּחַ ko̱ʹaḥ; or (Dan. 11:6) כּוֹחַ kowach; figuratively (capacity, means, produce); also ability, force, might, power(-ful), strength, substance, wealth.

34. Prince, Joseph (2009) DVD: God´s Secret on Tithing

35. Strong´s Dictionary ref. g5287 g5287. ὑπόστασις hypostasis; from a compound of 5259 and 2476; a setting under (support), i.e. (figuratively) concretely, essence, or abstractly, assurance (objectively or subjectively): — confidence, confident, person, substance, that which has foundation, is firm that which has actual existence a substance, real being

36. Strong´s Dictionary ref. g4102. πίστις pistis; from 3982; persuasion, i.e. credence; moral conviction (of religious truth, or the truthfulness of God or a religious teacher), especially reliance upon Christ for salvation; abstractly, constancy in such profession; by extension, the system of religious (Gospel) truth itself: — assurance, belief, believe, faith, fidelity

37. Vallotton, Kris (2017) Destined to Win, page 11

38. Strong´s Dictionary ref. h7797. שׂוּשׂ śûś; or שִׂישׂ siys; a primitive root; to be bright, i.e. cheerful: — be glad, x greatly, joy, make mirth, rejoice.

39. Strong´s Dictionary ref. h1523. גִּיל giyl; or (by permutation) גּוּל guwl; a primitive root; properly, to spin round (under the influence of any violent emotion), i.e. usually rejoice, or (as cringing) fear: — be glad, joy, be joyful, rejoice

40. Strong´s Dictionary ref. h1584. גָּמַר gâmar; a primitive root; to end (in the sense of completion or failure): — cease, come to an end, fail, perfect, perform.

ABOUT THE AUTHOR

Hilde Lundgaard Grimstad is Norwegian but is truly international at heart. As a teenager, she was already living in Australia as a Rotary exchange student for one year and made friends from all over the world. She became a Christian at the age of 21. Her life changed radically from that point onwards. World mission became her passion, and as a young believer she went on several mission trips. One of the highlights of these trips was that Hilde was among the first wave of Christians to share the Gospel in Albania after the fall of Communism. Another highlight was going to Ukraine to share the Gospel and give humanitarian aid to starving people.

She married at the age of 23, and she already gave birth to her first daughter at 25. Having a family never stopped Hilde and her husband from following their dreams and passion. Together with their four months old baby daughter, they went to India to attend a Discipleship Training School with Youth with a Mission. Hilde has always loved to study the Word of God, and after giving birth to their second daughter in 1996, she attended Bible school in what is now called Hillsong Oslo.

Hilde has demonstrated that there are many ways to be engaged in fulfilling the Great Commission. With two small children and a working husband, she did this through financially supporting missionaries and visiting their ministries to encourage them. She worked with projects and fundraisings for a Christian NGO: The Marita Foundation in Norway. Later, she was in charge of Humanitarian Aid and Development projects in North West Russia for her church, Oslo Christian Center, and she kept going on mission trips. She gave birth to her son in 2003, and their family was complete.

In 2005, her life took a new direction. She went back to university to get her Master´s degree at the Norwegian School of Management in Oslo. She now holds a Master of Science in Business and Economics with Honors.

In 2008, Hilde and her family moved to the Philippines for the first time. Her husband was heading a Norwegian listed company based in Manila. During this period, Hilde recognized the many talented Philippine artists and their products. The bags and jewelry made of recycled material in particular got her attention. They were made by women´s cooperatives in the slum areas and were providing crucial income for the survival of these families. She saw the opportunity of starting a new business while creating income opportunities for these women. Hilde´s shop concept littXtra.no was born. The family moved back to Norway in 2011, and Hilde established a web shop for littxtra.no, a gallery style store concept at their farm and a store in a shopping mall. She kept travelling back to the Philippines to purchase more products and to keep in touch with the mission network.

In 2015, the Philippines was once again calling on the Grimstad family. Another job opportunity had opened for Hilde´s husband in Manila. Hilde continued working with commercial projects, but very soon her focus shifted over to the teaching of the Word of God. She started the International Bible study group, Foundation Study, in 2016 and ever since her main focus has been teaching the Word of God. She also went to Myanmar to teach in Bible school and churches. The ladies in Foundation Study loved Hilde´s Bible study lessons and insisted that she compile them into a book; *Embraced, Empowered, Equipped* is the result.

Hilde is overwhelmed by the great feedback she has received on her book. Her dream is to have it translated into many languages to make her Bible study lessons accessible to believers who don´t have many Christian resources available in their own language. She will continue to travel and connect with missionaries, pastors and churches all over the world, and she might even write more books...

Printed in Great Britain
by Amazon

78217368R00178